THE AUTHOR

Hesketh Pearson was born in 1887 at Hawford, near Worcester, into an affluent conservative family. On leaving Bedford School he spent two years in a shipping office, used up a legacy roaming through North and South America, sold cars for his brother and finally, in 1911, became an actor with Sir Herbert Beerbohm Tree's company. There he met the actress Gladys Gardner and they were married the following year. After rising through the ranks in Mesopotamia and Iran during World War I, Pearson returned to the stage and also began his literary career, writing sketches, journalism, short stories and the scandalous fake *The Whispering Gallery: Leaves from a Diplomat's Diary,* which led to a notorious court case in 1927. It was not, however, until he was in his forties that Pearson at last discovered his true vocation when he wrote *Doctor Darwin* (1930) – the first of over twenty biographies which were to include *The Smith of Smiths* (1934), *The Fool of Love* (1934) on Hazlitt, *Tom Paine* (1937), *Bernard Shaw* (1942), *Oscar Wilde* (1946), *Dickens* (1949) and *Disraeli* (1951). 'I love people,' he wrote, 'who blow respectability and the Establishment to bits. Hence my portrait gallery.'

In 1951, after the death of his first wife, Hesketh Pearson married Joyce Ryder, who had lived beside him in London. He died in 1964.

SYDNEY SMITH
(from the Portrait by Henry P. Briggs)

THE SMITH OF SMITHS

being
The Life, Wit and Humour
of
SYDNEY SMITH

Hesketh Pearson

New Introduction by
Richard Ingrams

THE HOGARTH PRESS
LONDON

TO

MY WIFE

Published in 1984 by
The Hogarth Press
40 William IV Street, London WC2N 4DF

First published in Great Britain by Hamish Hamilton 1934
Hogarth edition offset, with additions and corrections, from original Hamish Hamilton edition

British Library Cataloguing in Publication Data

Pearson, Hesketh
The smith of Smiths: being the life, wit and humour of Sydney Smith.
1. Smith, Sydney, 1771–1845——
Biography 2. Authors, English——
Biography
I. Title
824'.7 PR5458

ISBN 0-7012-0568-7

Printed in Great Britain by
Cox & Wyman Ltd
Reading, Berkshire

CONTENTS

NEW INTRODUCTION

On January 26th, 1927 a young man was put on trial at the London Sessions charged with obtaining money by false pretences. The case, which was an unusual one, had attracted a great deal of attention in the papers and the public gallery was crammed. The background to the trial was this: the previous November, John Lane Ltd had caused a minor sensation when they published an anonymous book called *The Whispering Gallery: Leaves from a Diplomat's Diary*. This unnamed British diplomat turned out to be an immensely experienced and well-connected character. He had met and conversed with all the great men of the day from King Edward VII downwards. He had overheard discussions between Lloyd George and Asquith, he had weekended with Thomas Hardy and bumped into Bernard Shaw on several occasions. All these incidents he described in a brash and breezy way reminiscent of Frank Harris. But the book, once published, had immediately been attacked in the *Daily Mail* as a 'scandalous fake' and a series of 'monstrous attacks on public men'. Angry denials were issued by the various politicians quoted. Eventually it transpired that the book was not the work of a diplomat at all but had, in fact, been written by one Hesketh Pearson, an obscure young actor and freelance journalist. In a panic the publishers maintained that they had been hoodwinked into believing the book to be genuine and in response to a clamour in the press Pearson was brought to trial. Every pressure had been put on him to plead guilty but he refused. He was damned, he said, if he would admit to having wronged 'a pack of cads, cowards and humbugs like the Lanes'.

The tall, good-looking man in the dock came from a respectable middle-class background. His family were Worcestershire gentry and included a number of clergymen. He had been educated at Bedford School and served in Mesopotamia during the First World War, where he won the Military Cross. But his passion was for the stage and especially for Shakespeare. In 1911 he joined Beerbohm Tree's company at the Prince of Wales theatre and became an actor. By the time of the trial he had also written three books and a fair amount of journalism, mostly in the form of profiles. What persuaded him to write *The Whispering Gallery* is not altogether clear. Perhaps it was simply to make some money. Later in life he admitted that, at the time, he couldn't resist 'the sheer fun of creating a sensation and listening to all the comments it aroused'. At any rate, when he went into the dock he made no attempt to defend himself. Asked why he had kept up the pretence of a diplomat he answered in a rush of candour, 'because I was mad'. His attitude obviously made a deep impression on the jury which acquitted him after only a brief period of deliberation.

Besides showing something of Pearson's character, the *Whispering Gallery* episode is relevant here because it explains why *The Smith of Smiths* has two introductions in addition to this one. Pearson had published his first biography, *Doctor Darwin*, in 1930 but the shadow of the court case still hung over him and when he wrote his second, *The Smith of Smiths*, the publisher Hamish Hamilton demanded an introduction from a well-known name in order to add a note of respectability. This was to be the distinguished historian G. M. Trevelyan. But late in the day Trevelyan learned of Pearson's chequered past and withdrew his imprimatur on the grounds that he was a friend of Sir Rennell Rodd, a diplomat whom Pearson had at one point foolishly named as the author of the book. Trevelyan generously paid Pearson £300 by way of compensation – three times the amount of his advance – and G. K. Chesterton agreed to step into the breach. *The Smith of Smiths* was eventually published in 1934.

It was not until he was about forty that Pearson realised that his vocation was to write biography, though he always maintained that his years on the stage helped him to get under the skin of his subjects. At the time, in the early Thirties, biography was in the doldrums. Many writers, like Philip Guedalla and Emil Ludwig, deployed what Pearson called the 'Panoramic' style, a style which he parodied as follows: 'That month a loaded cab rolled across Belgrave Square, plunged into Chelsea and set a wide-eyed couple with a canary and a multitude of baggage before a newly painted door in Cheyne Row. Lord Grey, a trifle weary, repaired the gaps in his cabinet . . .' Others, following in the steps of Lytton Strachey, whom Pearson himself had much admired in his youth, adopted a more 'imaginative' approach, inferring at length the thoughts and emotions of their subjects on the basis of very little evidence. It was mainly as a result of his friendship with Hugh Kingsmill, himself a brilliant biographer and critic, that Pearson took Dr Johnson as his model and truth as his only objective. Kingsmill taught him to distinguish between the world of the Imagination (the world of the artist) and the world of the Will (the man of action). But unlike Kingsmill, Pearson believed one could write a good biography only if one was in sympathy with one's subject. For that reason he always chose people whom he admired. They included the romantic revolutionary Tom Paine, wits and satirists like W. S. Gilbert, Henry Labouchere and Oscar Wilde, and his life-long hero Bernard Shaw.

Of all his subjects Sydney Smith came closest to his own in character, and for that reason the book is probably his masterpiece. Even Oscar Wilde, from Pearson's point of view, had a number of flaws in his character which were thoroughly deplorable. Sydney needed no apologies. Only his religion Pearson found hard to stomach and, on the basis of no evidence, refused to accept that so sensible a person as Smith believed in the Divinity of Christ. Apart from that, they held most things in common, managing, like all the best people, to embody a mass of contradictions. They were both middle-class iconoclasts who deplored the hypocrisy of the Tory establishment without wishing completely to be deprived of the blessings which its existence guaranteed them. Both Smith and Pearson inveighed against the horrors of the public-school system; both in turn sent their sons to public schools. Even on religion Pearson was hardly consistent. He called himself an Atheist, but nothing made him angrier than any sign of disrespect towards his beloved Church of England. Above all, they shared the same ebullient nature and as far as one can tell both lived their lives in a state of almost constant high spirits and good humour.

Pearson always allowed his subjects to speak for themselves. 'The dramatist or biographer,' he once wrote, 'should remain in the background as spectator and recorder, not play the judge or moralist, distributing good or bad marks, condemning or praising his subjects.' Nothing more effectively brought a man to life than direct quotation. But it had been the misfortune of Smith, a man who put his best work into his conversation, that he had no Boswell to immortalise him. (It is worth recalling that to begin with a number of publishers turned this book down on the grounds of Smith's obscurity.) Pearson therefore ransacked his writings and the memoirs of his contemporaries in order to incorporate in his book all the best jokes and mots. The result was that for the first time Smith was made to live again and could be seen as one of the great English wits, or, as Chesterton preferred, the founder of the school of Nonsense.

In recognising the genius of Smith we ought not to overlook the achievement of his biographer. One reviewer of the first edition did precisely this, as Pearson observed at the time to his friend Kingsmill: 'The *Morning Post* has quite a good selling notice, though the writer seems to assume that the book was immaculately conceived – that is to say, he doesn't mention that it was written by anyone.' Pearson carried out his stated aim of remaining in the background so successfully that some literary critics dismissed him as a mere hack. But it should be noted that Graham Greene and Max Beerbohm, both master story-tellers, paid tribute to the skill with which he handled his material and his narrative. Another great admirer was P. G. Wodehouse.

The best thing about a Pearson biography is the author's high spirits. Looking back over their long years of friendship, Malcolm Muggeridge recalled the 'especial gusto which characterised everything he said and did'. He takes his reader along with him, getting him to share his enthusiasm. Occasionally slapdash, at time opinionated, he is never dull; and behind the jollity one can sense without too much difficulty the presence of a shrewd, warm-hearted and delightful man. 'Personally I would rather be dead than half alive,' he wrote in his memoirs. 'But I have enjoyed the experience of living so much that I now ask nothing of life but a quick death.' He died in 1964 at the age of seventy-seven, author of over twenty biographies. Muggeridge wrote in *The Times:* 'Pearson loved the English countryside and bells sounding across it: the English language and all who tried in however humble a capacity to use it worthily. He never could manage to finish reciting Wordsworth's verses on the death of James Hogg. The closing lines

How fast has brother followed brother,
From sunshine to the sunless lands

were too much for him. I shall always think of him stumbling over the poignancy of those exquisite verses, and hope that the land will, after all, turn out not to be sunless.'

Richard Ingrams, Aldworth 1984

ACKNOWLEDGMENT

I WISH to express my gratitude to Mr. Nowell Charles Smith, who has prepared, but not yet published, an authoritative text of Sydney Smith's correspondence from originals put at his disposal mainly by the late Lord Knutsford, and who has most unselfishly placed his annotated and corrected copy at my disposal, giving me permission to print as many of the unpublished passages as I pleased. But for his generous action, my portrait of Sydney Smith must have been incomplete. Though possibly the first, I shall certainly not be the last to appreciate his labours on what will prove to be the wittiest collection of letters in the English language.

I also wish to acknowledge the courtesy of Professor G. M. Trevelyan, who has allowed me to quote from the diary and correspondence of Lord Macaulay.

Of Mr. G. K. Chesterton's kindness in writing an Introduction, I shall say nothing because I could not say enough.

FOREWORD BY G. M. TREVELYAN

This book will enable a generation which has forgotten Sydney Smith, except as a name, to sample his wit and to realise the nature of his very unusual personality and character. Like Swift, he was in the wrong profession; he too, though conscientious in his performance of the duties of a clergyman, had other gifts and a different mentality from the clerical, a fact which adds piquancy to the story of his life and opinions.

His qualities as a political and social thinker and as a wit can be fairly adjudicated by those who read this book. For Mr Hesketh Pearson, though as a biographer he exercises his right to agree with his hero perhaps more often and more completely than his reader will always be able to do, belongs to the class of honest biographer. He never tries to make a case by concealment. Here is Sydney in his habit as he walked – and talked. The numerous quotations are fair samples of his thought, writings and speech. An honest Englishman is here honestly portrayed. One of the world's most singular and gifted men is here allowed to stand and unfold himself.

G. M. Trevelyan, 1933

INTRODUCTION

It is remarkable how little satisfactory and sympathetic study has been made of Sydney Smith. A hundred good books ought to have been born out of that author of a thousand good things. Mr. G. C. Heseltine wrote recently a very illuminating and notable sketch; but it was almost inevitably concerned largely with Sydney Smith's famous and spirited fight for religious liberty, especially in the case of Catholic Emancipation. In one aspect it is all the more to the credit of Sydney Smith that he fought so hard for the rights of a religion that he did not in the least understand. But it would seem that there have been many people since then who understood the fighting quite as little as he understood the faith. For we live alas, in an age that has lost faith in liberty, much more than it has lost faith in theology. But outside this special aspect and example, there has been nothing written of late at all fitted to express the fullness of the modern retrospect, upon one of the most remarkable of the makers of the great mood of liberty and liberality; which was until lately called the modern world, but which I fear can no longer be called modern. Mr. Hesketh Pearson has here fulfilled the need in its fullness, or what has been hitherto its emptiness; by dealing vividly not with one aspect, but with all aspects. Thus he shows us Sydney Smith in many mirrors of many minds, and not only in that of Wellington or Daniel O'Connell. Indeed, apart from many such glimpses in the text, the list of detached opinions is a much-needed biographical method. But the main impression is still that of a friend of freedom; urging it with far more fullness and power than men whose names came to be on the whole more famous and fashionable. For instance, Sydney Smith had almost all that Macaulay had; and a thousand things that Macaulay had not. In radiant and rapid exposition of the nineteenth-century philosophy, of secular sense and reverent religious indifference, *Peter Plymley's Letters* have just the same air of delivering a logical knock-out as Macaulay's Essays. But Sydney Smith did not only argue on behalf of freedom; he was free. He was free from all sorts of curious constraints that really restricted Macaulay, some of them, I am sure, sincere; some of them, I am afraid, a little insincere. For instance, whether or no Macaulay had a religion (and nobody ever discovered whether he had or not) it is certain that any religion he had sincerely held, would have been that of Sydney Smith; the free and fraternal benevolence, which recognised God as a matter of common sense; and really called itself Christian for the excellent reason that it would sound a little cranky to call itself Deist. And Sydney Smith had, whatever else he had, a deep, human, hearty and utterly sincere hatred of anything that sounded cranky. But Macaulay could never altogether forget that he was the son of a pillar of the Clapham Sect; and therefore there was a sort of primness, even in his tight-lipped pugnacity. Whatever were his religious sympathies, he still had sectarian sympathies. Now nothing is more notable about the generous and joyous impatience of Sydney Smith, than the fact that he hated the frenzies of sectarianism even more than the mummeries of Rome. For him the Methodists were simply madmen; and he said so; which is the ringing note of reality in all his record. He would have said that he was a loyal Anglican parson; his opponents might say he was a Pagan; but he was not only not a Puritan, but he was not a subconscious or submerged or secret Puritan. In his red blood was no such vinegar at all; for whatever we call the blood feeding such a brain, Christian or Pagan or Anglican, it had flowed through the heart of Herrick.

It was the same in the political comparison. He was a Whig, in the sense that he was often in practice one of the supporters of the Whigs; but he was never one of the Whigs.

He would have been the first to appreciate the bitter jest of Thackeray: 'I am not a Whig; but oh how I should like to be.' The aristocrats and well-paid officials who made up that Whig world, received him with delight; as any other kings might have received any other court jester. But at no point does any reader of his writings, public or private, feel that he was tied to the cause of the great Whig Party, in the curious way which is so characteristic of Macaulay to the last. Sydney Smith was never a Whig, even from the first. Sydney Smith was truly and exactly a Liberal; with all the truths and all the difficulties involved in the genuine love of Liberty. But, loving freedom, he felt himself free, as Macaulay and such men did not, to curse anything from the Clapham Sect to the Whig Cabinet.

But, above all, we see this in the department of his intellect; I will add of his imagination. For it is the real mark of his genius that he had a sort of imagination. If I may continue such a comparison merely as a convenience, it is quite impossible to imagine a contemporary like Macaulay, let alone a contemporary like Jeffrey, or Mackintosh, or Brougham, rushing instantly into wild extravagances to illustrate any topic or any truth! But in this Sydney Smith was the father of something that belonged to the future and not to the past.

It was inevitable, but it was misleading, that he should be called a wit; and even described as belonging to the age of the wits. He was in fact something much wilder than a humorist. He was, we might say, the real originator of Nonsense. He had really much more affinity with Lear and Lewis Carroll than with Luttrell and Rogers. Theirs was the old wit, at the best logical, and at the worst verbal. But Sydney Smith was a poet. His nonsense had imaginative laws of its own, and compels emotion by mere imagery, as does a great poem. To say that Brighton Pavilion looked as if St. Paul's Cathedral had come down and littered, is more than a logical sequence; it is an imaginative vista. To say that a bishop deserved to be preached to death by wild curates is not merely satire; it is a satisfaction of the fancy. And the memorable fact about Sydney Smith, as a man, is that all his friends and even foes attest that his fertility in these fancies was instant and incessant. Millions of such mad romances must have been thrown about among men who never recorded them. It is only fair to Macaulay, whose name I have taken in vain in these lines, to mention that Macaulay records one out of these thousand impromptu extravagances; that about the dubious Hindu visitor, 'who ought to have melted lead poured down his nostrils, if the good old Vedas were enforced as they ought to be'. That is the final and full impression of Sydney Smith; of a bubbling and boiling fountain of fancies and fun, which played day and night; and I doubt if any man in the modern world could have beaten him at that game; comic indeed, but of a sheer creative power.

G. K. CHESTERTON.

PREFACE

Sydney Smith by His Contemporaries

'A clergyman!!' – *William Charles Macready.*

'Smug Sydney.' – *Lord Byron.*

'The Smith of Smiths.' – *Lord Macaulay.*

'My noble-hearted husband.' – *Mrs. Sydney Smith.*

'Humour's pink primate, Sydney Smith.' – *Walter Savage Landor.*

'You can't say too much about Sydney.' – *Sir Walter Scott.*

'He is a very clever fellow, but he will never be a bishop.' – *George III.*

'A more profligate parson I never met.' – *George IV.*

'The loudest wit I e'er was deafened with.' – *Lord Byron.*

'The ancient and amusing defender of our faith.' – *Daniel O'Connell.*

'He exerted a great influence over my political career.' – *Lord Houghton.*

'After dinner he spoke to me for some time very kindly.' – *W. E. Gladstone.*

'I don't think the worse of his heart for his flighty way.' – *Thomas Campbell.*

'I never see Sydney Smith without thinking him too much of a buffoon.' – *Mr. Creevey.*

'Was there ever more sense combined with more hilarious jocularity?' – *Lord Cockburn.*

'At Sydney Smith's: the happiest day I remember to have ever spent.' – *Francis Horner.*

'I sat next to Sydney Smith, who was delightful . . . I don't remember a more agreeable party.' – *Benjamin Disraeli.*

'The power and diversity of Sydney Smith's wit was greater than that of any man I have ever known.' – *Sir Henry Holland.*

'A fellow of infinite fun (if not much humour) and of a fine digestion and some sense.' – *Thomas Carlyle.*

'As coarse as hemp.' – *Thomas Carlyle.*

'An odd mixture of Punch and Cato.' – *Lord Lansdowne.*

'To attempt to Boswell Sydney Smith's conversation would be out-Boswelling Boswell indeed.' – *Maria Edgeworth.*

'I think it the most argumentative, logical, ingenious, and by far the wittiest performance I ever met with.'–
R. B. Sheridan (on *Peter Plymley's Letters*).

'The lively talent, sound argument and genuine humour of the fifty pages which have so much interested me, could have been derived from no pen but one.'–
Rt. Hon. Thomas Grenville. (on *Letters to Archdeacon Singleton*).

'The only wit on record, whom brilliant social success had done nothing to spoil or harden.' – *Henry Fothergill Chorley.*

'His faunlike face is a sort of promise of a good thing when he does but open his lips.' – *Henry Crabb Robinson.*

'Nothing could exceed Sydney's wit and liveliness; he made Blanco ill from laughing.' – *Hon. Henry Edward Fox.*

'It is his condition to be witty, as it is that of Lady Seymour to be beautiful.' – *F. Guizot.*

'Have rather held out against him hitherto; but this day he conquered me; and I am now his victim, in the laughing way, for life . . . . There is this difference between Luttrell and Smith – that after the former, you remember what good things he said, and after the latter you merely remember how much you laughed.' – *Thomas Moore.*

'Sydney talks from the impulse of the moment, and his fun is quite inexhaustible.' – *Lord Macaulay.*

'I have a superstitious veneration for the cloth, which his free-and-easy wearing of it occasionally disturbs a little.' – *Frances Anne Kemble.*

'Who else could make such a mixture of odd paradox, quaint fun, manly sense, liberal opinion, striking language?' – *Francis Horner* (on Smith's lectures on Moral Philosophy).

'What a hideous, odd-looking man Sydney Smith is! with a mouth like an oyster, and three double chins.' – *Mrs. Brookfield.*

'Now I shall be able to do something for Sydney Smith.' – *Lord Grey* (on becoming Prime Minister).

'Sydney Smith has done more for the Whigs than all the clergy put together, and our not making him a bishop is mere cowardice.' – *Lord Melbourne.*

'In spite of innumerable affectations and oddities, he is certainly one of the wittiest and most original writers of our times.' – *Lord Macaulay.*

'Sydney beyond anything amusing. . . . Left Lord John's with Sydney and Luttrell, and when we got to Cockspur Street (having laughed all the way) we were all three seized with such convulsions of cachinnation at something (I forget what) which Sydney said, that we were obliged to separate, and reel each his own way with the fit.' – *Thomas Moore.*

'To a dissenter like myself . . . there was something very painful in the tone always taken by Sydney Smith about Church matters.' – *Harriet Martineau.*

'I wish you would tell Mr. Sydney Smith that of all the men I ever heard of and never saw, I have the greatest curiosity to see and the greatest interest to know him.' – *Charles Dickens.*

'The fanciful fun and inexhaustible humorous drollery of his conversation among his intimates can never be adequately rendered or reproduced.' – *Frances Anne Kemble.*

'Had England a hierarchy formed all of wits,
Whom, but Sydney, would England proclaim as its Primate?' – *Thomas Moore.*

'Sydney Smith passed ten days here and enlivened us extremely.' – *Lord Grey.*

'He drew such a ludicrous caricature . . . that Sir James Mackintosh rolled on the floor in fits of laughter.' – *Lord John Russell.*

'His kindliness was overflowing, and entirely took away the sting from the repartees which were perpetually bubbling up in his talk.' – *Lord Granville.*

'I looked upon him, as a Whig, at first with misgiving, but his honesty and kind-heartedness soon got the better of my antagonism, and we became intimate friends.' – *Rev. R. H. Barham.*

'Sydney Smith quizzed everybody, but hurt no one's feelings.' – *Harriet Martineau.*

'Sydney is, in his way, inimitable; and, as a conversational wit, beats all the men I have ever met.' – *Thomas Moore.*

'The truth is that Sydney Smith is naturally coarse, and a lover of scurrilous language.' – *Ist Earl of Dudley* (on an article by Smith in the *Edinburgh Review*).

'You have been laughing at me for the last seven years, and you never said anything which I wished unsaid.'– *Ist Earl of Dudley* (to Sydney Smith).

'The *Edinburgh Review* had been commenced in October, 1802, under the superintendence of the Rev. Sydney Smith, with whom, during his short residence in Scotland, he (Walter Scott) had lived on terms of great kindness and familiarity.' – *J. G. Lockhart.*

'His great delight was to produce a succession of ludicrous images. . . . It may be averred for certain that in this style he has never been equalled, and I do not suppose he will ever be surpassed.' – *Lord John Russell.*

'I have heard enough to satisfy me that he is a man of

genuine philanthropy and liberality of mind, upon the most *delicate* social subjects, and upon the main causes of poverty and abasement of the bulk of the people.' – *George Grote.*

'Sydney at breakfast made me actually cry with laughing. I was obliged to start up from the table.' – *Thomas Moore.*

'An irresistibly amusing companion.' – *George Ticknor.*

'He is the gayest man and the greatest wit in England; and yet, to those who know him, this is his least recommendation. His kind heart, sound sense, and universal indulgence, making him loved and esteemed by many to whom his wit was unintelligible. . . . My beloved and incomparable friend.' – *Lord Jeffrey.*

'He was an admirable joker; he had the art of placing ordinary things in an infinitely ludicrous point of view. I have seen him at Foston (his living near York) drive the servants from the room with the tears running down their faces, in peals of inextinguishable laughter: but he was too much of a jack-pudding.' – *Lord Brougham.*

'I wanted to tell you what deep respect I had for Sydney Smith. . . . He was the first in the literary circles of London to assert the value of *Modern Painters*, and he has always seemed to me equally keen-sighted and generous in his estimate of literary efforts. . . . There is no man (whom I have not personally known) whose image is so vivid in my constant affection.' – *John Ruskin.*

'A great luminary, such as we shall hardly see the like of again, and who has reigned without a rival in wit and humour for a great length of time. It is almost impossible to over-rate his wit, humour and drollery, or their effect in society. . . . If there was a fault in it, it was that it was too amusing. . . . A liberal, kind-hearted, charitable man.' – *Charles Greville* (on Sydney Smith's death).

' . . . old Lady Holland – whom I again see crying about dear Sydney Smith, behind that green screen as we last saw her together.' – *Charles Dickens* (after Sydney Smith's death).

From Various Sources:

Abraham Lincoln was one of Sydney Smith's warmest admirers, always reading and quoting passages from his writings.

Queen Victoria used to go into fits of laughter at the sayings of Sydney Smith, which were repeated to her by Lord Melbourne.

Sarah Siddons, who never jeopardised her deportment in society as a tragedy queen by lapsing into laughter, fell an easy prey to Sydney Smith's humour at their first meeting, developed convulsions, and had to be helped from the table.

THE SMITH OF SMITHS

CHAPTER I

SEEING ENGLAND

ABOUT the middle of the eighteenth century a young merchant of Eastcheap named Robert Smith sold his share of the business inherited from his father to his brother and set forth to see the world. Robert was of a roving disposition, anxious to see life in all its aspects and to crowd as many experiences as possible into his portion of it. Clearly one of the first things to be done was to fall in love. He sought out a pleasing object and commenced his first adventure. Maria Olier was the daughter of an exiled Huguenot. She was pretty and charming and good. Robert was dashing and handsome and well-to-do. The match seemed unexceptionable. A marriage was arranged and duly took place at St. George's, Bloomsbury.

But during the service Robert's mind began to wander. Marriage, he thought, meant settling down, the end of adventure, the birth of children and the beginning of responsibility. An impossible prospect for one who had not yet seen the world or experienced the thrill of travel. However, this difficulty could easily be overcome. At the conclusion of the ceremony he announced that he had to leave for America without delay, and bade farewell to his tearful bride at the door of the church. Mrs. Smith went home with her mother, and Robert, having come through his first adventure unscathed, crossed the ocean in search of others.

The best years of his life were spent in viewing the haunts of men and animals in various parts of the world and satisfying his lust for change and motion. At length he returned home, but not to peace and quiet. Having consummated his marriage, he decided to see England thoroughly, and his wife had no alternative but to see it with him. He bought, altered, spoilt and sold a score of residences in different parts of the country. No sooner had he purchased a house and spent both money and energy in ruining its appearance, than he got rid of it at a loss and departed for another district. Meanwhile his wife bore him five children – four sons and one daughter – at five different homes. They happened to be at Woodbridge in Suffolk on the 3rd of June, 1771, when their second child, Sydney, was born.

Something of the agitation inseparable from these constant removals communicated itself to the four boys, who quarrelled and argued interminably over every subject that arose out of their studies and were no more inclined to reach an agreement on any one point than their father was disposed to settle down in any one place. They differed as violently among themselves as the natives of different parishes might be expected to do. When they were old enough their father, in his migratory passages through England, scattered them at various scholastic establishments, and Sydney was dropped at a preparatory school in Southampton, where he was quite happy.

But he was far from happy at Winchester School, where he went in 1782. Their father, arresting for a moment his comet-like course, took counsel, and decided to send the boys to two public schools in sections of two. Under this arrangement 'Bobus', the eldest, went with Cecil to Eton, while Sydney went with Courtenay, the youngest, to Winchester. Here they suffered the usual public school training of the time; that is to say, they were starved, neglected, bullied by senior boys, thrashed by masters, made acquainted with all the popular forms of vice, and crammed with useless knowledge. Courtenay ran away twice. Sydney braved it out, but in the process contracted such a hearty loathing of the whole business that, when quite an old man, the mere mention of Winchester would make him shudder. In later years he never missed an opportunity of pointing out the criminal abuses and absurdities of public school life, and in one of his best-known essays he condemned the entire system, root and branch:

> 'At a public school,' he wrote, 'every boy is alternately tyrant and slave. The power which the elder part of these communities exercises over the younger, is exceedingly great – very difficult to be controlled – and accompanied, not unfrequently, with cruelty and caprice. . . . Now this system we cannot help considering as an evil – because it inflicts upon boys, for two or three years of their lives, many painful hardships, and much unpleasant servitude. These sufferings might perhaps be of some use in military schools; but to give to a boy the habit of enduring privations to which he will never again be called upon to submit – to inure him to pains which he will never again feel – and to subject him to the privation of comforts with which he will always in future abound – is surely not a very useful and valuable severity in education. It is not the life in miniature which he is to lead hereafter – nor does it bear any relation to it: he will never again be subjected to so much insolence and caprice ; nor ever, in all human probability, called upon to make so many sacrifices. . . . Such a system makes many boys very miserable, and produces those bad effects upon the temper and disposition which unjust suffering always does produce. . . . The morality of boys is generally very imperfect ; their notions of honour extremely mistaken; and their objects of ambition frequently very absurd. The probability then is that the kind of discipline they exercise over each other will produce (when left to itself) a great deal of mischief; and yet this is the discipline to which every child at a public school is not only necessarily exposed, but principally confined. . . . Submission to tyranny lays the foundation of hatred, suspicion, cunning and a variety of odious passions. We are convinced that those young people will turn out to be the best men who have been guarded most effectually, in their childhood, from every species of useless vexation, and experienced, in the greatest degree, the blessings of a wise and rational indulgence. . . .
>
> 'This system also gives to the elder boys an absurd and

pernicious opinion of their own importance, which is often with difficulty effaced by a considerable commerce with the world. The *head* of a public school is generally a very conceited young man, utterly ignorant of his own dimensions, and losing all that habit of conciliation towards others, and that anxiety for self-improvement, which results from the natural modesty of youth. Nor is this conceit very easily and speedily gotten rid of: we have often seen (if we mistake not) public-school importance lasting through the half of after-life, strutting in lawn, swelling in ermine, and displaying itself, both ridiculously and offensively, in the haunts and business of bearded men.'

On the subject of games, Sydney also had a word to say:

> 'There is a manliness in the athletic exercises of public schools which is as seductive to the imagination as it is utterly unimportant in itself. Of what importance is it in after-life whether a boy can play well or ill at cricket, or row a boat with the skill and precision of a waterman? If our young lords and esquires were hereafter to wrestle together in public, or the gentlemen of the Bar to exhibit Olympic games in Hilary Term, the glory attached to these exercises at public schools would be rational and important. But of what use is the body of an athlete when we have good laws over our heads – or when a pistol, a post-chaise or a porter can be hired for a few shillings? A gentleman does nothing but ride or walk; and yet such a ridiculous stress is laid upon the manliness of the exercises customary at public schools, exercises in which the greatest blockheads commonly excel the most – which often render habits of idleness inveterate, and often lead to foolish expense and dissipation at a more advanced period of life.'

It was the common belief in those days that almost every famous man had been educated at a public school. But 'it is very remarkable', said Sydney, 'that the most eminent men in every art and science have not been educated in public schools'; and he rattled off the names of nearly all the greatest Englishmen, from Shakespeare to Dr. Johnson.

As for the method of education at public schools, Sydney expressed absolute contempt for it. Schoolmasters, he said, encouraged their pupils to 'love the instrument better than the end – not the luxury which the difficulty encloses, but the difficulty – not the filbert, but the shell – not what may be read in Greek, but Greek itself'. There was no doubt that grammar, gerund-grinding, and the tyranny of the lexicon and the dictionary, had got the schoolboys of England in their grasp, and the boy 'was suffocated with the nonsense of the grammarians, overwhelmed with every species of difficulty disproportionate to his age, and driven by despair to peg-top or marbles'. Nor was there a greater object of compassion than 'a fine boy, full of animal spirits, set down in a bright sunny day, with a heap of unknown words before him, to be turned into English, before supper, by the help of a ponderous dictionary alone'. It was perfectly simple to see how much the average boy hated this sort of thing; and the real test was not what he did when he was thrashed, nor when the master's presence acted as a curb on his desires, 'but what he actually does when left in the midst of noisy boys, and with a recollection that, by sending to the neighbouring shop, he can obtain any quantity of unripe gooseberries upon credit'.

Forty years after he had left school, Sydney compiled a list of Popular Fallacies, one of which ran as follows: *Because I have gone through it, my son shall go through it also.* And this was how he dealt with it:

> 'A man gets well pummelled at a public school; is subject to every misery and every indignity which seventeen years of age can inflict upon nine and ten; has his eye nearly knocked out, and his clothes stolen and cut to pieces; and twenty years afterwards, when he is a chrysalis, and has forgotten the miseries of his grub state, is determined to act a manly part in life, and says, "I passed through all that myself, and I am determined my son shall pass through it as I have done"; and away goes his bleating progeny to the tyranny and servitude of the long chamber or the large dormitory. It would surely be much more rational to say, "Because I have passed through it, I am determined my son shall not pass through it; because I was kicked for nothing, and cuffed for nothing, and fagged for everything, I will spare all these miseries to my child." It is not for any good which may be derived from this rough usage; that has not been weighed and considered; few persons are

capable of weighing its effects upon character; but there is a sort of compensatory and consolatory notion, that the present generation (whether useful or not, no matter) are not to come off scot-free, but are to have their share of ill-usage; as if the black eye and bloody nose which Master John Jackson received in 1800, are less black and bloody by the application of similar violence to similar parts of Master Thomas Jackson, the son, in 1830. This is not only sad nonsense, but cruel nonsense. The only use to be derived from the recollection of what we have suffered in youth, is a fixed determination to screen those we educate from every evil and inconvenience, from subjection to which there are not cogent reasons for submitting. Can anything be more stupid and preposterous than this concealed revenge upon the rising generation, and latent envy lest they should avail themselves of the improvements time has made, and pass a happier youth than their fathers have done?'

In spite of the brutalities and stupidities with which they were surrounded, both Sydney and Courtenay did well at Winchester, and Sydney eventually became Prefect of Hall – the most responsible and covetable position in the School. Their holidays were more varied than those of other schoolboys, for the nomadic habits of their father ensured a regular shifting of scene. At one place only – Ledbury in Herefordshire – do we hear that Sydney spent much time as a child.

Early in 1789 Sydney was elected Scholar of New College, Oxford, and after a six months' stay at Mont Villiers, where his father sent him to learn French and where, for safety's sake, he was registered at one of the Jacobin clubs as 'Le Citoyen Smit', he settled down to hard work and plain living in the midst of a society where few worked and everyone drank too much. At the end of his second year he exchanged his Scholarship for a Fellowship of £100 a year, and from that moment his father never gave him a penny.

As he could not return hospitality, he would not accept it, and his life at Oxford was lonely and unhappy; he seldom referred to it in after years. His elder brother 'Bobus' was studying for the Bar; Cecil and Courtenay were being fitted out for the East; his mother's health had been undermined by years of suspense in the absence of her husband, by years of uncertainty in his presence, and by too many changes of address in periods of pregnancy; so Sydney was called upon to suffer for the rest of the family; he was the sole member of it whose interests were never considered and whose wishes were never consulted. To make matters worse, his brother Courtenay got into debt at Winchester, did not dare to tell his father, and implored Sydney to save him. Sydney undertook to pay the £30 out of his annual pittance of £100, and Courtenay sailed for India with a light heart.

> 'I did it with my heart's blood,' said Sydney many years later; 'it was the third of my whole income, for though I never in my life owed a farthing which I was unable to pay, yet my £100 a year was very difficult to spread over the wants of a college life.'

Too poor to make friends, too proud to borrow money, Sydney was thrown back on the classics and meditation. His opinion of university life was hardly more flattering than his opinion of public school life. Nearly forty years after he had left Oxford we find him writing of a friend who has sent his son to Cambridge:

> 'He has put him there to spend his money, to lose what good qualities he has, and to gain nothing useful in return. If men had made no more progress in the common arts of life than they have in education, we should at this moment be dividing our food with our fingers, and drinking out of the palms of our hands.'

Later still he expressed sympathy with a lady whose son was at Oxford – 'knowing, as I do, that the only consequences of a University education are the growth of vice and the waste of money'. He was delighted with a description of the two Universities as 'enormous hulks confined with mooring-chains, everything flowing and progressing around them', while they were stationary.

In 1792 Sydney took his degree. He was now compelled

to adopt a profession. He had been studying medicine and anatomy in his spare time at Oxford, and Dr. Christopher Pegge, whose lectures he had attended, advised him to become a doctor. Sydney's own inclinations were strongly towards the Bar – 'the law,' he said, 'is decidedly the best profession for a young man if he has anything in him' – but his father refused financial aid and summarily disposed of the question with: 'You may be a college tutor or a parson.' Sydney did not relish either prospect. 'Then you may go as a supercargo to China,' said his helpful parent. This was still less to his liking. None of the professions suggested by Smith senior promised high rewards for ambition, and Sydney was very ambitious. 'In the Church,' said he, 'a man is thrown into life with his hands tied, and bid to swim; he does well if he keeps his head above water.' Nevertheless, it was the only profession open to a scholarly and intelligent man with no private means; so into the Church he went.

CHAPTER II

FIRST FRIENDS

SYDNEY SMITH was ordained in 1794 and immediately became curate of Netheravon, near Amesbury, on Salisbury Plain – 'a pretty feature in a plain face', he called it. He was in sole charge of the parish for three years, and in addition had to take one service every Sunday at the neighbouring village of Fittleton. The condition of the poor was appalling and he set to work at once to better their lot. He established a Sunday school for the instruction of their children and an Industrial school to teach their girls how to knit, sew and darn. The struggle against ignorance and poverty was a severe one, but he was helped by the squire, Mr. Hicks-Beach, who spent about three months a year in the place and took a great fancy to his new curate.

The wretched state of the poor in his parish may be inferred from a few individual cases : A young girl got sixteen pounds of spinning work done a month and received four shillings for it. One man aged fifty-five was very unhealthy, worked hard for four shillings a week, and was beaten by a farmer with a large stick so viciously that, had he not been wearing a greatcoat, he would have been crippled. Another man supported a wife and four children on six shillings a week. Nearly all the people were dependent on parish relief and not a man received as much as ten shillings a week.

Sydney was asked by Mrs. Hicks-Beach to report on the situation, and his summary was so disquieting that no time was lost in starting the necessary work. At first the farmers and labourers resolutely refused to come to church, and he described his preaching as 'the voice of one crying in the wilderness', but by degrees he made friends of them and they came to gape through his sermons. Above all he attended to the immediate needs of the children, and with such effect that three generations later his name was remembered in the district.

His life was lonely. The chief event of the place was the arrival, once a week, of the butcher's cart from Salisbury. Sometimes, owing to the weather, it was delayed and the parish lived on vegetables. Now and again he had a visitor, and the three months' residence of the squire's family was of course a godsend, but for the most part he lived in complete solitude, exercising his brain with the study of theology and his body with long tramps on Salisbury Plain. 'Nothing can equal the profound, the immeasurable, the awful dullness of this place,' he complained, 'in which I lie, dead and buried, in hopes of a joyful resurrection in the year 1796.' Occasionally he paid flying visits to Bath to see his mother, now completely worn out by the unsettled habits of her husband, and once or twice he spent a holiday with the Hicks-Beaches at their home in Gloucestershire, though their care for his comfort was not always expressed in a practical way. 'Your offer of a horse to carry my portmanteau I cannot accept,' he wrote, 'and for two reasons. . . . The first is, you have no horse here; the next, I have no portmanteau.'

It was fortunate for Sydney that the squire had taken a liking for him. Hicks-Beach wanted his son Michael to spend a year or two at a German university before going to Oxford and asked Sydney to accompany the boy in the two-fold capacity of tutor and friend. Sydney jumped at the offer and in the spring of 1797 preached his last sermon at Netheravon, begging his listeners not to let the Sunday school fall into ruin by their own negligence. 'I have lived among your children,' he said, 'and have taught them myself, and have seen them improve, and I know it will make them better and happier men.'

By this time his father had tired of Bath and had established himself near Tiverton, surrounding his house with such a maze of bricks, mortar, planks, trenches and other material for re-building, that Sydney had great difficulty in effecting an entrance; but having done so he spent the summer there, learning German and making inquiries for a suitable university. In a letter to Hicks-Beach he suggested Weimar as the best destination for Michael and himself, because the Duke had assembled at his court the four heroes of German literature, Wieland, Goethe, Herder and Schiller, because the society was agreeable and had a literary turn, because the English were very well received and a young man anxious to improve himself would be welcomed with open arms, and 'because a young buck, or a fox-hunter, would be laughed at and neglected'.

Weimar was duly approved by Hicks-Beach and the autumn was spent in preparations for the trip. But Napoleon's activities on the continent made them alter their plans and after some months of uncertainty it was decided that they should go to Edinburgh instead, where Professors Dugald Stewart (Moral Philosophy), John Playfair (Mathematics), John Hill (Humanity), James Gregory (Medicine), and Joseph Black (Chemistry), were adding lustre to the University. They journeyed north by easy stages in the spring of 1798. We find them staying at Warwick Castle as guests of the Earl in May, going on from there to Birmingham, a 'place of loud noises and bad smells', and noting the sudden outburst of patriotism throughout the county: 'The merry yeomen of Warwickshire and Birmingham are all drunk.' They visited Manchester, 'a horrid, unfinished town', Liverpool, 'a wonderful scene of activity and enterprise', Matlock and Buxton, and reached the Lakes early in June. Sydney admired the beauty of Derwentwater, the grandeur of Ullswater, and the mountains round Windermere, but criticised the inns: 'People mistake this matter of simplicity strangely. Is it necessary to sit upon boards painfully hard, and put your feet upon malthouse floors, because you retire to a beautiful lake for 2 or 3 of the hot months of the year? There is surely some medium between mud and marble, huckaback and brocade.' They climbed Skiddaw, and Sydney wrote an account of the event to the parents of his pupil:

'Off we set, Michael, the guide and myself, at one in the morning to gain the summit of Skiddaw. I, who find it rather difficult to stick upon my horse on the plainest roads, did not find that facility increased by the darkness of the morning or the precipitous paths we had to ascend. I made no manner of doubt but that I should roll down into the town of Keswick the next morning and be picked up by the town beadle dead in a gutter; moreover I was moved a little for my reputation, for as I had a bottle of brandy in my pocket, placed there by the special exhortations of the guide and landlord, the Keswick coroner and jury would infallibly have brought me in *a Parson as died of drinking*. However, onward we moved, and arrived at the summit. The thermometer stood at 40, the wind was bitter, and the summit totally enveloped in thick clouds, which nearly wetted us through and totally cut off all view of the sun and the earth, too. Here we regaled upon biscuit and brandy, and waited for the dissipation of the vapor. The guide seemed to be about as much affected by the weather as Skiddaw itself, which mountain in height and brownness of complexion he something resembled. I was rueful enough, tho I really rejoiced in the novelty of the scene; but a more woebegone, piteous face than Michael put on you never saw – no tailor tried, cast and condemned for filching small parcels of cloth ever looked so unhappy. The wind, the complaisant wind, now puffed away the vapors at intervals and gave us a hasty view on different quarters of the magnificent scene which surrounded us. When the clearance was to the east, we looked over the level country of Northumberland, and saw the light of day rising from the German Ocean. Beneath us was Keswick, all quiet, and the solemn tranquil lake of Derwent – beyond these the Westmoreland mountains began to be tinged with the golden morning, or we caught the Isle of Man, the northern coast of Ireland, the Frith of Solway, or the hills of Cheviot well known to song and history. Above us was the blue heaven, and all under were the sons of men, scattered in fair cities and upon the hills and down in the dales, and over the whole face of the earth. And so we went down – and Michael grew warm and eat a monstrous breakfast, and was right pleased with his excursion, and all was well.'

They entered Edinburgh in the dust of a warm June evening and took lodgings at 38, South Hanover Street.

And now Sydney, at the age of 27, for the first time in his life, could really enjoy himself. He had money to spend; he was able to gratify his love of reason and practical knowledge by attending the lectures of Dugald Stewart on Moral Philosophy, the Clinical lectures of Dr. Gregory, and the lectures on Chemistry by Dr. Black; and his strong social instincts found full vent in a circle of young friends who, though ambitious, were not averse from hearing the chimes at midnight. The country round Edinburgh made such an impression on him that in the last year of his life it was still fresh in memory: 'Ah! what charming walks I had about Arthur's Seat, with the clear mountain air blowing in one's face. I often think of that glorious scene.' His admiration for the city itself was qualified: 'No smells were ever equal to Scotch smells. It is the School of Physic. Walk the streets and you would imagine that every medical man had been administering cathartics to every man, woman and child in the town. Yet the place is uncommonly beautiful, and I am in a constant balance between admiration and trepidation:

> Taste guides my eye, where e'er new beauties spread,
> While prudence whispers "look before you tread." '

The inhabitants of Edinburgh also made a deep impression on him. He must speak for himself:

> 'It requires a surgical operation to get a joke well into a Scotch understanding. Their only idea of wit, or rather that inferior variety of this electric talent which prevails occasionally in the north, and which, under the name of *wut*, is so infinitely distressing to people of good taste, is laughing immoderately at stated intervals. They are so imbued with metaphysics that they even make love metaphysically; I overheard a young lady of my acquaintance, at a dance in Edinburgh, exclaim, in a sudden pause of the music, "What you say, my Lord, is very true of love in the *aibstract*, but – " here the fiddlers began fiddling furiously, and the rest was lost. No nation has so large a stock of benevolence of heart: if you meet

with an accident, half Edinburgh immediately flocks to your door to inquire after your *pure* hand or your *pure* foot, and with a degree of interest that convinces you their whole hearts are in the enquiry. You find they usually arrange their dishes at dinner by the points of the compass: "Sandy, put the gigot of mutton to the south, and move the singet sheep's head a wee bit to the nor-wast." If you knock at the door, you hear a shrill female voice from the fifth flat shriek out "Wha's chapping at the door?" which is presently opened by a lassie with short petticoats, bare legs, and thick ankles. . . . Their temper stands anything but an attack on their climate; even the enlightened mind of Jeffrey cannot shake off the illusion that myrtles flourish at Craig Crook. In vain I have represented to him that they are of the genus *Carduus*, and pointed out their prickly peculiarities. In vain I have reminded him that I have seen hackney-coaches drawn by four horses in the winter, on account of the snow; that I had rescued a man blown flat against my door by the violence of the winds, and black in the face; that even the experienced Scotch fowls did not venture to cross the streets, but sidled along, tails aloft, without venturing to encounter the gale. Jeffrey sticks to his myrtle illusions, and treats my attacks with as much contempt as if I had been a wild visionary, who had never breathed his caller air, nor lived and suffered under the rigour of his climate, nor spent five years in discussing metaphysics and medicine in that garret of the earth – that knuckle-end of England – that land of Calvin, oat-cakes, and sulphur.'

In sending two brace of grouse to a friend, Sydney described them as 'curious, because killed by a Scotch metaphysician; in other and better language, they are mere ideas, shot by other ideas, out of a pure intellectual notion, called a gun'. Another national characteristic was duly noted: 'The most delicate and sensitive turpitude is always to be met with in Scotland: there are twenty people in Edinburgh whose manners and conduct are more perfect exponents of the King's health than the signatures of his physicians.' As for their theology, it was quite beyond him:

'It is in vain that I study the subject of the Scotch Church. I have heard it ten times over from Murray, and twenty times from Jeffrey, and I have not the smallest conception what it is about. I know it has something to do with oatmeal, but beyond that I am in utter darkness.'

But though he often poked fun at the Scots and their 'energetic and infragrant' capital, Sydney loved the place and the people and made many life-long friends among them, to one of whom he wrote: 'Never shall I forget the happy days I passed there, amidst odious smells, barbarous sounds, bad suppers, excellent hearts, and most enlightened and cultivated understandings!'

Not long after his arrival he was invited to preach in Charlotte Chapel, Rose Street, and he reported his first appearance in the pulpit to Mr. Hicks-Beach: 'I have the pleasure of seeing my audience nod approbation while they sleep.' But his efforts soon attracted the more alert minds of Edinburgh. Among others Dugald Stewart came to hear him and declared that his 'original and unexpected ideas gave me a thrilling sensation of sublimity never before awakened by any other oratory'. Two serious young men, Francis Horner and Lord Webb Seymour, after studying the works of Bacon for five hours, proceeded to Charlotte Chapel and heard Sydney preach 'a most admirable sermon on the true religion of practical justice and benevolence, as distinguished from ceremonial devotion, from fanaticism and from theology'. Another young man, Henry (afterwards Lord) Cockburn, was so much struck by the manner and matter of Sydney's address that, fifty years later, he could say:

> 'The best calm sermon I have heard was one preached in Edinburgh by Sydney Smith. It was a defence, upon grounds of mere reason and expediency, of the institution of death; the particular object being to show that the present brevity of life was best suited to the other circumstances of our condition. He held the MS. in his hand and read it exactly as an ordinary reader holds and reads from a printed book; but the thoughts had been so well considered, the composition was so proper, and the reading so quiet and impressive, that I doubt if there were a dozen dry eyes or unpalpitating hearts in the church; and every sentiment, and many of the expressions, and the whole scope and pathos of the discourse, are still fresh upon my mind at the distance of many years.'

Half a dozen of these sermons were published and dedicated to Lord Webb Seymour in these words: 'I know no man who, in spite of the disadvantages of high birth, lives to more honourable and commendable purposes than yourself.' In the course of the preface Sydney had a few words to say on the pulpit style of his fellow-preachers:

> 'Is it wonder that every semi-delirious sectary, who pours forth his animated nonsense with the genuine look and voice of passion, should gesticulate away the congregation of the most profound and learned divine of the Established Church, and in two Sundays preach him bare to the very sexton? Why are we natural everywhere but in the pulpit? No man expresses warm and animated feelings anywhere else with his mouth alone, but with his whole body; he articulates with every limb, and talks from head to foot with a thousand voices. Why this holoplexia on sacred occasions only? Why call in the aid of paralysis to piety? Is it a rule of oratory to balance the style against the subject, and to handle the most sublime truths in the dullest language and the driest manner? Is sin to be taken from men, as Eve was from Adam, by casting them into a deep slumber? Or from what possible perversion of common sense are we to look like field-preachers in Zembla, holy lumps of ice, numbed into quiescence and stagnation and mumbling?'

The general tendency of his sermons was what would then have been called subversive. In other words, he was on the side of humanity against its oppressors. He loved truth better than he loved Dundas, then the Tory tyrant of Scotland. He favoured some of the ideals (but scarcely one of the actions) of the French Revolution; he hated cruelty and injustice; and he resolutely refused, now and hereafter, to flatter authority in order to secure preferment. 'As long as God gives me life and strength,' he said, 'I will never cease to attack, in the way of my profession and to the best of my abilities, any system of principles injurious to the public happiness, whether they be sanctioned by the voice of the many, or whether they be not; and may the same God take that unworthy life away, whenever I shrink from the contempt and misrepresentation to which my duty shall call me to submit.' His remaining years witnessed to the sincerity of that challenge.

Meanwhile he was giving a good account of his tutorship. On June 30, 1798, he reported:

'Our beginning has been very auspicious; as far as we have hitherto gone, I am extremely pleased and satisfied with Michael. My first serious conversation with him was upon the subject of his toilette and the very great portion of time he daily consumed in adorning himself. This Michael took in high anger and was extremely sulky – and upon my renewing the conversation some time after, he was still more so. Without the smallest appearance of anger or vexation on my part, I turned his sulkiness into ridicule and completely laughed him into good humour. He acknowledged it was very foolish and unmanly to be sulky about anything, promised that he would hear any future remarks of mine upon his conduct with cheerfulness, and that he would endeavour to dress himself as quickly as he could, and to these promises he has certainly conformed himself. . . .

'Very soon after our arrival here, I checked his propensity of getting to bed so very early – he has since then generally sat up till between 10 and 11, and got up most mornings at about 6. The great apprehension I entertained of Michael was that he would hear everything I said to him with a kind of torpid silence, and that I should never be able to learn whether he acquiesced voluntarily or from compulsion in my proposals, or get him by any means to state candidly his objections and prefer openly and ingenuously his observations. From an entire ignorance of his opinions and disposition I should then have always been working in the dark. This difficulty, however, upon a better acquaintance with him has vanished; he talks over a subject boldly with me, and makes his objections like a man. . . . He very honestly confesses his love of horses and hounds and his dislike of study, but expresses his great willingness to fag as well as he can, and allows I have not been too hard upon him. In adjusting the time of study, my object was to occupy him fairly, without exciting his disgust. I think I have succeeded.'

Two months later he wrote:

'Michael takes a lesson in dancing every day. I get him now and then to shew me a step or two. I cannot bear the repetition of this spectacle every day, as it never fails to throw me into a fit of laughing little short of suffocation in which Michael joins and so ends the exhibition.'

Later he was forced to admit that Michael's progress in Latin was disappointing in comparison with his progress in music and dancing, but solaced the lad's anxious mother with: 'Talents are not to be measured by our progress in studies which we engage in contrary to, but by those which we undertake *with* our inclination.' He added that the place was growing upon them both, that they were very comfortably situated, and had thoughts of never leaving it. But by the next post he had another tale to tell.

Their landlady had been extremely civil throughout the summer months when lodgings were cheap and plentiful. With the approach of winter, however, the town became crowded and Sydney was told that unless he paid twelve guineas a month instead of nine he would have to leave. He objected, and the landlady displayed an unsuspected side of her character, calling him 'a Levite, a scourge of human nature and an extortioner', and giving him notice to go out instantly 'bag and baggage, without beat of drums or colours flying'. Sydney refused to stir. A battle of tongues ensued, in the course of which he threatened to carry the case 'through all the Courts of Justice in England, and from thence to Russia'. The threat impressed her; she began to climb down, admitting that she was apt to grow a little warm upon occasion, and was soon referring to his great kindness and generosity. Sydney took advantage of these cooler moments, made her sign an agreement in the presence of two witnesses, and was left in command on his carpet. Still, the atmosphere was not altogether harmonious and in the autumn of 1799 they moved to 19, Ann Street.

By now they were on excellent terms with one another, Sydney having completely won the confidence of Michael by laughing him out of love with the first lady who took his fancy and by seeing him safely through a drunken debauch. To prove his gratitude for these and many other good turns,

Michael freely criticised Sydney's sermons and behaved towards him invariably as one man to another. When Michael left for Oxford, his parents asked Sydney to remain in Edinburgh as tutor to their second son. At the same time he managed to obtain another pupil, and as he received £400 a year for each of them – 'the arbitrary value which I set upon the sacrifice of my own comfort' – the turn of the century saw him relatively prosperous.

It also saw him married. For many years he had been engaged to a friend of his sister, Catherine Pybus, and the moment he felt that he could decently support a wife he took the plunge. With the full consent of Catherine's mother (her father being dead) and the violent opposition of her brother (who objected equally to Sydney's poor prospects and political opinions) they were married in the parish church of Cheam, Surrey, on July 2, 1800. Sydney, being an honest churchman, perceived that one of his marriage vows could be accomplished on the spot, and he endowed his wife with all his worldly goods by flinging his entire fortune into her lap. It consisted of 'six small silver teaspoons, which from much wear had become the ghosts of their former selves'. Fortunately, his wife brought him a modest dowry, with, as immediate capital, a pearl necklace, which was quickly exchanged for £500, and they were able to buy the necessary plate, linen, etc., for the house Sydney had taken in Edinburgh – 46, George Street. Mr. Hicks-Beach, grateful for Sydney's beneficent influence over Michael, sent a cheque for £750, and altogether they had very little to complain about. They were a well-paired and happy couple, and remained so for forty-five years, until death divorced them.

In addition to the three men whose connection with Sydney's famous periodical the *Edinburgh Review* claims special treatment for them in the next chapter, his friendships with Dr. Thomas Brown, John Archibald Murray and Walter Scott must be mentioned. Thirty-three years after he left Edinburgh, he wrote of the first to a friend:

'Thomas Brown was an intimate friend of mine, and used to dine with me regularly every Sunday in Edinburgh. He was a Lake poet, a profound metaphysician and one of the most virtuous men that ever lived. As a metaphysician, Dugald Stewart was a humbug to him. Brown had real talents for the thing. You must recognise, in reading Brown, many of those arguments with which I have so often reduced you to silence in metaphysical discussions. Your discovery of Brown is amusing. Go on ! You will detect Dryden if you persevere, bring to light John Milton, and drag William Shakespeare from his ill-deserved obscurity!'

John Archibald Murray was a very different sort of person. Though not one of the original projectors of the *Edinburgh Review*, he acted in a semi-editorial capacity for the first few numbers with Jeffrey, Horner, Brougham and Smith, became a frequent contributor, and could always be relied on to take the editor's place during Jeffrey's occasional absences. His early career at the Bar was distinguished, but having private means he relaxed his efforts, and being of an easy-going disposition he made no attempt to fulfil the promise of his youth. He took part in the agitation for the Reform Bill and represented Leith in the House of Commons, succeeding Jeffrey as Lord Advocate. He introduced a number of Bills in the Commons, but soon wearied of political life, abandoned it, was knighted, and took his seat on the bench as Lord Murray. His hospitality was profuse and he was never so happy as when surrounded by his friends. Sydney quickly recognised a kindred spirit in him and they kept up a lively correspondence to the end of their days. He was constantly sending presents of game to his friends, and Sydney once assured him that 'even the rumour of grouse is agreeable'. Loving ease and comfort, no one was less in need of Sydney's advice: 'Why bore yourself with any profession if you are rich enough to do without it?' And at a period that was far too late in his life for advice on diet to be of much service to him, Sydney wrote:

'If you wish for anything like happiness in the fifth act of life, eat and drink about one half what you *could* eat and drink. Did I ever tell you my calculation about eating and

> drinking? Having ascertained the weight of what I could live upon, so as to preserve health and strength, and what I did live upon, I found that, between ten and seventy years of age, I had eaten and drunk forty four-horse wagon-loads of meat and drink more than would have preserved me in life and health! The value of this mass of nourishment I considered to be worth seven thousand pounds sterling. It occurred to me that I must, by my voracity, have starved to death fully a hundred persons. This is a frightful calculation, but irresistibly true; and I think, dear Murray, your wagons would require an additional horse each!'

Though their political views were strongly opposed, Walter Scott loved Sydney from the moment Jeffrey brought them together, and never tired of singing his praises as a wit, a writer and the most clubbable of men. In return, Sydney liked Scott as a man and admired him as a writer, but could not help laughing at his love of distinctions and his little snobberies. When, for example, Scott was making a laboured attempt to establish a pedigree, Sydney gravely referred to his own: 'My grandfather disappeared about the time of the assizes, and – we asked no questions.' He was a generous but discriminating critic of Scott's novels when they began to appear. Writing in 1819 to thank Constable for *The Bride of Lammermoor*, he spoke of it as 'the last novel of Walter Scott. It would be profanation to call him Mr. Walter Scott. I should as soon say Mr. Shakespeare or Mr. Fielding. . . . When I get hold of one of these novels, turnips, sermons and justice-business are all forgotten.' When *Ivanhoe* was published, Sydney wrote: 'I am sure he has five or six more such novels in him, therefore five or six holidays for the whole kingdom.' But when *The Monastery* followed within a few months, he said: 'I recommend one novel every year and more pains.' *The Pirate* drew this from him: 'All human themes have an end (except taxation), but I shall heartily regret my annual amusement if I am about to lose it.' And he advised: 'No more Meg Merrilies and Dominie Sampson – very good the first and second times, but now quite worn out, and always recurring. . . . One other such novel and there's an end; but who can last for ever? who ever lasted so long?' *Peveril of the Peak* was also not up to the mark, but 'his worst are better than what are called the successful productions of other persons'. *The Abbot* was 'far above common novels, but of very inferior execution to his others. . . . Meg Merrilies appears afresh in every novel'. *Kenilworth* and *The Fortunes of Nigel* he placed among Scott's happier efforts.

It was largely due to Sydney's presence in Edinburgh that Scott and a few others started the Friday Club. It was founded on the model of Johnson's Club and the members met for dinner (at £2 a head) every Friday in Fortune's Tavern. Among the original members were Professors Dugald Stewart and John Playfair, Sydney Smith, Walter Scott, John Archibald Murray, Henry Cockburn, Thomas Campbell, Francis Jeffrey, Francis Horner and Henry Brougham. The Club severely discouraged strangers, with the single exception of old James Watt, who was always welcome when visiting Edinburgh. Until his departure for London, Sydney was the predominant personality, and once at least he was the ringleader in an affair that might have distressed his graver clerical brethren had it been made public.

An apothecary named Gardiner had a shop in the house immediately to the east of the Assembly Rooms in George Street. Over the door was a head of the Greek doctor, Galen, which certain members of the Club had long itched to possess. But its position was elevated and seemingly well secured. One evening the character of Galen was discussed at the Club, and after the wine had been thoughtfully circulated several of the disputants raised the subject of his personal appearance. From that to the head over the apothecary's shop was an easy and natural step. The hours slipped by, the wine went to and fro, the less adventurous spirits stumbled off to bed, and four men were eventually left round the bottle to settle the question. They were: John Playfair (a professor, aged 56), Thomas Thompson (the Deputy Clerk Register and Clerk of Sessions, aged 36), Sydney Smith (a clergyman, aged 31), and Henry Brougham (a barrister, aged 24).

When the wine was finished, it almost seemed as if the meeting would close without coming to a decision. But Brougham was equal to the occasion. He made his famous punch mixture, a somewhat dangerous beverage of rum, sugar, lemons, marmalade, calves-foot jelly, water, and more rum. This had the desired effect. The professor, the Clerk of Sessions, the clergyman and the barrister sallied forth, and eventually found themselves at the apothecary's shop; or rather three of them found themselves there, the fourth, Brougham, having apparently got lost on the way. It was a formidable business which would have alarmed a band of sober professional burglars; but they were amateurs and their sobriety was questionable. The clergyman was hoisted on to the railings and was held in position by the professor, while the Clerk of Sessions valiantly attempted to mount the clergyman's back. These arduous and ticklish proceedings took some time, because the Clerk of Sessions, who was in constant danger of being impaled, objected to the casual advice which was being proffered him by the professor, who was swaying safely on the pavement.

In the midst of an animated discussion, the lights of the watch were descried some distance down the street; the Clerk of Sessions descended to earth with an agility which, exercised earlier, would have achieved the bust; the parson followed; the professor was already round the corner; and a few moments later Galen's head faced the watchmen alone. With the newcomers was a gentleman named Brougham, who had first egged his friends on, then given them the slip, and now played this trick upon them. Already he was marked out for success in politics.

CHAPTER III

A STORMY NIGHT

ONE stormy night in March, 1802, three men sat in a front room on the third floor of No. 18, Buccleuch Place, Edinburgh. Their names were: Francis Jeffrey, Henry Brougham and Sydney Smith. While the windows rattled and the doors shook and the wind roared in the chimney, they talked without pause, sometimes shouting when the gale outside made it necessary, and often laughing at the jokes of the parson, none more heartily than the parson himself. No one could have imagined from their frequent bursts of merriment that this meeting would mark an epoch, and that its outcome would revolutionise the minds of men and change the course of English history. Yet such was the case.

Consider the state of England at that time. The Catholics had not been emancipated; the Corporation and Test Acts had not been repealed; the Game Laws were horribly oppressive; man-traps and spring-guns were set all over the country; prisoners tried for their lives could have no counsel; Lord Eldon and the Court of Chancery were the scourge of the nation; libel was punished by the most brutal and vindictive imprisonments; the laws of debt and of conspiracy were on a barbarous footing; the Slave Trade was tolerated; Parliament stood for the interests of individual landowners while large sections of the public were unrepresented. All these and a thousand other evils were exposed by the *Edinburgh Review* and eventually righted by the political party to which it gave a conscience and a policy.

Sydney was the hero of that momentous and tempestuous

evening in March, 1802. The *Edinburgh Review* was his 'bold and sagacious idea'. Brougham was impressed, Jeffrey was despondent. Already Sydney had talked it over with Francis Horner and gained his support, but Jeffrey prophesied failure and odium. This started Sydney off. There would be no lack of contributors, he said. Was there anything Jeffrey himself did not know about literature? Here was Brougham, bursting with mathematical knowledge and a mine of information concerning the colonies. Could anyone give Horner points on political economy? Murray knew something about everything. Playfair, Stewart, Brown, Thompson, could all be relied on for occasional contributions. As for Sydney himself, he would write any number of articles on any number of subjects, and was quite ready to edit the whole. The success of the venture was already assured. They would raise a far greater storm in the world than the one that was raging outside at that moment. Sydney's enthusiasm was infectious and at last Jeffrey was talked over.

All the same there was some excuse for Jeffrey's pessimism. It was a daring and dangerous experiment. At that time it frequently spelt ruin for a man to be known to hold liberal opinions. He could not hope to rise in his profession; he was ridiculed by time-servers, hated by sycophants, and shunned by society. If he so much as hinted that the Catholics should be allowed to sit in Parliament, if he breathed a syllable against the senseless bigotry of the King, or suggested that the Slave Trade was iniquitous, he was assailed with all the Billingsgate of the French Revolution – Jacobin, Atheist, Incendiary, Regicide. Not a murmur against any abuse was permitted; to raise your voice against the monstrous punishments of the Game Laws, or against any injustice inflicted upon the poor by the rich, was enough to wreck your career and stamp you as blasphemous and seditious.

In addition to the storm of hatred and abuse which Jeffrey feared and foretold, there was also the taint of that particular trade. Professional journalism was not considered a decent occupation for a gentleman. Journalists were regarded as an inferior species and either avoided or insulted. It is difficult in these days to realise that only a century ago a Lord Chancellor scandalised his friends by inviting the editor of *The Times* to dinner. No one who had written for the press could be called to the Bar. A journalist was alternately a thing of nought and a danger to the community; in either case he was a low, mean, vulgar fellow, a hireling and a cad.

To allay Jeffrey's natural timidity, to secure their immunity from social stigma, and possibly because he revelled boyishly in an atmosphere of conspiracy, Sydney insisted that their incognito must at all costs be preserved. It was to be a 'hush-hush' enterprise. The subject could on no account be discussed in the street. They would have to meet in a dark room in a dark alley, where they would arrive singly, at different times, by different lanes, through back approaches, via circuitous routes. In fact, as the event proved, it was all conducted in such a mysterious manner that the chief conspirators instantly became marked men for life.

Their 'dark divans' were held at Willison's office in Craig's Close. Jeffrey's timidity and conviction of failure, his constant prophecies of professional ruin and social degradation, retarded publication of the first number until October; and if it had not been for Sydney's conviction of success, his assurance, light-heartedness, efficiency, good-nature, and complete personal ascendancy in the councils of the conspirators, there cannot be the least doubt that Constable, the publisher, who had been guaranteed four numbers as an experiment, would never have received the first.

Without being officially appointed as editor, Sydney took on the job for the first two numbers and revised all the articles, writing a good many himself. One of his slight revisions cost the *Review* a contributor, the redoubtable Dr. Thomas Brown, who strongly objected to being edited. Brougham, who at first supported Sydney's idea with enthusiasm, became troublesome and declined, in a pet, to have anything further to do with it. It seems that his contributions were too long, too political and too many. Sydney hinted that some should be cut, others altered and several omitted. Brougham became violent; Sydney remained firm; there were scenes, reconciliations, fiery assertions, compromises. At length Brougham, finding he could not get his own way, withdrew. But he returned the moment the first number met with resounding success. Sydney, always reasonable, welcomed him back and together they settled down to the pleasant pursuit of author-baiting. With the primary object of shocking a famous authoress, Sydney recalled an evening of their collaboration:

'We *were* savage,' he told Harriet Martineau many years later: 'I remember how Brougham and I sat trying one night how we could exasperate our cruelty to the utmost. We had got hold of a poor nervous little vegetarian, who had put out a poor silly little book; and when we had done our review of it, we sat trying to find one more chink, one more crevice, through which we might drop one more drop of verjuice, to eat into his bones.'

They certainly enjoyed themselves. 'We take it for granted that Mr. Ritson supposes Providence to have had some share in producing him', wrote Brougham – 'though for what inscrutable purposes we profess ourselves unable to conjecture', added Sydney.

Let us pause for a while to consider the character of Sydney's remarkable collaborator. Henry Brougham was born in Edinburgh in the year 1778. Though claiming to be descended from two noble families, his pedigree cannot be traced with certainty beyond a Cumberland gentleman who bought a Westmorland property in the seventeenth century. Henry was sent to the High School at Edinburgh at the age of seven, where he did well, and entered the University in 1792. Here he distinguished himself in the debating societies, studied mathematics and physics, read law, and indulged in such riotous sports as twisting knockers off the doors of law-abiding citizens. His vacations were spent in walking-tours at home and abroad. Having passed advocate on June 1, 1800, he went the southern circuit, acted as counsel for poor prisoners for the sake of practice, behaved in a boisterous and eccentric fashion, and tormented the judge of assize. Being admitted a member of Lincoln's Inn, he settled in London in 1805, read English law, and lived on the articles he wrote for the *Edinburgh Review*. His versatility as a reviewer was amazing; he could write on any subject at any length, and was actually responsible for eighty articles in the first twenty numbers.

He entered Parliament in 1810 and became a figure of note by repeatedly attacking Slavery. He made his reputation as an advocate with his defence of Leigh Hunt and his brother, and as a politician with his vigorous attack on Castlereagh, who was forced as a consequence to withdraw the 'Orders in Council'. He quickly became very popular with the commercial classes, and his prestige in the country at large was assured when he took the side of the Princess of Wales against her husband, the Regent. As Queen she appointed Brougham her attorney-general. There is no doubt that he could have prevented the scandal of the Queen's trial by making known to her Lord Liverpool's offer of £50,000 a year if she would live abroad; but he saw a splendid opportunity of enhancing his reputation, withheld the information and was rewarded. His speech for the defence lasted two days and the peroration, which he had written over carefully seven times, made a sensation. As a result of the trial his popularity went beyond all bounds, and the 'Brougham's Head' became a common tavern sign throughout the country.

When the Whigs came to power in 1830 he was made Lord Chancellor, in which office he brought about considerable improvements in the Court of Chancery, the abolition of the Court of Delegates, the substitution for it of the Judicial Committee of the Privy Council, and the institution of the Central Criminal Court. He was also responsible for the present system of County Courts.

His public activities were endless. He organised the Society for the Diffusion of Useful Knowledge, which published cheap editions of educational works. He considered that the upper classes required scientific training, and he founded the London University. He forced Parliament to vote grants and developed a system of national education. He played a leading part in the Reform Bill crisis and was foremost among those who fought for the abolition of slavery and the emancipation of the Catholics. There was, in fact, a period in his life, after the passage of the Reform Bill, when he had reached a point of popularity unapproached by any man of his age except the Duke of Wellington, and when he was the greatest personal force in the history of English politics, Gladstone alone excepted.

Against this coloured background of virtuous achievement, we must set the man as seen by his friends and colleagues. He was a megalomaniac, being firmly convinced that there was nothing he could not do better than anyone else; he could write better than any author, criticise better than any reviewer, speak better than any orator, sum up evidence better than any judge, understand arithmetic better than any mathematician, govern the country better than any Prime Minister, make laws better than any legislator. There was nothing in the wide world he could not do better than it had ever been done, better than it was ever likely to be done. Yet beneath this colossal self-confidence lurked the devil of jealousy. *He* knew he was superior to all men, but no one seemed to agree with him. Why did Jeffrey engage new contributors to the *Edinburgh Review* when he, Brougham, could beat them all at their own subjects? The thought maddened him; he wrote furious letters to the editor; and thereafter Jeffrey kept him in the dark whenever additions were made to the staff. His envy of other men's productions (how dared they write books which he could have written so much better?) made his criticisms unbalanced and contemptuous; and when a young man named Macaulay began his career on the *Review*, gaining golden opinons from readers and colleagues alike, Brougham's rage and envy knew no limits:

he cut the upstart dead when they met, and conceived such a hatred for this new rival that several people, including the object of his wrath, had serious doubts of his sanity.

It was the same in politics. His driving power did much to carry the Reform Bill and his clearance of arrears in the Court of Chancery was regarded as a legal miracle, but he was not satisfied with the praise universally bestowed upon his achievements. He made the most extravagant claims, boasting that he alone was responsible for the successful passage of the Reform Bill, and that he had saved the country from chaos and civil war. He even went so far as to report a long scene between himself (as hero of the crisis), Lord Grey and the King, which was afterwards discovered to be a pure invention. His memory was prodigious and his vitality superhuman. 'If he would stint himself to doing twice as much as two of the most active men in London, it would do very well,' remarked Sydney Smith. His greatest speech was made on the second reading of the Reform Bill, and his love of showmanship was such that, at the conclusion of his well-studied peroration, he lifted up his voice in prayer and fell upon his knees. Throughout his speech he had kept himself going on draughts of mulled port, and as he remained in a kneeling posture his friends assumed that the drink had gone to his head and that he was not in command of his legs. Much to his annoyance, therefore, they picked him up and set him on the woolsack.

Wishing to be Prime Minister he did his utmost to create discord between Lord Grey and the Whigs, and when Lord Melbourne took office he betrayed the confidence of his chief to *The Times*, bringing on himself this severe rebuke from the new Prime Minister:

> 'You domineered too much, you interfered with other departments, you encroached upon the province of the Prime Minister, you worked, as I believe, with the press in a manner unbecoming the dignity of your station, and you formed political views of your own and pursued them by means which were unfair towards your colleagues.'

The King was not sorry to see the last of him, for his levity in court was a public scandal, his social pleasantries shocked the women, his buffoonery and horseplay were scarcely in accord with the dignity of his office, and once, in a moment of inexcusable elation, he had taken the Great Seal with him on a tour of Scotland.

He had a thirst for admiration that no flattery could quench, and so anxious was he to impress others with a sense of his superiority that he could neither talk nor live at ease. Finding himself neglected and partially disgraced in England, he applied for a certificate of naturalisation in France, in order to qualify as a deputy to the National Assembly; but when it was explained to him that as a French citizen he would lose his English citizenship and with it his rank, offices and emoluments, he withdrew the application. Anxious to know what the papers would say about him, he spread a report that he had met his death in a carriage-accident, and was stunned by some of the less laudatory reviews of his career; but when Sir Robert Peel was thrown from his horse and killed, the general grief made Brougham so jealous that he went about saying: 'Let every statesman take care to ride like a sack, that he may die like a demi-god.'

Spiteful, capricious, treacherous, unscrupulous, overbearing, changing with every wind, violently supporting one day what he had violently assailed another, now charming his friends, now attacking them; there can be little wonder that Macaulay thought him a demon and that his arrival during a performance of *The Messiah* was hailed by Sydney Smith with the words: 'Here comes counsel on the other side.' Later, Sydney summed him up more carefully:

> 'His labour for any particular purpose is unwearied, and his activity to promote his ends inexhaustible. He leaves no corner unsearched, no stone unturned, no human being uncoaxed and uncanvassed, or, if needs be, unthreatened and unalarmed. . . . If he had been born in Italy in the fifteenth century, he would have convulsed that country from Venice to Calabria, and gained an immense historical reputation by

scattering war, fraud, misery, stratagem, and spoil, over that fine portion of the world.'

It is difficult to feel sympathy with a man who believed he was not as other men are, and fortunately Brougham did not ask for sympathy. Admiration, the wonder and applause of men – these were his desiderata. His gaunt, ungainly figure, his awkward, ungraceful gestures, his rough, unamiable features, were barriers to the attainment of his heart's desire; but somehow people forgot them when he began to speak; and if it had not been for that restless and unappeasable something in his nature which made him the prey of emotions less gifted men could curb or overcome, he would assuredly have been the greatest figure in English political history.

At the age of ninety, a lonely, disappointed, irritable and bitter old man, he died at Cannes, which he had found a fishing-village and left a fashionable resort. He is chiefly remembered to-day for a curious carriage, specially built for him, which excited much wonder by its unusual shape – 'an old little sort of garden chair' – the forerunner of all 'broughams'.

. . . .

If in the passage of years Sydney Smith thought less and less of Brougham, his affection and admiration for Francis Horner increased with time. No two men could have been more unlike one another. Sydney was always bursting with good spirits, Horner was chiefly concerned about the melioration of his character. Born in 1778 and educated at the High School and University of Edinburgh, Horner determined to go to the Bar and stayed for a while in England in order to rid himself of his broad Scottish accent. Disliking the practice of the Scots Court, he was admitted a student of Lincoln's Inn early in 1802. He made his first appearance at the Bar of the House of Lords in 1804, but was so nervous that he could hardly speak. He became a member of Parliament in 1806 and was called to the English Bar in 1807. Lord Grenville offered him the post of Financial Secretary to the Treasury, but he declined it on the ground that he did not wish to take any political office until he was rich enough to live at ease out of office.

By degrees he made his name as a speaker and was always heard with respect on such subjects as the Slave Trade, the Corn Laws, Catholic Emancipation, and above all economics. He was the first man to make the doctrines of political economy intelligible to the House of Commons. Suddenly, in the summer of 1816, his health failed and he went to Pisa, where he died early the following year. Though his oratorical powers were not great, and his intellect not above the average – his reputation resting almost entirely on his knowledge of bullion, currency and kindred subjects – he had gained a great reputation in the House by his simplicity and uprightness of character, dissimilar in every respect from that of his rival, Brougham, and when the news of his early death was received, Parliament suspended its sittings and voted to his memory a monument in Westminster Abbey.

Soon after his arrival in Edinburgh, Sydney made Horner's acquaintance. Several friends of sound heart but enfeebled understanding had warned Sydney against the young man because of his violent political opinions, and Sydney, rightly interpreting this to mean that he was a person who thought for himself, quickly sought him out. They became warm friends almost at once. There was something very remarkable in Horner's countenance – 'the commandments were written on his face,' said Sydney. It was a grave, handsome face, its chief feature causing Sydney to speak of him as 'the Knight of the Shaggy Eyebrows'. Sydney also told him that there was not a crime he might not commit with impunity, as no judge or jury who saw him would give the smallest degree of credit to any evidence against him; and when Jeffrey was about to introduce a lady to him, Sydney sent a serious warning: 'Let him see her under the influence of your presence, or he will impregnate her. There is a fecundity in his very look; his smiles are seminal.'

Horner's life was spent in self-improvement and thinking a

good deal about mankind. So conscientious was he that he toiled over his articles for the *Edinburgh Review*, correcting and re-correcting them, as if the well-being of the world depended on the result. He would have been shocked by Sydney's careless remark, 'I never read a book before reviewing it; it prejudices a man so,' and not very much amused after realising that it was a joke. One evening Sydney and Lord Dudley pretended to justify the conduct of the English Government in stealing the Danish fleet; they argued with such gravity that Horner got up and left the room in a state of indignation. They threw up the window and with loud peals of laughter implored him to return as they had only been joking. But he went on his way with a set face, and it took them a fortnight of serious behaviour before they were forgiven.

When Horner was ill he was advised by the doctor to give his mind a rest and confine himself to amusing books, but on searching his library it appeared that he had no amusing books, the nearest to any work of that description being *The India Trader's Complete Guide.* Sydney complained that he was 'so extremely serious about the human race that I am forced to compose my face half a street off before I meet him,' and when Sydney proposed as a motto for the *Edinburgh Review* 'We cultivate literature on a little oatmeal', Horner thought it too flippant and suggested a grave motto from Publius Syrus, who no one but himself had read, and this was at last adopted. Yet, in spite of their temperamental disparity, they remained the best of friends, and when they were both living in London Horner spent his happiest hours at Sydney's house, ending one of his letters, in which he declared that old friends were better than new, with the words: 'I cling to Smith.'

Though not remarkably good-tempered, nor particularly lively and agreeable, it was his simplicity and goodness that appealed to Sydney, who wrote of Horner's rapid rise in public esteem:

> 'He verifies an observation I have often made, that the world do not dislike originality, liberality, and independence,

so much as the *insulting arrogance* with which they are almost always accompanied. Now Horner pleases the best judges, and does not offend the worst.'

Horner's untimely death was a severe blow to Sydney, who felt it more keenly than any sorrow he had then experienced, or, with one exception, was ever to experience; and he put on record those aspects of his friend's nature which had so quickly aroused his affection and admiration:

'Having known him well before he had acquired a great London reputation, I never observed that his fame produced the slightest alteration in his deportment: he was as affable to me, and to all his old friends, as when we were debating metaphysics in a garret in Edinburgh. I don't think it was in the power of ermine, or mace, or seals, or lawn, or lace, or any of those emblems and ornaments with which power loves to decorate itself, to have destroyed the simplicity of his character. I believe it would have defied all the corrupting appellations of human vanity: Serene, Honourable, Right Honourable, Sacred, Reverend, Right Reverend, Lord High, Earl, Marquis, Lord Mayor, Your Grace, Your Honour, and every other vocable which folly has invented and idolatry cherished, would all have been lavished on him in vain.'

Speaking also of Horner's kindness, his consideration for others, Sydney made this observation:

'I mention these things because men who do good things are so much more valuable than those who say wise ones; because the order of human excellence is so often inverted, and great talents considered as an excuse for the absence of obscure virtues.'

The third of Sydney's collaborators in his great design of creating an entirely new type of journalism may be described as the Father of Editors, the first of a famous line, Francis Jeffrey. Born in 1773 and educated at the Edinburgh High School, his early years showed little promise of after-fame and were spent in practising composition. In 1791 he went to Queen's College, Oxford, but disliked the place and found his companions uncongenial and dissipated. While there he lost his Scottish accent and acquired in its place an unpleasant semi-English one, a high-keyed, metallic, clipped utterance, that was peculiarly his own. Returning to Edinburgh, he prepared for the Scottish Bar, but, having no standing in society, he was unhappy and lived much alone, practising composition and writing criticisms of his own performances. In those days Dundas controlled the whole system of government and patronage in Scotland; and as Jeffrey had been turned into a Whig by his father's gloomy Toryism, he had no chance of preferment. He was admitted to the Bar in 1794, but was unsuccessful and suffered acute fits of depression. Almost in despair he married on an income of less than £100 a year – and then the *Edinburgh Review* was launched.

Constable, the publisher, was given the first three numbers free; but its success was so great that Sydney determined to put the enterprise on a business footing before he left Edinburgh, and arranged with Constable that the editor should receive £300 a year and contributors ten or twelve guineas a sheet. Brougham admitted that the *Review* owed its success 'to the wise advice which Smith administered to Constable at the conclusion of his short reign as *quasi*-editor'. Its success was equally due to Sydney's wisdom in nominating Jeffrey for the post of editor and influencing him to take it; for Jeffrey soon made it the leading organ of public opinion throughout Great Britain, its independence alone making it both feared and respected. Jeffrey exercised his editorial powers very freely and often came into conflict with his contributors, but his personal charm and tactful manner smoothed over all difficulties and he never lost a friend in his life.

In person he was diminutive, rather under five feet in height. Sydney said he was so small that it was difficult to see him, that he would have been killed during an election had he been more visible, and once wrote to him: 'Magnitude to you must be such an intoxicating idea, that I have no doubt you would rather be gigantic in your errors than immense in no respect whatever.' What Jeffrey lacked in volume he made up for in volubility. Once he had started talking, nothing could stop him. He spoke with great rapidity and argued about everything under the sun. When some politician forgot his speech in the House and had to sit down, Sydney reported the incident to Jeffrey, adding: 'How very much it must surprise you that anybody stops who has begun to speak!' Little wonder that in course of time his throat began to give him trouble – 'So much wine goes down it, so many million words leap over it, how can it rest?' was Sydney's explanation. 'Tell me . . . yes or no, *simpliciter*,' begged Sydney again and again when he wanted a short answer to a straight question.

His cataract of words could, however, be very amusing. He was a wonderful mimic and could alter his voice and face and even give the impression of commanding height when impersonating the leading 'characters' at the Bar or on the Bench. He once kept Thomas and Jane Carlyle in fits of laughter for a whole evening, calling up with the aid of attitude, gesticulation, accent, facial expression, the personalities he had known. There was real genius in the entertainment, for the words, all his own and spontaneously suggested by the histrionic effort of *being* the parts, flowed from him as from the pen of a creative artist. He could assume twenty faces, each quite dissimilar, and speak with twenty voices, each different from the rest. The stage lost another Garrick when Jeffrey took to criticism.

By nature he was too analytical; he found it easier to blame than to praise, to point out what was wrong than what was right. Sydney told him that it would do him a lot of good to be humbled and frightened, and 'if you could be alarmed into the semblance of modesty, you would charm everybody; but remember my joke against you about the moon and the solar system – "Damn the solar system! – bad lights – planets too distant – pestered with comets – feeble contrivance; could make a better with great ease".' Sydney returned to the charge more than once: 'I exhort you to restrain the violent tendency of your nature for analysis and to cultivate synthetical propensities. What's the use of virtue? What's the use of wealth? What's the use of honour? What's a guinea but a damned yellow circle? What's a chamberpot but an infernal hollow sphere? The whole effort of your mind is to destroy. Because others build slightly and eagerly, you employ yourself in kicking down their houses, and contract a sort of aversion for the more honourable, useful and difficult task of building well yourself.' After one of Jeffrey's periodical trouncings of Wordsworth, Sydney wrote: 'Do not such repeated attacks wear in some little degree the shape of persecution?'

But in certain respects Sydney found him too timid: 'Your letter restricts me so on the subject of raillery that I find it impossible to comply with your conditions. . . . The reasons for your extreme prudery I do not understand, nor is it necessary that I should do so.' The explanation of this apparent contradiction in Jeffrey's nature is simple enough: he lacked enthusiasm. It was his job as a critic, he felt, to pull a man's work to pieces, but there was no point in attacking a nation for behaving in a particular sort of way or a sect for believing in a particular sort of thing. The nation and the creed might prove to be right – in any case it was dangerous to attack them and still more dangerous to make fun of them, as Sydney so often did – but the individual whose work you were trouncing was fair game – and, what was more to the purpose, safe game. Also, to denounce a people or a religion signified a burning sense of right and wrong; but to ridicule a poet or a political opponent implied nothing except enjoyment of the sport. Jeffrey was all brain and no belief; and when Sydney Smith, fired with resentment against injustice or filled with contempt at the spectacle of human stupidity, sent in one of his satirical articles in which a race or a faith was held up to scorn, Jeffrey was seriously alarmed. There was perhaps a note of irony in Sydney's remark that he envied his friend 'the good temper with which you attack prejudices that drive me almost to the limits of insanity'.

Though full of liveliness, there was little heartiness about Jeffrey. He never laughed aloud; when amused he sniggered;

but he had such a pleasant, easy manner that no one could help feeling at home with him and liking him. He was popular with the women, especially pretty women, with whom he kept up a sort of mock flirtation; they admired his delicate, attractive, dainty little figure, and they could perceive the tenderness and sensitiveness that lay concealed beneath his urbane manner and sometimes arrogant style of speech. Kind-hearted he certainly was; no author in distress applied to him for money in vain, even when he did not particularly like the applicant's work; and once, an article of his having led to a duel with Moore at Chalk Farm, it was discovered that he had not loaded his pistol. Fortunately the duellists were arrested before they commenced operations, became life-long friends, and not long after Jeffrey offered Moore £500 when the poet was in difficulties.

As a critic of literature, judged by modern standards, he was less satisfactory. He considered that Rogers and Campbell were the only two poets of his day whose work would be immortal, and he cried (not with laughter) over the sentimental passages in the novels of Dickens. Luckily, the influence of the *Edinburgh Review* was felt in other fields than those of literature. Brougham spoke of the vast reforms and improvements in all our institutions, social as well as political, which it had effected; and Sydney wrote to Jeffrey in 1825: 'It must be to you, as I am sure it is to me, a real pleasure to see so many improvements taking place, and so many abuses destroyed – abuses upon which you, with cannon and mortars, and I with sparrow-shot, have been playing for so many years.'

In 1829 Jeffrey was elected Dean of the Faculty of Advocates, being so popular that no one cared to oppose him, and retired from the *Edinburgh Review*. Sydney was constantly urging his friend's claims to recognition on the Whig leaders and when the party came to power in 1830 Jeffrey was made Lord Advocate. He represented Edinburgh in Parliament from 1832 to 1834, but the worry and work of his office oppressed him; he was not a success in the House; he hated living in London; people pestered him to frank their letters ('I am made a mere post office of!' he complained); he became utterly miserable, and gradually his health broke down altogether. In 1834 he accepted a judgeship in the Court of Sessions and took his seat on the Bench as Lord Jeffrey. 'His robes, God knows, will cost him little,' Sydney remarked; 'one buck rabbit will clothe him to the heels.' He died, as cheerfully as possible, in 1850.

Much could be said about him, but all that need be added here is that Sydney loved him and Hazlitt admired him, that Carlyle thought him 'a beautiful little man', and that Macaulay wrote in his diary a comparison between Jeffrey and Sydney Smith which ends with these words: 'In ability I should say that Jeffrey was higher, but Sydney rarer. I would rather have been Jeffrey; but there will be several Jeffreys before there is a Sydney.'

CHAPTER IV

THE BLUE AND BUFF

FOR twenty-five years Sydney Smith wrote articles for the *Edinburgh Review*, and the famous blue and buff cover was seen on bookstalls for a century after he laid down his pen. At this date it may safely be said that of all the articles that appeared in a paper which revolutionised both politics and journalism, those by Sydney are the most modern in tone and incomparably the most amusing. He was perhaps the first to realise that one could only quicken an Englishman's intelligence by tickling his sense of humour; by making his countrymen laugh he made them think. Professor Saintsbury compared him with Voltaire, giving the palm of absolute simplicity to Sydney. There had been no one at all like him in England before, and there has been no one to compare with him since. Some of his peculiar qualities will shortly be indicated. But first let us hear him on the subject of his own contributions. Writing to Jeffrey in 1819 he summed up the matter thus:

'You must consider that Edinburgh is a very grave place, and that you live with Philosophers who are very intolerant of nonsense. I write for the London, not for the Scotch market, and perhaps more people read my nonsense than your sense. The complaint was loud and universal of the extreme dullness and *lengthiness* of the *Edinburgh Review*. Too much, I admit, would not do of my style; but the proportion in which it exists enlivens the *Review* if you appeal to the whole public, and not to the 8 or 10 grave Scotchmen with whom you live. I am a very ignorant, frivolous, half-inch person; but, such as I am, I am sure I have done your *Review* good, and *contributed* to bring it into notice. Such as I am, I shall be, and cannot promise to alter; such is my opinion of the effect of my articles. . . . Almost anybody of the sensible men who write for the *Review* would have written a much wiser and more profound article than I have done upon the Game Laws; but I am quite certain nobody would obtain more readers for his essay upon such a subject and I am equally certain that the principles are right, and that there is no lack of sense in it.

'So I judge myself, but after all the practical appeal is to you. If you think my assistance of no value, I am too just a man to be angry with you upon that account; but while I write, I must write in my own way.'

Now let us see why so many people liked and so many others hated that way of his, and why Sydney speaks to us to-day in a language we can understand better than that of his successors on the *Edinburgh Review*, Carlyle and Macaulay.

In the early years of the nineteenth century there was in England a Society for the Suppression of Vice. It consisted, as all such societies do, of busybodies, of men and women who felt that the poorer classes were getting out of hand, possibly as a result of the French Revolution. Sydney instantly perceived the class feeling that was at the back of the Society's activities and saw the harm of such an association: 'We have no doubt but that the immediate effect of a voluntary combination for the suppression of vice, is an involuntary combination in favour of the vices to be suppressed.' It was obvious, too, that 'the fear of God can never be taught by constables, nor the pleasures of religion be learnt from a common informer'. Besides, such a Society would have to justify its existence: 'Men, whose trade is rat-catching, love to catch rats; the bug-destroyer seizes on his bug with delight; and the suppressor is gratified by finding his vice.' Nevertheless, if the object of the Society had been to stamp out the vice of cruelty irrespective of class, there would have been some reason for its existence. Sydney described the situation with care:

> 'Of cruelty to animals, let the reader take the following specimens: Running an iron hook in the intestines of an animal; presenting this first animal to another as his food; and then pulling this second creature up and suspending him by the barb in his stomach. Riding a horse till he drops, in order to see an innocent animal torn to pieces by dogs. Keeping a poor animal upright for many weeks, to communicate a peculiar hardness to his flesh. Making deep incisions into the flesh of another animal while living, in order to make the muscles more firm. Immersing another animal, while living, in hot water.
>
> 'Now we do fairly admit, that such abominable cruelties as these are worthy the interference of the law: and that the Society should have punished them, cannot be matter of surprise to any feeling mind. – But stop, gentle reader! these cruelties are the cruelties of the Suppressing Committee, not of the poor. You must not think of punishing these. – The first of these cruelties passes under the pretty name of *angling*; and therefore there can be no harm in it – the more particularly as the President himself has one of the best preserved trout streams in England. – The next is *hunting*; – and as many of the Vice-Presidents and of the Committee hunt, it is not possible there can be any cruelty in hunting. The next is a process for making *brawn* – a dish never tasted by the poor, and therefore not to be disturbed by indictment. The fourth is the mode of *crimping* cod; and the fifth of boiling lobsters; all high-life cruelties, with which a justice of the peace has no business to meddle. The real thing which calls forth the sympathies, and harrows up the soul, is to see a number of boisterous artisans baiting a bull or a bear; not a savage hare, or a carnivorous stag – but a poor, innocent, timid bear – not pursued by magistrates, and deputy lieutenants, and men of education – but by those who must necessarily seek their relaxation in noise

and tumultuous merriment – by men whose feelings are blunted, and whose understanding is wholly devoid of refinement. . . . A man of ten thousand a year may worry a fox as much as he pleases – may encourage the breed of a mischievous animal on purpose to worry it; and a poor labourer is carried before a magistrate for paying sixpence to see an exhibition of courage between a dog and a bear! Any cruelty may be practised to gorge the stomachs of the rich – none to enliven the holidays of the poor. We venerate those feelings which really protect creatures susceptible of pain, and incapable of complaint. But heaven-born pity nowadays calls for the income tax and the court guide, and ascertains the rank and fortune of the tormentor before she weeps for the pain of the sufferer. . . . The trespass, however, which calls forth all the energies of a suppressor, is the sound of a fiddle. That the common people are really enjoying themselves is now beyond all doubt; and away rush Secretary, President, and Committee, to clap the cotillon into the Compter, and to bring back the life of the poor to its regular standard of decorous gloom. The gambling-houses of St. James's remain untouched. The peer ruins himself and his family with impunity; while the Irish labourer is privately whipped for not making a better use of the excellent moral and religious education which he has received in the days of his youth!'

In short Sydney advised them to 'denominate themselves a Society for suppressing the vices of persons whose income does not exceed £500 per annum'.

It is pleasant to turn from the hypocrisy of vice suppressors to the pagan pleasures of the rich. No one enjoyed good dinners, good company and good service, more than Sydney, who was a born epicurean. This was how he set the scene for one of his articles:

'An excellent and well-arranged dinner is a most pleasing occurrence, and a great triumph of civilised life. It is not only the descending morsel, and the enveloping sauce – but the rank, wealth, wit and beauty which surround the meats – the learned management of light and heat – the silent and rapid services of the attendants – the smiling and sedulous host, proffering gusts and relishes – the exotic bottles – the embossed plate – the pleasant remarks – the handsome dresses – the cunning artifices in fruit and farina! The hour of dinner, in short, includes every thing of sensual and intellectual gratification which a great nation glories in producing.

'In the midst of all this, who knows that the kitchen chimney caught fire half an hour before dinner! – and that a poor little wretch, of six or seven years old, was sent up in the midst of the flames to put it out?'

He then summarised the evidence given before Parliament concerning the chimney-boys, and put the case in favour of roasting small children:

'We come now to burning little chimney-sweepers. A large party are invited to dinner – a great display is to be made – and about half an hour before dinner there is an alarm that the kitchen chimney is on fire! It is impossible to put off the distinguished personages who are expected. It gets very late for the soup and fish, the cook is frantic – all eyes are turned upon the sable consolation of the master chimney-sweeper – and up into the midst of the burning chimney is sent onc of thc miscrable little infants of the brush! There is a positive prohibition of this practice, and an enactment of penalties in one of the acts of Parliament which respect chimney-sweepers. But what matter acts of Parliament, when the pleasures of genteel people are concerned? Or what is a toasted child, compared to the agonies of the mistress of the house with a deranged dinner?'

Having completed the evidence, he explained why the condition of the poor was not really a laughing matter, and noted the existence of a 'set of marvellously weak gentlemen, who discover democracy and revolution in every effort to improve the condition of the lower orders, and to take off a little of the load of misery from those points where it presses the hardest.'

Professor Saintsbury has recorded his opinion that Sydney's essays on Methodism gave far more offence to the religious public of evangelical persuasion than all his jokes on bishops or his arguments for Catholic emancipation; and that, owing to the strong influence which then, as now, Nonconformists possessed in the councils of the Liberal party, these essays prevented the Whig leaders, when they came to power, from giving Sydney the highest ecclesiastical preferment. Sydney certainly frightened his editor by his jocular treatment of Methodists.

> 'I do not understand what you can mean by levity of quotation,' he wrote to Jeffrey; 'I attack these men because they have foolish notions of religion. The more absurd the passage the more necessary it should be displayed – the more urgent the reason for making the attack at all.'

One must remember that, with Sydney, reason and religion were practically synonymous terms, and therefore what appeared to him as unreasonable was irreligious. The Gospel, he said, had no enthusiasm. His attitude was made clear at the outset of his attack. Referring to the Arminian and Calvinistic Methodists and the evangelical clergy of the Church of England, he said:

> 'We shall use the general term of Methodism to designate these three classes of fanatics, not troubling ourselves to point out the finer shades and nicer discriminations of lunacy, but treating them all as in one general conspiracy against common sense, and rational orthodox Christianity.'

He then began simply to quote their own reports of revelations, miraculous conversions, fits, raptures, ecstasies, and what-not; leaving them to parody themselves, which they did very effectively. But it was when he dealt with their Indian Missions that the fun became fast and furious. The headings he gave to the extracts from their accounts were neat and extremely irritating. Beneath the words *Brother Carey's Piety at Sea*, we read:

> 'Brother Carey, while very sea-sick, and leaning over the ship to relieve his stomach from that very oppressive complaint, said his mind was even then filled with consolation in contemplating the wonderful goodness of God.'

Another extract, entitled by Sydney *Effects of Preaching to an Hindoo Congregation*, ran:

> 'I then told them of Christ, his death, his person, his love, his being the surety of sinners, his power to save, etc., and exhorted them earnestly and affectionately to come to him. Effects were various; one man came before I had well done, and wanted to sell stockings to me.'

Underneath the words *Feelings of a Hindoo Boy upon the Eve of Conversion*, we learn that there was a general stir amongst some of the native children, which afforded the missionaries great encouragement, and that one of the boys was overheard to say in prayer:

> 'The Lord Jesus Christ was so good as to die for us poor souls: Lord, keep us all this day! Oh hell! gnashing, and beating, and beating! One hour weeping, another gnashing.'

The following confession was headed by the reviewer *Account of Success in 1802 – Tenth Year of the Mission*:

> 'Wherever we have gone we have uniformly found, that so long as people did not understand the report of our message they appeared to listen; but the moment they understood something of it, they either became indifferent, or began to ridicule.'

Sydney gave dozens of such extracts, but one more will suffice – *A Brahman converted:*

> 'Dec. 11. Lord's Day. A Brahman came from Nuddea. After talking to him about the Gospel, which he said he was very willing to embrace, we sent him to Kristno's. He ate with them without hesitation, but discovered such a thirst for Bengalee rum as gave them a disgust.
>
> 'Dec. 13. This morning the Brahman decamped suddenly.'

Conversion was often attended by inconveniences. One convert was dragged from his house; his hands were tied; his face, eyes and ears were clogged with cow-dung; and in this state he was left for several hours to meditate upon the glories of his new-found faith. Yet the missionaries were able to report that only one thing kept many of the natives from being baptised in the name of Jesus Christ – no barber could be found to shave them.

Sydney came to the conclusion that the Methodists were

> 'quite insane and ungovernable; they would deliberately, piously and conscientiously expose our whole Eastern empire to destruction, for the sake of converting half a dozen Brahmans, who, after stuffing themselves with rum and rice, and borrowing money from the missionaries, would run away and cover the Gospel and its professors with every species of impious ridicule and abuse. . . . Why are we to send out little detachments of maniacs to spread over the fine regions of the world the most unjust and contemptible opinion of the Gospel? The wise and rational part of the Christian ministry find they have enough to do at home to combat with passions unfavourable to human happiness, and to make men act up to their professions. But if a tinker is a devout man, he infallibly sets off for the East.'

Naturally these attacks did not go unanswered. One John Styles came to the rescue of the Methodists; and his *Strictures on Two Critiques in the Edinburgh Review* produced a third and yet more stinging article from Sydney, who, after a passing reference to 'the sacred and silly gentleman before us', quickly warmed to his work. 'Whoever wishes to keep the intervals between churches and lunatic asylums as wide as possible,' he began, are, according to Mr. Styles, 'nothing better than open or concealed enemies of Christianity.' Mr. Styles had complained of his levity in attacking the Methodists, but

> 'it is not the practice with destroyers of vermin to allow the little victims a veto upon the weapons used against them. . . . We are convinced a little laughter will do them more harm than all the arguments in the world. . . . Besides, he should remember the particular sort of ridicule we have used, which is nothing more than accurate quotation from the Methodists themselves. It is true that this is the most severe and cutting ridicule to which we could have had recourse; but whose fault is that?'

As the argument developed Sydney began to generalise: 'Wherever Methodism extends its baneful influence, the character of the English people is constantly changed by it. Boldness and rough honesty are broken down into meanness, prevarication and fraud.' When so foolish a set of men were let loose in India, who could be surprised that 'the natives almost instinctively duck and pelt them'?

Of course, Mr. Styles had arraigned the indolence of the Church of England. To this Sydney retorted:

> 'It is not in human nature that any persons who possess power can be as active as those who are pursuing it. The fair way to state the merit of the two parties is to estimate what the exertions of the lachrymal and suspirious clergy would be if they stepped into the endowments of their competitors. The moment they ceased to be paid by the groan – the instant that Easter offerings no longer depended upon jumping and convulsions – Mr. Styles may assure

himself that the character of his darling preachers would be totally changed; their bodies would become quiet and their minds reasonable.'

Stung to fury, Mr. Styles, a stranger to India, had made an error which his antagonist was not the man to overlook:

'In speaking of the cruelties which their religion entails upon the Hindoos, Mr. Styles is peculiarly severe upon us for not being more shocked at their piercing their limbs with *kimes*. This is rather an unfair mode of alarming his readers with the idea of some unknown instrument. He represents himself as having paid considerable attention to the manners and customs of the Hindoos; and, therefore, the peculiar stress he lays upon this instrument is naturally calculated to produce, in the minds of the humane, a great degree of mysterious terror. A drawing of the *kime* was imperiously called for; and the want of it is a subtle evasion, for which Mr. Styles is fairly accountable. As he has been silent on this subject, it is for us to explain the plan and nature of this terrible and unknown piece of mechanism. A *kime*, then, is neither more nor less than a false print in the *Edinburgh Review* for a *knife*; and from this blunder of the printer has Mr. Styles manufactured this Dædalian instrument of torture, called a *kime*! We were at first nearly persuaded by his arguments against *kimes;* we grew frightened; – we stated to ourselves the horror of not sending missionaries to a nation which used *kimes*; – we were struck with the nice and accurate information of the Tabernacle upon this important subject: – but we looked in the errata, and found Mr. Styles to be always Mr. Styles – always cut off from every hope of mercy, and remaining for ever himself.'

Quite apart from the fact that Methodists were utterly disqualified from the job of converting 'pagans who cut themselves with cruel *kimes*', there was the further question of whether missionary work was advisable at all:

'Let us ask, too, if the Bible is universally diffused in Hindostan, what must be the astonishment of the natives to find that we are forbidden to rob, murder, and steal; we who, in fifty years, have extended our empire from a few acres about Madras, over the whole peninsula, and sixty millions of people, and exemplified in our public conduct every crime of which human nature is capable. What matchless impudence to follow up such practice with such precepts! If we have common prudence, let us keep the gospel at home, and tell them that Machiavelli is our prophet, and the god of the Manicheans our god.'

Fortunately the powers on the spot recognised the danger, and Sydney took a hearty farewell of his evangelical brethren in these words:

'The Board of Control (all Atheists and disciples of Voltaire, of course) are so entirely of our way of thinking, that the most peremptory orders have been issued to send all the missionaries home upon the slightest appearance of disturbance. Those who have sons and brothers in India may now sleep in peace. Upon the transmission of this order, Mr. Styles is said to have destroyed himself with a *kime*.'

Another subject dealt with at some length by Sydney was the convict settlement at Botany Bay. In the light of later history, some of his remarks are amusing. To begin with, he did not believe that the prospect of transportation would prove a deterrent to crime.

'The ancient avocation of picking pockets will certainly not become more discreditable from the knowledge that it may eventually lead to the possession of a farm and a thousand acres on the river Hawkesbury. . . . There is some risk that transportation will be considered as one of the surest roads to honour and wealth; and that no felon will hear a verdict of *not guilty* without considering himself as cut off in the fairest career of prosperity.'

Then there was a serious drawback to peopling a country with convicts; vice was bound to spread, because the felon, immediately he landed, met his brother of the road, the foot-pad of his heart, 'the man whose hand he has often met in the same gentleman's pocket'. As a colony it had the grave disadvantage of distance, and the time would come when it would

> 'of course involve us in many of those just and necessary wars, which deprive Englishmen so rapidly of their comforts, and make England scarcely worth living in. . . . Are we to spend another hundred millions of money in discovering its strength and to humble ourselves again before a fresh set of Washingtons and Franklins?'

Sydney was sceptical as to its natural resources; the country had not been more generously populated simply because the soil was poor:

> 'It is difficult to suppose any other causes powerful enough to resist the impetuous tendency of man to obey that mandate for increase and multiplication, which has certainly been better observed than any other declaration of the Divine Will ever revealed to us.'

Recently there had been a bad Governor: 'It is common, we know, to send a person who is somebody's cousin; but, when a new empire is to be founded, the Treasury *should* send out into some other part of the town, for a man of sense and character.' Still, there were more important things than that: 'A good government is an excellent thing; but it is not the first in the order of human wants. The first want is to subsist; the next to subsist in freedom and comfort; first to live at all, then to live well.'

Some time before the appearance of his article a committee

of the House of Commons had recommended the encouragement of distilleries:

> 'but, as it was merely a measure for the increase of human comforts, it was stuffed into the improvement baskets and forgotten. There has been in all governments a great deal of absurd canting about the consumption of spirits. We believe the best plan is to let people drink what they like and wear what they like, to make no sumptuary laws either for the belly or the back.'

The passage of a century has merely emphasised the value of his warning.

From the convicts of Australia to the gentlemen of England was an easy step for Sydney; and, though he lived among the latter, he was no more afraid of the one than the other. In those days country gentlemen preserved their game with the help of certain mechanical contrivances known as man-traps and spring-guns. The first mangled the poacher, the second killed him. Sydney felt that as 'pointers have always been treated by the legislature with great delicacy and consideration', it was time that poachers should be shown some mercy, though, of course, no one would dream of suggesting that they should receive equal treatment with dogs. Although he knew that 'the rulers who ride the people never think of coaxing and patting till they have worn out the lashes of their whips and broken the rowels of their spurs', still he felt that 'the happiness of the common people, whatever gentlemen may say, ought every now and then to be considered'. So he set to work to teach the gentlemen a lesson in common humanity. Naturally they loathed him for it, and expressed their loathing pretty openly; so he taught them another lesson; in fact, he gave them the benefit of four articles in the *Edinburgh Review*.

Preservers of game had decided, he said, that since

poachers and game could not exist at one and the same time, 'the least worthy of God's creatures must fall – the rustic without a soul – not the Christian partridge, not the immortal pheasant, not the rational woodcock, or the accountable hare'. Then there was the law of trespass. Pointers, of course could trespass with impunity, but they were animals 'faithfully ministerial to the pleasures of the upper classes of society'. Not so the poor.

> 'Is there upon earth,' he cried, 'such a mockery of justice as an act of Parliament, pretending to protect property, sending a poor hedge-breaker to gaol, and specially exempting from its operation the accusing and the judging squire, who, at the tail of the hounds, have that morning, perhaps, ruined as much wheat and seeds as would purchase fuel a whole year for a whole village?'

He warned the gentlemen that their 'cruel laws and childish passion for amusement' were spreading vice and misery among the lower orders of mankind, and that 'the efficient maximum of punishment is not what the legislature chooses to enact but what the great mass of mankind think the maximum ought to be'. He reminded them that 'the greatest curse under heaven (witness Ireland) is a peasantry demoralised by the barbarity and injustice of their rulers'. He jeered at the notion that gentlemen would not live in the country unless they could preserve game:

> 'How absurd it would be to offer to the higher orders the exclusive use of peaches, nectarines and apricots, as the premium of rustication – to put vast quantities of men into prison as apricot eaters, apricot buyers, and apricot sellers – to appoint a regular day for beginning to eat, and another for leaving off – to have a lord of the manor for greengages – and to rage with a penalty of five pounds against the unqualified eater of the gage! And yet the privilege of shooting a set of wild poultry is stated to be the

bonus for the residence of country gentlemen. . . . If gentlemen cannot breathe fresh air without injustice, let them putrefy in Cranborne Alley.'

And finally he pictured England's green and pleasant land under the dominion of the Game Laws:

'There is a sort of horror in thinking of a whole land filled with lurking engines of death – machinations against human life under every green tree – traps and guns in every dusky dell and bosky bourn – the *feræ naturæ*, the lords of manors eyeing their peasantry as so many butts and marks, and panting to hear the click of the trap and to see the flash of the gun. How any human being, educated in liberal knowledge and Christian feeling, can doom to certain destruction a poor wretch, tempted by the sight of animals that naturally appear to him to belong to one person as well as another, we are at a loss to conceive. We cannot imagine how he could live in the same village, and see the widow and orphans of the man whose blood he had shed for a trifle. We consider a person who could do this to be deficient in the very elements of morals – to want that sacred regard to human life which is one of the corner stones of civil society. If he sacrifice the life of man for his mere pleasures, he would do so, if he dared, for the lowest and least of his passions. He may be defended, perhaps, by the abominable injustice of the Game Laws – though we think and hope he is not. But there rests upon his head, and there is marked in his account, the deep and indelible sin of *blood-guiltiness*.'

Sydney, by the way, was under no illusions about the poor; he did not make the mistake of idealising their condition or themselves; and when people talked about their virtuous marriages, the privilege a labourer felt at being able to support his home as husband and father and to lay out his life in the service of wife and children, Sydney quickly destroyed the picture:

'This is viewing life through a Claud Lorraine glass, and decorating it with colours which do not belong to it. A ploughman marries a ploughwoman because she is plump; generally uses her ill; thinks his children an encumbrance; very often flogs them; and, for sentiment, has nothing more nearly approaching to it than the ideas of broiled bacon and mashed potatoes.'

But that was no reason why one should not take their side against oppressive and antiquated laws, to which politicians so often referred when they spoke about 'the wisdom of our ancestors – the usual topic whenever the folly of their descendants is to be defended'. Among other grave injustices he exposed the cruel treatment to which untried prisoners were then subjected. While waiting for their trial and unable to find bail, poor prisoners were made to work on a new invention called the tread-mill.

'Is it no punishment to such a man to walk up hill for six months?' asked Sydney; 'and yet there are gentlemen who suppose that the common people do not consider this as punishment! – that the gayest and most joyous of human beings is a treader, untried by a jury of his countrymen, in the fifth month of lifting up the leg, and striving against the law of gravity, supported by the glorious information which he receives from the turnkey that he has all the time been grinding flour on the other side of the wall! . . . Gentlemen punishers are sometimes apt to forget that the common people have any mental feelings at all, and think, if body and belly are attended to, that persons under a certain income have no right to likes and dislikes.'

When, as frequently happened, the prisoner was found not guilty, he had nothing to recompense him but the memory of several months of undeserved and unprofitable torment: 'The verdict of the jury has pronounced him steady in his morals; the conduct of the justices has made him stiff in his joints.'

Another example of 'folly sanctioned by antiquity' was that prisoners accused of felony were not allowed counsel, which meant that they were unable to procure witnesses to their innocence. When the subject was brought up in the House of Commons someone argued that the practice of employing counsel would be a grave expense to the prisoner. Whereupon Sydney wrote a speech, to be delivered to prisoners in such trying circumstances:

> 'You are going to be hanged to-morrow, it is true, but consider what a sum you have saved! Mr. Scarlett or Mr. Brougham might certainly have presented arguments to the jury, which would have insured your acquittal; but do you forget that gentlemen of their eminence must be recompensed by large fees, and that, if your life had been saved, you would actually have been out of pocket above £20? You will now die with the consciousness of having obeyed the dictates of a wise economy; and with a grateful reverence for the laws of your country, which prevent you from running into such unbounded expense – so let us now go to prayers.'

This barbarous law had remained unrepealed simply because the majority of felons were poor people. 'When a gentleman suffers,' said Sydney, 'public attention is awakened to the evils of laws.' But 'gentlemen are rarely hung. If they were so, there would be petitions without end for counsel'. He appealed to the judges to use their influence on the side of humanity: 'It is surely better to be a day longer on the circuit, than to murder rapidly in ermine.' Alas! judges were but human: 'Some have been selected for flexible politics – some are passionate – some are in a hurry – some are violent churchmen – some resemble ancient females – some have the gout – some are eighty years old – some are blind, deaf, and have lost the power of smelling.' How could poor tongue-tied prisoners expect such judges to protect them?

It was said that no prisoner had ever urged the disadvantage of having no counsel. Sydney replied that when a man was accused of a crime he did not find fault with the established system of jurisprudence, but brought forward facts and arguments to prove his own innocence: 'The fraudulent baker at Constantinople, who is about to be baked to death in his own oven, does not complain of the severity of baking bakers, but promises to use more flour and less fraud.' One exponent of the prevailing system, Sir John Singleton Copley, actually argued that the employment of counsel for prisoners would introduce a most deplorable element of wrangling and bickering between defending and prosecuting counsel, which, where a man's life was in the balance, would seriously detract from the dignity of the occasion.

> 'Can anything be more preposterous than this preference of taste to justice, and of solemnity to truth?' asked Sydney. 'What an eulogium of a trial to say, "I am by no means satisfied that the jury were right in finding the prisoner guilty; but everything was carried on with the utmost decorum! The verdict was wrong; but there was the most perfect propriety and order in the proceedings. The man will be unfairly hanged; but all was genteel!" '

In conclusion Sydney had a suggestion to make:

> 'Howard devoted himself to his country. It was a noble example. Let two gentlemen on the Ministerial side of the House (we only ask for two) commit some crimes, which will render their execution a matter of painful necessity. Let them feel, and report to the House, all the injustice and inconvenience of having neither a copy of the indictment, nor a list of witnesses, nor counsel to defend them. We will venture to say that the evidence of two such persons would do more for the improvement of the criminal law than all the orations of Mr. Lamb or the lucubrations of Beccaria. Such evidence would save time, and bring the

question to an issue. It is a great duty, and ought to be fulfilled – and in ancient Rome would have been fulfilled.'

It is a little difficult to reconcile the writer of the above extracts with the man who strongly recommended solitary confinement in gaols; yet the fact remains that his two articles on *Prisons* stress the necessity of making them as unpleasant as possible. The first article begins:

'There are, in every county in England, large public schools maintained at the expense of the county, for the encouragement of profligacy and vice, and for providing a proper succession of housebreakers, profligates and thieves. They are schools, too, conducted without the smallest degree of partiality or favour; there being no man (however mean his birth or obscure his situation) who may not easily procure admission to them. The moment any young person evinces the slightest propensity for these pursuits, he is provided with food, clothing and lodging, and put to his studies under the most accomplished thieves and cut-throats the county can supply. There is not, to be sure, a formal arrangement of lectures, after the manner of our Universities; but the petty larcenous stripling, being left destitute of every species of employment, and locked up with accomplished villains as idle as himself, listens to their pleasant narrative of successful crimes, and pants for the hour of freedom, that he may begin the same bold and interesting career.'

The second article ends:

'In prisons which are really meant to keep the multitude in order, and to be a terror to evil doers, there must be no sharing of profits – no visiting of friends – no education but religious education – no freedom of diet – no weavers' looms or carpenters' benches. There must be a great deal of solitude; coarse food; a dress of shame; hard, incessant, irksome, eternal labour; a planned and regulated and unrelenting exclusion of happiness and comfort.'

Certainly the discipline in the prisons of those days was extremely lax, and Sydney saw them, relatively speaking, as so many palaces for the poor. This was how he suggested a sentence might be passed:

'Prisoner at the Bar, you are fairly convicted by a jury of your country of having feloniously stolen two pigs, the property of Stephen Muck, farmer. The Court having taken into consideration the frequency and enormity of this offence, and the necessity of restraining it with the utmost severity of punishment, do order and adjudge that you be confined for six months in a house larger, better, better aired, and warmer than your own, in company with 20 or 30 young persons in as good health and spirits as yourself. You need do no work; and you may have anything for breakfast, dinner and supper, you can buy. In passing this sentence, the Court hope that your example will be a warning to others; and that evil-disposed persons will perceive, from your suffering, that the laws of their country are not to be broken with impunity.'

He believed that 'prisons are a mere invitation to the lower classes to wade, through felony and larceny, to better accommodations than they can procure at home', and that 'where the happiness of prisoners is so much consulted, we should be much more apprehensive of a conspiracy to break into, than to break out of, prison'. This should all be altered. A prison must be 'a place of sorrow and wailing, which should be entered with horror, and quitted with earnest resolution never to return to such misery. . . . This great point effected, all other reformation must do the greatest good.' Female prisoners should be under the care of a matron with proper assistants: 'Where this is not the case, the female part of the prison is often a mere brothel for the turnkeys.' Prison

Inspectors would be useless because (1) they would have fat salaries, (2) they would be taken from the retainers of government officials, and (3) they would never put their noses inside a prison. Great attention must be paid to religious instruction, but tracts were worse than useless, as most of them were written on the assumption that thieves were inferior in common sense to children of five:

> 'The story generally is that a labourer with six children has nothing to live upon but mouldy bread and dirty water; yet nothing can exceed his cheerfulness and content – no murmurs – no discontent: of mutton he has scarcely heard – of bacon he never dreams: furfurous bread and the water of the pool constitute his food, establish his felicity, and excite his warmest gratitude. The squire or parson of the parish always happens to be walking by and overhears him praying for the king and the members for the county, and for all in authority; and it generally ends with their offering him a shilling, which this excellent man declares he does not want, and will not accept! These are the pamphlets which Goodies and Noodles are dispersing with unwearied diligence. It would be a great blessing if some genius would arise who had a talent of writing for the poor. He would be of more value than many poets living upon the banks of lakes – or even (though we think highly of ourselves) of greater value than many reviewing men living in the garrets of the north.'

Doubtless Sydney would highly approve of modern prisons, which are largely run along the lines he indicated; but it is possible that if he had been able to feel more sympathy with the works of the Lake poets, of which he was so scornful, he would have had less sympathy with the idea of solitary confinement.

Late in life, when preparing his essays for publication in book form, Sydney was surprised that he had said so little about war.

'I am sorry that I did not, in the execution of my self-created office as a reviewer, take an opportunity . . . to descant a little upon the miseries of war. . . . There is more of misery inflicted upon mankind by one year of war than by all the civil peculations and oppressions of a century. Yet it is a state into which the mass of mankind rush with the greatest avidity, hailing official murderers, in scarlet, gold and cocks' feathers, as the greatest and most glorious of human creatures. It is the business of every wise and good man to set himself against this passion for military glory, which really seems to be the most fruitful source of human misery.'

It is true that he did not give as much attention to the crime of war as he did to the crimes of peace, but whenever the opportunity arose he seized it. Extended quotation from one book was followed by the words:

'We are always glad to bring the scenery of war before the eyes of those men who sit at home with full stomachs and safe bodies, and are always ready with vote and clamour to drive their country into a state of warfare with every nation of the world.'

He resented flippancy on so grave a topic, and once referred to a review by Brougham dealing with the conduct of the war in 1809 as 'not in good taste; he should have put on an air of serious concern, not raillery and ridicule; things are too serious for that. But it is very able. It is long yet vigorous like the penis of a jackass'.

One of Sydney's most celebrated passages occurred in an article on America, wherein he strongly advised that country not to be led into war by a love of glory:

'We can inform Jonathan what are the inevitable consequences of being too fond of glory: – TAXES upon every article which enters into the mouth, or covers the back, or is placed under the foot – taxes upon every thing which it is pleasant to see, hear, feel, smell, or taste – taxes upon warmth, light, and locomotion – taxes on every thing on earth, and the waters under the earth – on every thing that comes from abroad, or is grown at home – taxes on the raw material – taxes on every fresh value that is added to it by the industry of man – taxes on the sauce which pampers man's appetite, and the drug that restores him to health – on the ermine which decorates the judge, and the rope which hangs the criminal – on the poor man's salt and the rich man's spice – on the brass nails of the coffin, and the ribands of the bride – at bed or board, couchant or levant, we must pay. – The schoolboy whips his taxed top – the beardless youth manages his taxed horse, with a taxed bridle, on a taxed road: – and the dying Englishman, pouring his medicine, which has paid 7 per cent, into a spoon that has paid 15 per cent – flings himself back upon his chintz bed, which has paid 22 per cent – and expires in the arms of an apothecary who has paid a licence of a hundred pounds for the privilege of putting him to death. His whole property is then immediately taxed from 2 to 10 per cent. Besides the probate, large fees are demanded for burying him in the chancel; his virtues are handed down to posterity on taxed marble; and he is then gathered to his fathers – to be taxed no more.'

Many years afterwards, he preached a sermon in St. Paul's Cathedral on the accession of Queen Victoria, when he denounced war with a passionate eloquence rare at any time, unique in his.

Sydney seldom reviewed novels and plays. But he wrote enthusiastically and at length about Lister's novel, *Granby*, giving his reasons for thinking it good:

'The main question as to a novel is – did it amuse? were you surprised at dinner coming so soon? did you mistake eleven for ten? and twelve for eleven? were you too late to dress? and did you sit up beyond the usual hour? If a novel produces these effects, it is good; if it does not – story, language, love, scandal itself cannot save it. It is only meant to please; and it must do that or it does nothing. Now *Granby* seems to us to answer this test extremely well; it produces unpunctuality, makes the reader too late for dinner, impatient of contradiction, and inattentive – even if a bishop is making an observation, or a gentleman, lately from the Pyramids or the Upper Cataracts, is let loose upon the drawing-room.'

He had but a single stricture to make on the work: one of the characters struck the hero, which called forth this comment from the reviewer.

'Nobody should suffer his hero to have a black eye, or to be pulled by the nose. The Iliad would never have come down to these times if Agamemnon had given Achilles a box on the ear. We should have trembled for the Aeneid if any Tyrian nobleman had kicked the pious Aeneas in the 4th book. Aeneas may have deserved it; but he could not have founded the Roman Empire after so distressing an accident.'

He was not much impressed by the French works that came his way. Of Madame de Staël's *Delphine* he remarked: 'The morality of all this is the old morality of Farquhar, Vanbrugh and Congreve – that every witty man may transgress the seventh commandment, which was never meant for the protection of husbands who labour under the incapacity of making repartees.' And: 'We may decorate a villain with graces and felicities for nine volumes, and hang him in the last page. This is not teaching virtue, but gilding the gallows, and raising up splendid associations in favour of being hanged.' Elsewhere he spoke of the ritual connected with capital punishment among the Danes, which was so considerable that the common people committed murder to 'enjoy such inestimable advantages, and the government was positively obliged to make hanging dull as well as deadly before it ceased to be an object of popular ambition'.

In another review he called attention to the declamatory habits of Gallic authors, 'beginning, in the true French style, with "*Oh, toi!*", and going on with what might be expected to follow such a beginning'. A Frenchman named J. Fievée had visited England and published a book on its inhabitants. Sydney gave it a terrific trouncing, admitting, however, that it was extremely valuable in one sense: 'The height of knowledge no man has yet scanned, but we have now pretty well fathomed the gulf of ignorance.' Only one of the Frenchman's statements had any real foundation:

> 'Mr. Fievée alleges against the English that they have great pleasure in contemplating the spectacle of men deprived of their reason. And indeed we must have the candour to allow that the hospitality which Mr. Fievée experienced seems to afford some pretext for this assertion.'

Sydney, by the way, was not among those who thought that the English had nothing to learn from the French:

> 'There is nothing which an Englishman enjoys more than the pleasure of sulkiness – of not being forced to hear a word from anybody which may occasion to him the necessity of replying. It is not so much that Mr. Bull disdains to talk, as that Mr. Bull has nothing to say. His forefathers have been out of spirits for six or seven hundred years, and seeing nothing but fog and vapour, he is out of spirits too; and when there is no selling or buying, or no business to settle, he prefers being alone and looking at the fire. If any gentleman were in distress, he would willingly lend a helping hand; but he thinks it no part of neighbourhood to talk to a person because he happens to be near him. In short, with many excellent qualities, it must be

acknowledged that the English are the most disagreeable of all the nations of Europe – more surly and morose, with less disposition to please, to exert themselves for the good of society, to make small sacrifices, and to put themselves out of their way. They are content with Magna Charta and Trial by Jury; and think they are not bound to excel the rest of the world in small behaviour, if they are superior to them in great institutions.'

Reviewing a tragedy in five acts by M. G. Lewis, Sydney had several complaints to make, one of which proves that the drama lost an acute critic when the church gained an ambitious curate:

'Ottilia at last becomes quite furious, from the conviction that Cæsario has been sleeping with a second lady, called Estella; whereas he has really been sleeping with a third lady, called Amelrosa.'

Sydney was extremely fond of travel-books, and dealt with a number of them. The two which provoked his best comments may be mentioned here. His review of a book on Ceylon contained these passages:

'Among the great variety of birds, we were struck with Mr. Percival's account of the honey-bird, into whose body the soul of a common informer appears to have migrated. It makes a loud and shrill noise, to attract the notice of anybody whom it may perceive; and thus inducing him to follow the course it points out, leads him to the tree where the bees have concealed their treasure; after the apiary has been robbed, this feathered scoundrel gleans his reward from the hive.'

'The usual stories are repeated here of the immense size and voracious appetite of a certain species of serpent. The best history of this kind we ever remember to have read was of a serpent killed near one of our settlements in the East Indies; in whose body they found the chaplain of the garrison, all in black, the Rev. Mr. – (somebody or other, whose name we have forgotten), and who, after having been missing for above a week, was discovered in this very inconvenient situation.'

The most amusing essay Sydney ever wrote appeared in the *Edinburgh Review* in 1826. Its subject was a volume entitled *Wanderings in South America*, by Charles Waterton. The writer pictured himself in these extracts more vividly than any contemporary was able to paint him:

'He (Mr. Waterton) appears in early life to have been seized with an unconquerable aversion to Piccadilly, and to that train of meteorological questions and answers which forms the great staple of polite English conversation. . . . He seems to love the forests, the tigers, and the apes – to be rejoiced that he is the only man there; that he has left his species far away: and is at last in the midst of his blessed baboons!'

'Being a *Wourali* poison fancier, Mr. Waterton has recorded several instances of the power of his favourite drug. A sloth poisoned by it went gently to sleep, and died! a large ox, weighing one thousand pounds, was shot with three arrows; the poison took effect in 4 minutes, and in 25 minutes he was dead. The death seems to be very gentle, and resembles more a quiet apoplexy, brought on by hearing a long story, than any other kind of death.'

'Snakes are certainly an annoyance; but the snake, though high-spirited, is not quarrelsome; he considers his fangs to be given for defence, and not for annoyance, and never inflicts a wound but to defend existence. If you tread upon him, he puts you to death for your clumsiness, merely because he does not understand what your clumsiness means; and certainly a snake, who feels fourteen or fifteen stone stamping upon his tail, has little time for reflection, and may be allowed to be poisonous and peevish.

American tigers generally run away – from which several respectable gentlemen in Parliament inferred, in the American war, that American soldiers would run away also!

'The description of the birds is very animated and interesting; but how far does the gentle reader imagine the campanero may be heard, whose size is that of a jay? Perhaps 300 yards. Poor innocent, ignorant reader! unconscious of what Nature has done in the forests of Cayenne, and measuring the force of tropical intonation by the sounds of a Scotch duck! The campanero may be heard three miles! – this single little bird being more powerful than the belfry of a cathedral, ringing for a new dean – just appointed on account of shabby politics, small understanding, and good family! . . .

'It is impossible to contradict a gentleman who has been in the forests of Cayenne; but we are determined, as soon as a campanero is brought to England, to make him toll in a public place, and have the distance measured. The toucan has an enormous bill, makes a noise like a puppy dog, and lays his eggs in hollow trees. How astonishing are the freaks and fancies of nature! To what purpose, we say, is a bird placed in the woods of Cayenne with a bill a yard long, making a noise like a puppy dog, and laying eggs in hollow trees? The toucans, to be sure, might retort, to what purpose were gentlemen in Bond Street created? To what purpose were certain foolish prating Members of Parliament created? – pestering the House of Commons with their ignorance and folly, and impeding the business of the country? There is no end of such questions. So we will not enter into the metaphysics of the toucan.'

'One species of the goatsucker cries, "Who are you? who are you?" Another exclaims, "Work away, work away." A third, "Willy, come go, Willy, come go." A fourth, "Whip-poor-Will, Whip-poor-Will." It is very flattering to us that they should all speak *English*! – though we cannot much commend the elegance of their selections.'

'Just before his third journey, Mr. Waterton takes leave of Sir Joseph Banks, and speaks of him with affectionate regret. "I saw" (says Mr. W.), "with sorrow, that death was going to rob us of him. We talked of stuffing quadrupeds; I agreed that the lips and nose ought to be cut off, and stuffed with wax." This is the way great naturalists take an eternal farewell of each other!'

'The sloth, in its wild state, spends its life in trees, and never leaves them but from force or accident. The eagle to the sky, the mole to the ground, the sloth to the tree; but what is most extraordinary, he lives not *upon* the branches, but *under* them. He moves suspended, rests suspended, sleeps suspended, and passes his life in suspense – like a young clergyman distantly related to a bishop. Strings of ants may be observed, says our good traveller, a mile long, each carrying in its mouth a green leaf the size of a sixpence! he does not say whether this is a loyal procession, like Oak-Apple Day, or for what purpose these leaves are carried; but it appears, while they are carrying the leaves, that three sorts of ant-bears are busy in eating them.'

'Every animal has his enemies. The land tortoise has two enemies – man and the boa constrictor. The natural defence of the land tortoise is to draw himself up in his shell, and to remain quiet. In this state, the tiger, however famished, can do nothing with him, for the shell is too strong for the stroke of his paw. Man, however, takes him home and roasts him – and the boa constrictor swallows him whole, shell and all, and consumes him slowly in the interior, as the Court of Chancery does a great estate.'

'The Yorkshire gentlemen have long been famous for their equestrian skill; but Mr. Waterton is the first among them of whom it could be said that he has a fine hand upon a crocodile.'

'Mr. Waterton, though much given to sentiment, made a Labairi snake bite itself, but no bad consequences ensued – nor would any bad consequences ensue if a court martial were to order a sinful soldier to give himself a thousand lashes. It is barely possible that the snake had some faint idea whom and what he was biting.'

'Insects are the curse of tropical climates. The *bête rouge* lays the foundation of a tremendous ulcer. In a moment you are covered with ticks. Chigoes bury themselves in your flesh, and hatch a large colony of young chigoes in a few hours. They will not live together, but every chigoe sets up a separate ulcer, and has his own private portion of pus. Flies get entry into your mouth, into your eyes, into your nose; you eat flies, drink flies, and breathe flies. Lizards, cockroaches, and snakes, get into the bed; ants eat up the books; scorpions sting you on the foot. Everything bites, stings, or bruises; every second of your existence you are wounded by some piece of animal life that nobody has ever seen before. . . . An insect with eleven legs is swimming in your teacup, a nondescript with nine wings is struggling in the small beer, or a caterpillar with several dozen eyes in his belly is hastening over the bread and butter! All nature is alive, and seems to be gathering all her entomological hosts to eat you up, as you are standing, out of your coat, waistcoat, and breeches. Such are the tropics. All this reconciles us to our dews, fogs, vapours, and drizzle – to our apothecaries rushing about with gargles and tinctures – to our old, British, constitutional coughs, sore throats and swelled faces.'

'We come now to the counterpart of St. George and the Dragon. Every one knows that the large snake of tropical climates throws himself upon his prey, twists the folds of his body round the victim, presses him to death, and then eats him. Mr. Waterton wanted a large snake for the sake of its skin; and it occurred to him that the success of this sort of combat depended upon who began first, and that if he could contrive to fling himself upon the snake, he was just as likely to send the snake to the British Museum, as the snake, if allowed the advantage of prior occupation, was to eat him up. The opportunities which Yorkshire squires have of combating with the boa constrictor are so few, that Mr. Waterton must be allowed to tell his own story in his own manner. . . .

'When the body of the large snake began to smell, the vultures immediately arrived. The king of the vultures first gorged himself, and then retired to a large tree while his subjects consumed the remainder. It does not appear that there was any favouritism. When the king was full, all the mob vultures ate alike; neither could Mr. Waterton perceive that there was any division into Catholic and Protestant vultures, or that the majority of the flock thought it essentially vulturish to exclude one-third of their numbers from the blood and entrails.'

CHAPTER V

HIS SPIRITUAL HOME

DURING his stay in Scotland, Sydney Smith usually spent the summer months out of Edinburgh. He and Michael toured the Highlands and Wales, though their ascent of Skiddaw had put them off any further feats of mountaineering, and they spent several weeks of one holiday season with the Hicks-Beaches at Williamstrip Park, Fairford. Few people can have disliked the country so much as Sydney. 'It is a place with only one post a day. . . . In the country I always fear that creation will expire before tea-time.' Rural interests were not his interests; he regarded 'being kicked up and down Pall Mall as a more reasonable exercise than riding a high-trotting horse'. Shooting was not for him: 'When I take a gun in my hand, I am sure the safest place for a pheasant is just opposite the muzzle.' Though he probably never held a rod in his hand, he admitted that angling was not without merit: 'I give up fly-fishing; it is a light, volatile, dissipated pursuit. But ground-bait, with a good steady float that never bobs without a bite, is an occupation for a bishop, and in no way interferes with sermon-making.' As for the so-called charm of the simple life, 'Whenever I enter a village, straightway I find an ass.'

We are not, therefore, surprised to find him writing to Jeffrey from Gloucestershire:

> 'After a vertigo of one fortnight in London, I am now undergoing that species of hybernation or suspended existence called a pleasant fortnight in the country. I behave myself quietly and decently as becomes a corpse, and hope to regain the rational and immortal part of my composition about the 20th of this month.'

A few weeks later he explained his continued rustication; 'I have been waiting for Mrs. Beach to be delivered of a son, that I may be delivered from the country.'

But now the time had come for Sydney to enter his spiritual home. At the urgent solicitation of his wife, who felt there was no future for him in Scotland, he took his family to London in the summer of 1803. They now had a daughter, who was called Saba (after a king in the 72nd Psalm) on the ground that anyone with the surname of Smith ought to have an uncommon Christian name by way of compensation. Sydney left Edinburgh with a heavy heart; there were to be no more of those marvellous evenings when Jeffrey would argue that black was white, and Brougham would perorate, and Brown would become abstruse, and Stewart would discuss mind and matter, and Playfair would get excited about mathematics, and Scott would tell stories, and Murray would rhapsodise on food and drink, and Horner would talk of the soul, and Sydney himself would make everyone laugh. It was all over now; youth was passing; responsibilities were beginning; life had to be started afresh; a clergyman had to get a living; but he knew that he would be 'like a full-grown tree transplanted – deadly sick at first, with bare and ragged sinews, shorn of many a root'.

They took lodgings at 77 Upper Guildford Street, but in a little time moved to their first London home, No. 8 Doughty Street, Mecklenburgh Square.[1] Francis Horner had preceded them to London, and Sydney was soon the centre of a new circle of friends, which included Sir Samuel Romilly, James Scarlett (afterwards Lord Abinger), Sir James Mackintosh, John Whishaw, Henry Grattan, John William Ward (afterwards Lord Dudley), Samuel Rogers, Henry Luttrell and 'Conversation' Sharp. These, together with Lords Holland and Lansdowne, Richard Porson, Henry Hallam, David Ricardo, John Hoppner and others, belonged to a club

[1] The house is still standing and the tablet on it is the only visible memorial in the streets of London to the greatest of English wits and the most humorous wit in English.

which had been founded in 1798 at a party given by Mackintosh and christened by 'Bobus' Smith 'the King of Clubs'. 'Bobus' had now followed his two other brothers to India, and Sydney took his place in the Club, which met monthly at the Crown and Anchor tavern in the Strand. Later it moved to the Freemason's Tavern, then to Grillion's Hotel in Albemarle Street, and finally to the Clarendon Hotel, where it met for the last time in 1823. It was very exclusive, no stranger being admitted unless recommended by four members, and the membership was confined to thirty persons, all residing in England. Sydney went so far as to suggest, in one case, a further qualification: 'We have admitted a Mr. Baring, importer and writer, into the King of Clubs, upon the express promise that he lends £50 to any member of the Club when applied to. I proposed this amendment to his introduction, which was agreed to without a dissenting voice.' According to some of the guests, the talk was not spontaneous enough; several members were in the habit of preparing their contributions to the discussion, and even polishing up the repartees with which they hoped to dazzle the table. No doubt Sydney was having a dig at his fellow-members when he asked Lady Holland to speak severely to Sir Samuel Romilly about the levity and impropriety of his conversation at the Club, adding: 'Ward and I talk of leaving the Club if a more chaste line of dialogue is not adhered to.' At any rate, the general feeling was that the Club eventually perished from too much wit, from the effort of living up to its conversational standard.

In addition to these meetings of the Club, Sydney and Mackintosh had little gatherings at their own houses every week when Rogers, Horner, Scarlett, Hoppner, Sharp and Sir Thomas Lawrence always made up the party; and the same friends were constantly meeting at Mickleham, Sharp's house near Dorking, Sydney's fondness for this place causing him to be nicknamed 'the Bishop of Mickleham'.

Meanwhile Sydney was not earning enough in his profession to live on, and the family funds were low. His wife had just inherited some jewels from her mother, which she decided to sell. During the negotiations with the jeweller, Sydney expressed serious anxiety 'lest mankind should recover from their illusion and cease to value such glittering baubles before they could be sold'; however, mankind kept its head, and after the sale he was equally uneasy in his mind at having helped to continue the illusion by accepting so large a price for them.

Mrs. Smith had two children during their stay in Doughty Street; the first died almost at once ('children,' said Sydney, 'are horribly insecure: the life of a parent is the life of a gambler'), and the second, Douglas, gave his parents many anxious moments both before and after birth.

> 'I am sure you will be glad to hear of Mrs. Sydney first. I have been expecting that she would be brought to bed every night for the last eight days, but to the amazement of the obstetric world she is still as pregnant as the Trojan horse. I will advertise you of her delivery.'

A day or two after Jeffrey received this letter, the child was born, and Sydney sat up several nights by the bedside expecting every moment would be its last, and spent the daytime in keeping his wife's spirits up. His eldest daughter recalled that all through these years he was the life and soul of the family, behaving more like a wildly happy boy than a clerical parent. He told them stories, romped with them, played with their toys, stuffed them with grapes, and maintained such a level of hilarious merriment that their childhood was passed in happiness and laughter.

In spite of outward appearances, his early years in London were anxious ones. He preached occasionally, but 'the greater part of the congregation thought me mad' and 'the clerk was as pale as death in helping me off with my gown, for fear I should bite him'. Sometimes he and his wife went out to dinner at the houses of the rich, but their arrival in a hackney coach, with straw on the floor, which clung to Mrs. Smith's gown after she had entered the hall, and the grins of the footmen, did not help to make their poverty bearable. When he went alone, he walked all the way through dirty streets, carrying his dress shoes in his pocket and changing into them on arrival. At first the servants stared at such eccentric behaviour, but he made them laugh at something or other, and they got used to him. He never changed his opinions for the sake of social popularity, but spoke his mind freely before any duke or lord who happened to be present, which did not increase his chances of preferment. Also it was known that he had written certain articles in the *Edinburgh Review*, and this made him extremely unpopular with the political party in power, their aristocratic supporters and sycophantic hangers-on. His elder brother 'Bobus' gave him a certain amount of financial help, or his position would quickly have become critical.

At last his luck turned. He met Sir Thomas Bernard, who liked Sydney as well as his opinions, and managed to get him appointed preacher every other Sunday evening at the Foundling Hospital, of which Sir Thomas was Treasurer. For this he received £50 a year. Another friend who owned a chapel then occupied by a sect of Dissenters offered it to him if he could get permission from the vicar of the parish to preach there. But the vicar suspected that Sydney's preaching might draw off part of his own congregation, refused his consent, and the Dissenters remained in possession. It was a severe rebuff, but a little later Sydney became morning preacher at Berkeley Chapel, John Street, Mayfair, which his sermons quickly filled to overflowing, and, on alternate Sundays, at Fitzroy Chapel (now St. Saviour's Church), Fitzroy Square. His popularity as a preacher grew, and he was asked to deliver a sermon in the Temple Church. He chose Toleration as his subject, and made a strong appeal in favour of Catholic Emancipation. Most of the congregation were furious – one of them, Lord Henley, said he deserved the Star Chamber for it – and attempts were made to prevent him from preaching again in Berkeley Chapel. Unintimidated, he published the sermon that had caused so much offence. But long before this he had realised the hopelessness of his position: 'You ask me about my prospects. I think I shall remain long as I am,' he told Jeffrey. 'I have no powerful friends. I belong to no party – I do not cant – I abuse canting everywhere – I am not conciliating – and I have not talents enough to force my way without these laudable and illaudable auxiliaries.'

A living seemed out of the question; yet something had to be done to support his growing family; and being of an intensely hospitable nature he was anxious to take a larger house in a more central position. Already he had chosen one, but to furnish it properly he would require at least £200. Again Sir Thomas Bernard came to the rescue, with a proposal that he should give a series of lectures on Moral Philosophy at the Royal Institution, of which Sir Thomas had been one of the founders and was now the Treasurer. Though Sydney knew very little about Moral Philosophy except what he had learned from Brown and Stewart, he had more than his share of common sense, and for the sake of that £200 would have lectured on anything. It was arranged that he should give twenty lectures for £50.

Very happy at the prospect of making some money at last, Sydney went for long walks in the fields about Primrose Hill, deep in the throes of composition. The first lecture was delivered on Nov. 10th, 1804, and met with such success that he became the talk of the town. The excitement increased with each lecture, and at last the crowds that came to hear him were so considerable that Albemarle Street and the neighbourhood were blocked with carriages, not a seat was to be had for love or money an hour before the lecture was due to commence, the aisles were packed with standing people, and the doors of the hall had to be left open so that listeners in the lobbies could hear the discourse.

Sydney was surprised and delighted with his success, which he described as 'the most successful swindle of the season'. The lectures, he said, had created 'such an uproar as I never remember to have been excited by any other literary imposture'. And he wrote to Jeffrey:

> 'My lectures are just now at such an absurd pitch of celebrity that I must lose a good deal of reputation before the public settles into a just equilibrium respecting them. I am most heartily ashamed of my own fame, because I am conscious I do not deserve it, and that the moment men of sense are provoked by the clamour to look into my claims, it will be at an end.'

Yet there were some good things in his lectures. Sir Robert Peel, then a boy, retained throughout life a vivid recollection of the speaker's manner and matter. Sydney was an impressive elocutionist. He had a rich flexible voice, and could heighten his comic effects and deepen the eloquent passages without the least effect of strain. At one moment the audience was convulsed with laughter, at another hushed with intense interest. A few of the more characteristic passages in his lectures must not be omitted from his biography. One sentence in particular has since been considerably abbreviated and is now (as 'a square peg in a round hole') one of the most famous phrases in the language. This is how it originally came from Sydney:

> 'If you choose to represent the various parts in life by holes upon a table, of different shapes – some circular, some triangular, some square, some oblong – and the persons acting these parts by bits of wood of similar shapes, we shall generally find that the triangular person has got into the square hole, the oblong into the triangular, and a square person has squeezed himself into the round hole. The officer and the office, the doer and the thing done, seldom fit so exactly that we can say they were almost made for each other.'

He had recently been writing about wit in an *Edinburgh Review* article. There he had said that the essence of wit is surprise, and that in all cases of wit there is an apparent incongruity and a real relation. He had given an example: Louis XIV, being continually harassed by the solicitations of a veteran officer for promotion, said one day, loud enough to be heard by the veteran: 'That gentleman is the most troublesome officer I have in my service.' Said the officer: 'That is precisely the charge which your Majesty's enemies bring against me.' Sydney elaborated this view of wit in his lectures, and came to this remarkable conclusion:

> 'It is imagined that wit is a sort of inexplicable visitation, that it comes and goes with the rapidity of lightning, and that it is quite as unattainable as beauty or just proportion. I am so much of a contrary way of thinking, that I am convinced a man might sit down as systematically and as successfully to the study of wit as he might to the study of mathematics: and I would answer for it that by giving up only six hours a day to being witty he should come on prodigiously before midsummer, so that his friends should hardly know him again.'

Turning to humour he said:

> 'As you increase the incongruity, you increase the humour; as you diminish it, you diminish the humour. If a tradesman of a corpulent and respectable appearance, with habiliments somewhat ostentatious, were to slide down gently into the mud, and dedecorate a pea-green coat, I am afraid we should all have the barbarity to laugh. If his hat and wig, like treacherous servants, were to desert their falling master, it certainly would not diminish our propensity to laugh; but if he were to fall into a violent passion, and abuse everybody about him, nobody could possibly resist the incongruity of a pea-green tradesman, very respectable, sitting in the mud, and threatening all the passers-by with the effects of his wrath. Here, every incident heightens the humour of the scene: – the gaiety of his tunic, the general respectability of his appearance, the rills of muddy water which trickle down his cheeks, and the harmless violence of his rage! But if, instead of this, we were to observe a dustman falling into the mud, it would hardly attract any attention, because the opposition of ideas is so trifling, and the incongruity so slight.'

Sydney suffered more than anyone from an illusion common to most Englishmen, the cause of which he explained as follows :—

'There is an association in men's minds between dullness and wisdom, amusement and folly, which has a very powerful influence in decision upon character, and is not overcome without considerable difficulty. The reason is, that the *outward* signs of a dull man and a wise man are the same, and so are the outward signs of a frivolous man and a witty man; and we are not to expect that the majority will be disposed to look to much *more* than the outward sign.'

He described a genius in these words:

'The meaning of an extraordinary man is that he is *eight* men, not one man; that he has as much wit as if he had no sense, and as much sense as if he had no wit; that his conduct is as judicious as if he were the dullest of human beings, and his imagination as brilliant as if he were irretrievably ruined.'

At about that time Sydney was finding his father a little troublesome. The cause of the quarrel is unknown, but at its conclusion he reported to Jeffrey:

'I am at last reconciled to my father. He was very ill, very much out of spirits, and tired to death with the quarrel the moment he discovered I ceased to care a halfpenny about it. I made him a slight apology – just sufficient to save his pride, and have as in duty bound exposed myself for these next 7 or 8 years to all that tyranny, trouble and folly with which I have no manner of doubt at the same age I shall harass my children.'

Possibly, therefore, the following passage from one of his lectures had a slight autobiographical tinge:

'The Scythians always ate their grandfathers; they behaved very respectfully to them for a long time, but as soon as their grandfathers became old and troublesome, and began to tell long stories, they immediately ate them. Nothing could be more improper, and even disrespectful, than dining off such near and venerable relations; yet we could not with any propriety accuse them of bad taste in morals.'

The success of the first series of lectures was so great that galleries had to be erected in the hall of the Institution for the second series, and the lecturer was allowed to name his own terms. He asked for £120 and got it. On the proceeds he took and furnished No. 18 Orchard Street, Portman Square, at which house a son (who died early) and a daughter (Emily) were added to the family. He was now able to extend his hospitality, and every week he gave a supper to about two dozen people, at which there was a great deal of noise and laughter. There was nothing ostentatious about his receptions; he never pretended to be more affluent than he was; the suppers were simple and the company various; he lived up to his maxim: 'Avoid shame, but do not seek glory – nothing so expensive as glory.'

His taste in pictures was peculiar. One day he purchased a number at an auction sale and brought them home in triumph. His wife looked at them and shook her head; his friends looked at them and then looked sadly at him; they were simply a lot of very cheap and badly-executed copies of old masters. Sydney displayed them in different lights; they did not improve. He displayed them at different angles; worse and worse. He descanted on their exceptional merits, pointing out this wonderful effect, that lovely colour, their undoubted antiquity (proved by their mouldy and mildewed appearance), and concluding that, if they were not by old masters, they certainly deserved to be. His friends refused to be convinced or to show the least enthusiasm, and at last, much to his wife's relief, he sent them off to another auction sale, taking the precaution to describe one of them as 'a beautiful landscape by Nicholas de Falda, a pupil of Valdeggio, the only painting of that eminent artist'.

It is perhaps unnecessary to add that the aesthetic sense was not very highly developed in Sydney. He admired prettiness in scenery, but hated anything that looked at all bare or barren. He never expressed his feeling for nature more exactly than in one of his lectures:

> 'The sudden variation from the hill country of Gloucestershire to the Vale of Severn, as observed from Birdlip, or Frowcester Hill, is strikingly sublime. You travel for twenty or five-and-twenty miles over one of the most unfortunate,

> desolate countries under heaven, divided by stone walls, and abandoned to screaming kites and larcenous crows: after travelling really twenty and to appearance ninety miles over this region of stone and sorrow, life begins to be a burden, and you wish to perish. At the very moment when you are taking this melancholy view of human affairs, and hating the postilion, and blaming the horses, there bursts upon your view, with all its towers, forests and streams, the deep and shaded Vale of Severn. Sterility and nakedness are thrown in the background: as far as the eye can reach, all is comfort, opulence, product, and beauty: now it is an ancient city or a fair castle rising out of the forests, and now the beautiful Severn is noticed winding among the cultivated fields, and the cheerful habitations of men. The train of mournful impressions is quite effaced, and you descend rapidly into a vale of plenty, with a heart full of wonder and delight.'

He loved everything that was bright and infinitely preferred gaslight to any masterpiece of painting. He bought pictures merely in order to decorate his rooms, and when they looked too gloomy he brightened them up: 'Look at that sea-piece now; what would you desire more? It is true the moon in the corner was rather dingy when I first bought it; so I had a new moon put in for half a crown, and now I consider it perfect.' He horrified a connoisseur who was expatiating on the glories of a masterpiece. 'Immense breadth of light and shade!' exclaimed the connoisseur. 'Yes,' agreed Sydney, 'about an inch and a half.'

All through these six years of his life in London he kept up a regular correspondence with Jeffrey, giving him the news of the hour, chiefly political, discussing the affairs of the *Edinburgh Review*, and sometimes making those serio-comic remarks of which he was a master and which, hidden in the midst of letters dealing with current topics, must be rescued by his biographer from the mass of less attractive matter that surrounds them. Let us dip into the letters of this period and see Sydney Smith in his habit as he lived, a man who combined wit and humour in such a rare abundance that Shakespeare's Falstaff alone is his superior, and no one is his equal in the English language.

First he had to report that 'it is the universal opinion of all the cleverest men I have met with here that our *Review* is uncommonly well done, and that it is perhaps the first in Europe'. He begged Jeffrey to come and stay with Horner, himself and his family, at Oxford for the long vacation: 'We would settle the fate of nations, and believe ourselves (as all three or four men who live together do) the sole repositories of knowledge, liberality and acuteness.' Again he wrote plaintively: 'When are we to drink copiously of warm rum and water to a late hour in the morning?' A few months later he was informed that some paper had printed an attack on him which he had not yet read:

> 'One of the charges against me, I understand, is that I am ugly; but this is mere falsehood, and a plain proof that the gentleman never can have seen me. I certainly am the best-looking man concerned with the *Review*, and this John Murray has been heard to say behind my back. Pray tell the said John Murray that three ladies, apparently pregnant and much agitated, have been here to inquire his direction, calling him a base, perfidious young man.'

Of a lady to whom he had just been introduced, he wrote:

> 'She is, for a woman, well-informed and very liberal: neither is she at all disagreeable; but the information of very plain women is so inconsiderable that I agree with you in setting no very great store by it. I am no great physiognomist, nor have I much confidence in a science which pretends to discover the inside from the out; but where I have seen fine eyes, a beautiful complexion, grace and symmetry, in women, I have generally thought them amazingly well-informed and extremely philosophical. In contrary instances, seldom or ever. Is there any accounting for this?'

Another lady aroused his enthusiasm:

> 'Tell Murray that I was much struck with the politeness of Miss Markham the day after he went. In carving a partridge I splashed her with gravy from head to foot; and though I saw three distinct brown rills of animal juice trickling down her cheek, she had the complaisance to swear that not a drop had

reached her. Such circumstances are the triumphs of civilised life.'

After his lectures he was able to say:

> 'As for London, whatever be its other demerits, it is at least the best place for an adventurer. In 3 years I have doubled my income. What should I have done if I had been led by the idle love of daisies?'

He complained of the dilatory methods of the publisher of the *Review*:

> 'That sebacic quadruped Constable has omitted to send quarterly tributes of reviews to Horner and me – to me, the original proposer of the *Review*, and to Horner, the frumentarious philosopher! If he is ever guilty of a similar omission, he shall be pulled down from his present exalted eminence to such distress that he shall be compelled to sell indecent prints in the open air in order to gain a livelihood.'

He also complained of the editorial methods of Jeffrey:

> 'I think you have spoilt many of my jokes; but this, I suppose, every writer thinks, whose works you alter; and I am unfortunately, as you know, the vainest and most irritable of human beings.'

Brougham had been sent on a mission to Portugal in 1806, returning in December of that year:

> 'Brougham is just returned from Portugal. It is rumoured that he was laid hold of by the Inquisition, and his buttocks singed with wax tapers, on account of the *Edinburgh Review*. They were at first about to use flambeaux, conceiving him to be you; but upon recurring to the notes they have made of your height, an error was discovered of two feet, and the lesser fires only administered.'

The excitements of London sometimes caused an interval in their correspondence, and one of Sydney's letters began:

> 'I hope you are not angry with me for having so long delayed to write to you. In this pleasing and detestable place I neglect every duty and have no more virtue left in me than hath an antient harlot.'

But there was good news for Jeffrey to make up for the lapse:

> 'You have earned a very high reputation here, and you may eat it out in turbot at great people's houses if you please; tho' I well know you would prefer the quiet society of your old friends.'

Owing to the success of his lectures he was able to help an old Edinburgh friend, Dr. Reeve, whose merits as a physician he pressed upon the committee of the Royal Institution. Then he wrote advising Reeve to accept the offer to lecture, if he received it,

> 'because he must be a very clumsy gentleman if, in lecturing upon the moral and physical nature of man, he cannot take an opportunity of saying that he lives at No. 6 Chancery Lane, and that few people are equal to him in the cure of fevers.'

Another letter of this period, written from Bath, introduces us to the most important friend he made in London:

> 'War, my dear Lady Holland, is natural to women, as well as men – at least with their own sex. A dreadful controversy has broken out in Bath, whether tea is most effectually sweetened by lump or pounded sugar; and the worst passions of the human mind are called into action by the pulverists and the lumpists. I have been pressed by ladies on both sides to speak in favour of their respective theories, at the Royal Institution, which I have promised to do.'

When Sydney first set foot in Holland House he was extremely nervous. The reputation of the place was, at the least, awe-inspiring. Everybody of distinction in the worlds of literature, science, painting and politics, was received there, from the Prince of Wales to the poet of the hour. Sheridan, Fox, Byron, Grey, Lansdowne, Russell, Humphry Davy, Canova, Wilkie, von Humboldt, Washington Irving, Talleyrand, Metternich, Bentham, Romilly, Brougham, Rogers, Luttrell – the list could be extended to include every name of note in that age, though the more violent Tories kept away because the Hollands were Whigs and stood for Progress and the march of mind. Sydney probably owed his introduction to the fact that his brother 'Bobus' had married Lord Holland's aunt. At any rate, he went, saw, was conquered, and eventually, after a period of shyness and fiddling with his watch-chain and shuffling with his feet, became the conqueror. From the moment he began to feel at ease, it was for him an enchanted palace, where wit and beauty reigned supreme, where the art of feeding and drinking was practised to perfection, where liberal sentiments and faultless breeding were in exquisite harmony, and where civilisation had reached its apogee. London was his spiritual home, and Holland House its sanctuary.

> 'Some of the best and happiest days of my life I have spent under your roof,' he wrote in 1810 to Lady Holland, 'and though there may be in some houses, particularly in those of our eminent prelates, a stronger disposition to pious exercises and as it were devout lucubrations, I do not believe all Europe can produce as much knowledge, wit and worth as passes in and out of your door under the nose of Thomas the porter.'

Yet the reputation of Holland House at this period was small compared with the immense social prestige it had acquired twenty years later, when, according to Macaulay, it was 'celebrated for its rare attractions to the furthest ends of the civilised world.' Three members of the famous circle claim our immediate though brief attention.

The third Lord Holland was born in 1773, and was quickly made acquainted with one form of oppression, which may have influenced his attitude towards all forms of oppression for the rest of his life. As a boy at Eton he was ordered to toast bread with his fingers for a senior boy's breakfast. Finding this method neither pleasant nor practical, he obtained a fork; but his fag-master resented the novelty, broke it over his head, and forced him to go on toasting bread with his fingers, which retained a withered appearance to the end of his days. After leaving Oxford he spent some years abroad, meeting many people of note, from Gibbon to Talleyrand, and eloping with Lady Webster, a Jamaica heiress, whose husband divorced her. Lord Holland married her after the birth of their first son.

Though he had the advantage of constant association with his famous uncle, Charles James Fox, Lord Holland did not distinguish himself as a speaker in the Upper House. He suffered from hesitation, due to a rush of ideas to the head, or confused utterance, due to the same cause. He was at his best in Holland House, where he could debate at ease, split hairs in comfort, and then split the filaments into filaments still finer. Not ambitious by nature, he was made so by his wife, who ruled him autocratically. He was notable for his extreme cheerfulness of disposition, for his kindness to all around him, for his toleration of all opinions, for his keen sense of the ridiculous, for his anecdotes of political debates which were enlivened by admirable mimicry of the chief speakers, for the fact that, though seldom free from gout, he never lost his temper or appeared irritable, for the way in which he put people at their ease, for the skilful manner in which he started a conversation, kept it going, and prevented anyone from monopolising it, for the charm and courtesy of his manner, and for his contagious good humour. It was the universal opinion that he was the pleasantest host who ever presided over a hospitable feast.

Of his public life it is enough to say that for forty years he was the champion of oppressed races and persecuted sects, that he was not subject to the prejudices of his class, that he was always on the side of the Commons against the Lords, that, though a planter, he was strongly opposed to the Slave Trade, and that, though a landlord, he fought whole-heartedly against the Corn Laws.

His wife was unlike him in almost every respect. Quick-tempered, imperious, irritable, fanatical, superstitious, much given to lamentation, to fierce hatreds and affections, she ruled Holland House and its visitors with a tyrannical insolence that would have emptied her salon if she had not balanced these qualities with extreme generosity and warm-heartedness, absolute loyalty to friends, a keen interest in the thoughts and doings of other people, and a real genius for mixing her guests. It was also well within her power to change from provocation to flattery at a moment's notice and heal the wound she had just made.

While her husband looked rather like Mr. Pickwick and possessed not a little of his benevolent simplicity, she had the air of Queen Elizabeth with a good deal of her character. Her manner was haughty and she ordered lords about like footmen. 'Lay that screen down, Lord Russell; you will spoil it,' was a typical command. Once she ordered Lord Melbourne to change his seat at dinner; he left the house in a fury – but he came back. People sitting near her were expected to pick up her fan whenever she dropped it; and Count d'Orsay, who had retrieved it several times in succession one evening, suggested that he should remain on the floor for the purpose. 'Now, Macaulay, we have had enough of this,' she would say, breaking into his talk and tapping her fan sharply on the table; 'give us something else.' The fact that others were delighted with such an order, even though they might fall under her displeasure later, helped to strengthen her authority over all. 'Your poetry is bad enough,' she informed Samuel Rogers, 'so pray be sparing of your prose.'

She refused to sit down to dinner with her husband until he had changed a waistcoat she disliked, would not let him use his crutches when he was suffering agonies from gout because he was allowing necessity to develop into a habit, and sometimes ordered the servants to take away his plate or wheel him off to bed in the middle of a story he was telling – all of which he bore with the utmost good humour. When she was invited out to dinner, she insisted on placing the most entertaining people in her immediate neighbourhood. People submitted to her dictatorial manners from sheer astonishment. She was hated by young women; her acid humour made them quail; and she never approved of their clothes, nor of their faces if they were pretty.

She travelled like royalty with a retinue of servants, and long after the introduction of railways she persisted in travelling 'by land', as it was called. She liked to make a slow and stately progress through the countryside, and when she did at last go by train she made the driver limit the speed to less than twenty miles an hour, to the annoyance of the other passengers. Yet this proud, imperious woman was frightened out of her wits by the sound of thunder; she would close all the shutters, draw all the curtains, and order candles to be lit in broad daylight to mitigate the flashes of lightning. The mere mention of cholera made her shake; she refused to eat any ice because she had been told that it was bad for cholera; and when a few cases were reported from Glasgow she said that the town ought to be surrounded with troops to prevent all intercourse between it and the rest of the country. The howling of a dog made her jump and she believed that the noise portended her death.

Her enthusiasm led her into all sorts of extravagant actions. She adored Napoleon and after Waterloo spoke of him as 'Poor dear man!'; she sent papers and plums to him both at Elba and St. Helena; his last hours were comforted by '*les pruneaux de Madame Holland*'; and he left her a snuff-box in his Will. But she was equally kind to uncelebrated friends who were ill or to poets who were in need, and she treated her servants well. When one of her pages was ill, she made her guests sit by his bedside to amuse him, much to their embarrassment – and his.

Once Sydney Smith had thoroughly established himself at Holland House he was the only person who was ever allowed to take liberties with her. 'Ring the bell, Sydney,' she commanded. 'Oh, yes,' he returned, 'and shall I sweep the floor?' He even went so far as to help himself to pats of butter from her own special dish.

Such were the master and mistress of Holland House: an equable lord, a fitful lady. The third member of the household to be noticed was as much a part of the establishment as the Hollands themselves. This was John Allen, their physician, adviser, librarian and friend. He was born near Edinburgh in 1771, studied medicine and surgery there, became friendly with Jeffrey, Smith and the rest, and wrote for the *Edinburgh Review*. In 1802 Lord Holland wanted a physician to accompany him on a long continental tour. Two or three people, including Sydney Smith, recommended Allen, and from that moment until the day of his death in 1843 he remained with the family. Lady Holland bullied him outrageously, but he bore it all in silence. Macaulay was never able to understand how Allen could stoop to be ordered about like a footman and treated like a negro slave, and he records a scene at the house of Samuel Rogers in 1833, when Lady Holland was in a furious temper and rude to everybody present. None of them treated her with much respect, and Sydney made merciless sport of her. Suddenly Allen came to her defence, flew into a rage with them all, and was especially angry with Sydney, 'whose guffaws were indeed tremendous'. After their departure Rogers praised the way in which Allen had fired up in defence of Lady Holland, but Tom Moore confided to Macaulay that Allen was bursting with envy to see the rest of them so free, while he was conscious of his own slavery, and that one could give him credit for nothing but attachment to his dinners. There was some truth in this, but Moore was still smarting from Lady Holland's rudeness and did not care to remember that she could inspire affection as easily as resentment.

Allen was strongly opposed to all religions and Sydney often made jokes about his scepticism. 'Pray for me,' he once wrote to Lady Holland, 'but don't let Allen do so.' Still, it appears from one of Sydney's recollections that Allen retained an open and inquiring mind: 'During one wet summer I used the anti-liquid prayer and Allen put up a barometer in the vestry, remaining there during the rest of the service to watch the effects, but I am sorry to say he did not find them very satisfactory.' Allen was a stout, strong man, with a large head, a broad face, bright eyes, and huge legs. 'Allen's legs are enormous,' said Sydney; 'they are clerical! He has the creed of a philosopher and the legs of a clergyman; I never saw such legs – at least belonging to a layman.'

Politically he was a republican and took part in a dinner to celebrate the fall of the Bastille. (In parenthesis it may be observed that the amount of food consumed by English gentlemen in honour of certain events in the French Revolution, if distributed to the Parisian mob at a judicious moment, would have prevented the fall of the Bastille.) He hated Napoleon, but hated the Bourbons still more, and at their restoration he lost all interest in contemporary politics, becoming immersed in historical research and writing an *Inquiry into the Rise and Growth of the Royal Prerogative in England.* Byron thought Allen the best informed and one of the ablest men he had ever known, and there is no doubt that he had accumulated vast quantities of facts and was a sort of walking encyclopædia.

His principal job in Holland House was to prepare the lists of guests, to arrange what rooms they were to occupy, to sit at the foot of the table, and to carve the dinner, which service he usually performed to the accompaniment of caustic comments by Lady Holland. He went with her everywhere and was usually invited with the Hollands when they dined with friends. He was never allowed to leave Holland House, except for a few hours each week when he had to visit Dulwich College, of which he was elected Warden in 1811 and Master in 1820. 'You may depend upon it you will never be happy when you are Disallenised,' Sydney warned Lady Holland; 'I endeavour sometimes to think of you and Allen separately, but find it quite impossible; you are become one idea and cannot be divided by the most subtle thinkers in Edinburgh.'

CHAPTER VI

CATHOLICS

IN the summer of 1807 Sydney Smith took his family to the village of Sonning, near Reading, where he had hired a cottage for several months. One of their neighbours was Sir William Scott (afterwards Lord Stowell) who is chiefly remembered for a famous phrase: 'The elegant simplicity of the three per cents.' Happily he lived up to another of his sayings – 'A dinner lubricates business' – and in spite of his strong Toryism frequently entertained Sydney at his house. He could not help admiring this strange, amusing clergyman, who, though ambitious, refused to barter his soul for a bishopric, and told him candidly that if he wanted to be rich he must change his politics. Sydney smiled, and went on driving nails into his clerical coffin.

For, indeed, at this very moment he was preparing his biggest bombshell for the Tory party. He had been meditating a book for more than two years, but had been at a loss for a subject. Recent events in the political world had now given him one.

In January, 1806, William Pitt had expired, praying for his country according to one account, asking for a pork pie according to another. Popular feeling was in favour of Fox as the only possible successor, but the King hated Fox, and a coalition of 'All the Talents' was formed as a compromise under the leadership of Lord Grenville, with Fox at the Foreign Office. 'All the Talents' did their best to abolish the Slave Trade, restore peace to Europe, deal justly with Ireland and put an end to political corruption; but in the midst of their endeavours Fox died, and the remaining talents were not strong enough to counter the influence of the Court. In March, 1807, the Grenville cabinet proposed that Catholic officers should serve in the army. This annoyed the King to such an extent that he instantly demanded a promise from his ministers that, under no circumstances whatever, would they introduce measures for Catholic relief or even mention the subject to him again. 'All the Talents' resented such an arbitrary demand, promptly resigned, and for over twenty years the hands of the clock were held back by such men as Canning, Perceval, Sidmouth, Liverpool and Castlereagh – a period of corruption, jobbery, bigotry and petty tyranny, unequalled in English history since the Revolution of 1688.

Sydney Smith, though far from friendly to the Catholic faith, hated political and religious persecution, and wrote such a scathing indictment of the average Protestant attitude to the question of Catholic emancipation that, after the circulation of his pamphlet, the way was paved for the removal of all the disabilities under which the Catholics had laboured for generations. Far more than to any other cause, the Catholics in Great Britain and Ireland could attribute the general feeling in favour of their emancipation, when at last it was manifested, to the common sense, wit and ridicule of Sydney Smith.

His work appeared in the form of 'Letters' written by one Peter Plymley to his brother Abraham, a country clergyman. The first was published in the summer of 1807 and its effect, we are told, was like a spark on a heap of gunpowder. Four more came out before the end of the year, followed by a further five in 1808, when they were collected and issued as a pamphlet, which quickly ran through sixteen editions. The Government did its utmost to discover the real name of the author, but failed, and the secret was never divulged. There was, however, little doubt in the minds of people like Byron, Sheridan, the Hollands, Lords Grey and Grenville, to say nothing of Sydney's intimate friends, that only one living man could write with the brilliance of Swift and with a humour that Swift lacked. Grenville rallied Holland on the affectation of concealing the author's name, and Holland reminded Grenville that the only author to whom they both thought it could be compared in English lost a bishopric for his wittiest performance, adding that, if they could discover the author, and ever had a bishopric in their gift, they should prove that the Whigs were more grateful and more liberal than the Tories.

Sydney himself kept up the pretence of ignorance pretty well, even with friends. Writing to Lady Holland, he said:

> 'Mr. Allen has mentioned to me the letters of a Mr. Plymley, which I have obtained from the adjacent market-town, and read with some entertainment. My conjecture lies between three persons – Sir Samuel Romilly, Sir Arthur Pigott, or Mr. Horner, for the name is evidently fictitious. I shall be very happy to hear your conjectures on this subject on Saturday, when I hope you will let me dine with you at Holland House.'

A year later, after a visit to Scotland, he wrote:

> 'I found a great number of philosophers in Edinburgh in a high state of obscurity and metaphysics. Dugald Stewart is extremely alarmed by the repeated assurances I made that he was the author of "Plymley's Letters" – or generally considered so to be.'

Thirty odd years later he explained the inclusion of the 'Letters' in a complete edition of his works:

> 'Somehow or another, it came to be conjectured that I was the author: I have always denied it; but finding that I deny it in vain, I have thought it might be as well to include the Letters in this Collection.'

It is not possible in these days to conceive the ignorance, stupidity and barbarous bigotry of the English nation with regard to the Catholic faith a little more than a century ago. There are, of course, certain modern forms of imbecility on the same scale but not on the same sort of subject, and these will not be visible to the naked and normal eye for another century, when the fashion in lunacy will have changed. An exact parallel is therefore impossible; but if, say, an Englishman had tried to persuade his countrymen in the year 1917 that the Germans were gentlemen, he would have been in much the same position as Sydney, who tried to persuade his countrymen in 1807 that the Catholics were civilised. He realised at the outset that it was useless to expect England to treat the Irish Catholics as human beings by appealing merely to her sense of fairplay; so he determined to frighten her into justice with the bogey of Bonaparte, and, lest anyone should question his methods, he revealed his sinister design with engaging candour:

> 'To talk of not acting from fear is mere parliamentary cant. From what motive but fear, I should like to know, have all the improvements in our constitution proceeded? I question if any justice has ever been done to large masses of mankind from any other motive. . . . If I say, Give this people what they ask because it is just, do you think I should get ten people to listen to me? . . . The only way to make the mass of mankind see the beauty of justice, is by showing to them in pretty plain terms the consequence of injustice.'

He disclaimed all connection with politics:

> 'If I could see good measures pursued, I care not a farthing who is in power; but I have a passionate love for common justice, and for common sense, and I abhor and despise every man who builds up his political fortune upon their ruin.'

For this reason his sympathies did not lie with the Percevals and Cannings of the reigning administration. Spencer

Perceval was Chancellor of the Exchequer. He had obtained the sinecure office of Surveyor of the Meltings and Clerk of the Irons, had attempted to obtain the revenues of the Duchy of Lancaster for life (though the attempt had been foiled), had procured the reversion of his brother's office of Registrar to the Court of Admiralty, and had burked a Parliamentary inquiry into reversions generally. In his favour it was said that he was a faithful husband and a kind father.

'These are, undoubtedly, the first qualifications to be looked to in a time of the most serious public danger,' remarked Peter Plymley, 'but somehow or other (if public and private virtues must always be incompatible), I should prefer that he destroyed the domestic happiness of Wood or Cockell, owed for the veal of the preceding year, whipped his boys, and saved his country.'

Another aspect of Perceval:

'I cannot for the soul of me conceive whence this man has gained his notions of Christianity: he has the most evangelical charity for errors in arithmetic, and the most inveterate malice against errors in conscience. While he rages against those whom in the true spirit of the Gospel he ought to indulge, he forgets the only instance of severity which that Gospel contains, and leaves the jobbers, and contractors, and money-changers at their seats, without a single stripe.'

The Foreign Secretary, Canning, was no better:

'Providence has made him a light, jesting, paragraph-writing man, and that he will remain to his dying day – call him a legislator, a reasoner, and the conductor of the affairs of a great nation, and it seems to me as absurd as if a butterfly were to teach bees to make honey.'

Still, there was one appeal that ought to weigh even with

politicians of this order. Irish Catholics were disqualified by their religion from every post of honour or value in the State, and were prevented from making money in other ways:

> 'There is a religion, it seems, even in jobs; and it will be highly gratifying to Mr. Perceval to learn that no man in Ireland who believes in seven sacraments can carry a public road, or bridge, one yard out of the direction most beneficial to the public, and that nobody can cheat the public who does not expound the scriptures in the purest and most orthodox manner. This will give pleasure to Mr. Perceval: but, from his unfairness upon these topics, I appeal to the justice and the proper feelings of Mr. Huskisson. I ask him if the human mind can experience a more dreadful sensation than to see its own jobs refused, and the jobs of another religion perpetually succeeding? I ask him his opinion of a jobless faith, of a creed which dooms a man through life to a lean and plunderless integrity. He knows that human nature cannot and will not bear it; and if we were to paint a political Tartarus, it would be an endless series of snug expectations, and cruel disappointments. . . . Besides, look at human nature : – what is the history of all professions? Joel is to be brought up to the Bar: has Mrs. Plymley the slightest doubt of his being Chancellor? Do not his two shrivelled aunts live in the certainty of seeing him in that situation, and of cutting out with their own hands his equity habiliments? And I could name a certain minister of the Gospel who does not, in the bottom of his heart, much differ from these opinions. Do you think that the fathers and mothers of the holy Catholic Church are not as absurd as Protestant papas and mammas? The probability I admit to be, in each particular case, that the sweet little blockhead will in fact never get a brief; – but I will venture to say, there is not a parent from the Giant's Causeway to Bantry Bay who does not conceive that his child is the unfortunate victim of the exclusion, and that nothing short of positive law could prevent his own dear

pre-eminent Paddy from rising to the highest honours of the State. So with the army, and parliament; in fact, few are excluded; but, in imagination, all; you keep twenty or thirty Catholics out, and you lose the affections of four millions.'

The English were permanently bedridden with Erin-phobia: 'The moment the very name of Ireland is mentioned, the English seem to bid adieu to common feeling, common prudence, and common sense, and to act with the barbarity of tyrants, and the fatuity of idiots.' Meanwhile we played a different game with the rest of the world:

'Our conduct to Ireland, during the whole of this war, has been that of a man who subscribes to hospitals, weeps at charity sermons, carries out broth and blankets to beggars, and then comes home and beats his wife and children. We had compassion for the victims of all other oppression and injustice, except our own.'

The situation was fraught with danger. Bonaparte, by tolerating all creeds, was conquering Europe on common sense:

'To deny the Irish this justice now, in the present state of Europe, and in the summer months, just as the season for destroying kingdoms is coming on, is (beloved Abraham), whatever you may think of it, little short of positive insanity.'

But how did England propose to meet such a foe? Peter dealt with the situation in a parable:

'Here is a frigate attacked by a corsair of immense strength and size, rigging cut, masts in danger of coming by the board, four foot water in the hold, men dropping off very fast; in this dreadful situation how do you think the Captain acts (whose name shall be Perceval)? He calls all hands upon deck; talks to them of King, country, glory, sweethearts, gin, French prison, wooden shoes, old England, and hearts of oak: they give three cheers, rush to their guns, and, after a tremendous conflict, succeed in beating off the enemy. Not a syllable of all this: this is not the manner in which the honourable Commander goes to work: the first thing he does is to secure 20 or 30 of his prime sailors who happen to be Catholics, to clap them in irons, and set over them a guard of as many Protestants; having taken this admirable method of defending himself against his infidel opponents, he goes upon deck, reminds the sailors, in a very bitter harangue, that they are of different religions; exhorts the Episcopal gunner not to trust to the Presbyterian quarter master; issues positive orders that the Catholics should be fired at upon the first appearance of discontent; rushes through blood and brains, examining his men in the Catechism and 39 Articles, and positively forbids everyone to sponge or ram who has not taken the Sacrament according to the Church of England. Was it right to take out a captain made of excellent British stuff, and to put in such a man as this? Is not he more like a parson, or a talking lawyer, than a thoroughbred seaman? And built as she is of heart of oak, and admirably manned, is it possible, with such a captain, to save this ship from going to the bottom?'

Over and over again we had been saved from a French invasion of Ireland by lucky winds: 'Such is the miserable and precarious state of an anemocracy, of a people who put their trust in hurricanes, and are governed by wind.'

We had allowed Catholic soldiers to enlist in our army, promising to respect their faith, and were now forcing them to attend Church of England services. Peter Plymley asked:

'How would my admirable brother, the Rev. Abraham Plymley, like to be marched to a Catholic chapel, to be sprinkled with the sanctified contents of a pump, to hear a number of false quantities in the Latin tongue, and to see a number of persons occupied in making right angles upon the breast and forehead?'

There had been a period in our history when we had treated the Scots and their religion in the same senseless manner: 'The Percevals of those days called for blood: this call is never made in vain, and blood was shed'; but we could not prevent 'that metaphysical people from going to heaven their true way, instead of our true way. . . . The true and the only remedy was applied; the Scotch were suffered to worship God after their own tiresome manner, without pain, penalty, and privation'. For that matter our attitude to Dissenters was just as silly. True, we allowed them to vote, to enter Parliament, and to fill certain offices; 'but no eel in the well-sanded fist of a cook-maid, upon the eve of being skinned, ever twisted and writhed as an orthodox parson does when he is compelled by the gripe of reason to admit anything in favour of a Dissenter.' Anyone who was not a member of the Established Church carried a social stigma:

> 'I solemnly believe blue and red baboons to be more popular here than Catholics and Presbyterians; they are more understood, and there is a greater disposition to do something for them. When a country squire hears of an ape, his first feeling is to give it nuts and apples; when he hears of a Dissenter, his immediate impulse is to commit it to the county jail, to shave its head, to alter its customary food, and to have it privately whipped. This is no caricature but an accurate picture of national feelings, as they degrade and endanger us at this very moment.'

Incidentally, since we could not be happy unless we were persecuting someone, why did we not pick on a sect that was too weak to be dangerous? By this expedient we could enjoy the same opportunity for cruelty and injustice without being exposed to the same risks. Peter suggested to his brother that

William Wilberforce 'and the patent Christians at Clapham' should be the victims. Why not force them to go to operas, melodramas and pantomimes, and in other ways gratify our love of insolence and power?

> 'Cruelty and injustice must, of course, exist: but why connect them with danger? Why torture a bulldog, when you can get a frog or a rabbit? I am sure my proposal will meet with the most universal approbation. Do not be apprehensive of any opposition from ministers. If it is a case of hatred, we are sure that one man will defend it by the Gospel: if it abridges human freedom, we know that another will find precedents for it in the Revolution.'

In fact our laws were rooted in prejudice: 'Every law which originated in ignorance and malice, and gratifies the passions from whence it sprang, we call the wisdom of our ancestors: when such laws are repealed, they will be cruelty and madness; till they are repealed, they are policy and caution.' And Peter was forced to this conclusion: 'When I hear any man talk of an unalterable law, the only effect it produces upon me is to convince me that he is an unalterable fool.' The very name of Progress frightened the average Briton out of his wits: 'Turnpike roads, navigable canals, inoculation, hops, tobacco, the Reformation, the Revolution – there are always a set of worthy and moderately-gifted men who bawl out death and ruin upon every valuable change which the varying aspect of human affairs absolutely and imperiously requires.'

It had been suggested that the Catholics ought to be grateful for small mercies, that they were asking for more freedom because they had already been given a little, that they would never have dared to ask for perfect justice if they had not received partial justice. Peter met this with another parable:

> 'There is a village (no matter where) in which the inhabitants, on one day in the year, sit down to a dinner prepared

at the common expense: by an extraordinary piece of tyranny (which Lord Hawkesbury would call the wisdom of the village ancestors), the inhabitants of three of the streets, about a hundred years ago, seized upon the inhabitants of the fourth street, bound them hand and foot, laid them upon their backs, and compelled them to look on while the rest were stuffing themselves with beef and beer; the next year the inhabitants of the persecuted street (though they contributed an equal quota of the expense) were treated precisely in the same manner. The tyranny grew into a custom; and (as the manner of our human nature is) it was considered as the most sacred of all duties to keep these poor fellows without their annual dinner: the village was so tenacious of this practice, that nothing could induce them to resign it; every enemy to it was looked upon as a disbeliever in Divine Providence, and any nefarious churchwarden who wished to succeed in his election had nothing to do but to represent his antagonist as an abolitionist, in order to frustrate his ambition, endanger his life, and throw the village into a state of the most dreadful commotion. By degrees, however, the obnoxious street grew to be so well peopled, and its inhabitants so firmly united, that their oppressors, more afraid of injustice, were more disposed to be just. At the next dinner they are unbound, the year after allowed to sit upright, then a bit of bread and a glass of water; till at last, after a long series of concessions, they are emboldened to ask, in pretty plain terms, that they may be allowed to sit down at the bottom of the table, and to fill their bellies as well as the rest. Forthwith a general cry of shame and scandal: "Ten years ago, were you not laid upon your backs? Don't you remember what a great thing you thought it to get a piece of bread? How thankful you were for cheese-parings? Have you forgotten that memorable era, when the lord of the manor interfered to obtain for you a slice of the public pudding? And now, with an audacity only equalled by your ingratitude, you have the impudence to ask for knives and forks, and to request, in terms too plain to be mistaken, that you may sit down to table with the rest, and be indulged even with beef and beer: there are not more than half a dozen dishes which we have reserved for ourselves; the rest has been thrown open to you in the utmost profusion; you have potatoes, and carrots, suet dumplings, sops in the pan, and delicious toast and water, in incredible quantities. Beef, mutton, lamb, pork, and veal are ours; and if you were not the most restless and dissatisfied of human beings, you would never think of aspiring to enjoy them." '

The truth of the matter was that Protestants enjoyed their position of social superiority over Catholics:

'You may not be aware of it yourself, most reverend Abraham, but you deny their freedom to the Catholics upon the same principle that Sarah your wife refuses to give the receipt for a ham or a gooseberry dumpling: she values her receipts, not because they secure to her a certain flavour, but because they remind her that her neighbours want it – a feeling laughable in a priestess, shameful in a priest; venial when it withholds the blessings of a ham, tyrannical and execrable when it narrows the boon of religious freedom.'

In order to maintain this childish sense of superiority, there was a Protestant conspiracy to keep alive every superstition that made the Catholics appear odious:

'I thought that the terror of the Pope had been confined to the limits of the nursery, and merely employed as a means to induce young master to enter into his small clothes with greater speed, and to eat his breakfast with greater attention to decorum. For these purposes, the name of the Pope is admirable; but why push it beyond?'

Speaking for himself, Peter felt sure that

'after a Catholic justice had once been seen on the bench, and it had been clearly ascertained that he spoke English, had no tail, only a single row of teeth, and that he loved port wine – after all the scandalous and infamous reports of his physical conformation had been clearly proved to be false – he would be reckoned a jolly fellow, and very superior in flavour to a sly Presbyterian. Nothing, in fact, can be more uncandid and unphilosophical than to say that a man has a tail, because you cannot agree with him upon religious subjects; it appears to be ludicrous: but I am convinced it has done infinite mischief to the Catholics, and made a very serious impression upon the minds of many gentlemen of large landed property'.

Perhaps it would have been better if the administration of 'All the Talents' had made a little experiment before attempting to repeal any of the laws against the Catholics:

'They should have caused several Catholics to have been dissected after death by surgeons of either religion; and the report to have been published with accompanying plates. If the viscera, and other organs of life, had been found to be the same as in Protestant bodies; if the provisions of nerves, arteries, cerebrum, and cerebellum, had been the same as we are provided with, or as the Dissenters are now known to possess; then, indeed, they might have met Mr. Perceval upon a proud eminence, and convinced the country at large of the strong probability that the Catholics are really human creatures, endowed with the feelings of men, and entitled to all their rights. But instead of this wise and prudent measure, Lord Howick, with his usual precipitation, brings forward a Bill in their favour, without offering the slightest proof to the country that they were anything more than horses and oxen.'

It was improbable, however, that even such an experiment

would have convinced the general public, for such a wave of credulity was passing over the country, such a tempest of loyalty had set in, 'that the 47th proposition in Euclid might now be voted down with as much ease as any proposition in politics'; and therefore if any leading politician hated the abstract truths of science as much as he hated concrete truth in human affairs, now was the time 'for getting rid of the multiplication table, and passing a vote of censure upon the pretensions of the *hypotenuse*'.

In such an age of mediocrity, absurdity and bigotry, anything was possible:

> 'I have often thought, if the *wisdom of our ancestors* had excluded all persons with red hair from the House of Commons, of the throes and convulsions it would occasion to restore them to their natural rights. What mobs and riots would it produce! To what infinite abuse and obloquy would the capillary patriot be exposed; what wormwood would distil from Mr. Perceval, what froth would drop from Mr. Canning; how our Lord Hawkesbury would work away about the hair of King William and Lord Somers, and the authors of the great and glorious Revolution; how Lord Eldon would appeal to the Deity and his own virtues, and to the hair of his children: some would say that red-haired men were superstitious; some would prove they were atheists; they would be petitioned against as the friends of slavery, and the advocates for revolt; in short, such a corrupter of the heart and understanding is the spirit of persecution, that these unfortunate people (conspired against by their fellow-subjects of every complexion), if they did not emigrate to countries where hair of another colour was persecuted, would be driven to the falsehood of perukes, or the hypocrisy of the Tricosian fluid.'

But why were we treating the Irish Catholics so shamefully? What was our object? Did it profit us in any way? The answer was that, if we gave the Catholics equal rights with the

Protestants, we would lose the affections of the Orangemen. The Catholics must be kept in subjection in order that 'Sir Phelim O'Callaghan may continue to whip Sir Toby M'Tackle, his next-door neighbour, and continue to ravish his Catholic daughters'. Naturally the Sir Phelims would be annoyed, but they would become accustomed to their deprivations by degrees.

> 'To a short period of disaffection among the Orangemen, I confess I should not much object: my love of poetical justice does carry me as far as that; one summer's whipping, only one: the thumb-screws for a short season; a little light easy torturing between Lady-day and Michaelmas; a short specimen of Mr. Perceval's rigour. I have malice enough to ask this slight atonement for the groans and shrieks of the poor Catholics, unheard by any human tribunal, but registered by the Angel of God against their Protestant and enlightened oppressors.'

As a matter of sober fact, if our object really was to convert the Catholics to the Protestant religion, we should adopt a totally different kind of strategy:

> 'If a rich young Catholic were in Parliament, he would belong to White's and to Brooke's, would keep racehorses, would walk up and down Pall Mall, be exonerated of his ready money and his constitution, become as totally devoid of morality, honesty, knowledge, and civility as Protestant loungers in Pall Mall, and return home with a supreme contempt for Father O'Leary and Father O'Callaghan. I am astonished at the madness of the Catholic clergy, in not perceiving that Catholic emancipation is Catholic infidelity; that to entangle their people in the intrigues of a Protestant Parliament, and a Protestant court, is to ensure the loss of every man of fashion and consequence in their community. The true receipt for preserving their religion, is Mr. Perceval's receipt for destroying

it: it is to deprive every rich Catholic of all the objects of secular ambition, to separate him from the Protestant, and to shut him up in his castle with priests and relics.'

But the point that Peter Plymley was most anxious to drive home was that our treatment of the Catholics made Ireland a source of serious danger to the Empire. Bonaparte had only to land an army in Cork, and the country would rise against us to a man.

'We are told, in answer to all our arguments, that this is not a fit period – that a period of universal war is not the proper time for dangerous innovations in the constitution: this is as much as to say, that the worst time for making friends is the period when you have made many enemies; that it is the greatest of all errors to stop when you are breathless, and to lie down when you are fatigued. Of one thing I am quite certain: if the safety of Europe is once completely restored, the Catholics may for ever bid adieu to the slightest probability of effecting their object. Such men as hang about a court not only are deaf to the suggestions of mere justice, but they despise justice; they detest the word *right*; the only word which rouses them is *peril*; where they can oppress with impunity, they oppress for ever, and call it loyalty and wisdom.'

Assuming, then, that the worst were to happen, and that we were invaded as a consequence of our folly, did brother Abraham really believe that the English yeomen and farmers would be a match for the conquerors of Europe?

'As for the spirit of the peasantry in making a gallant defence behind hedgerows, and through plate-racks and hen-coops, highly as I think of their bravery, I do not know any nation in Europe so likely to be struck with the panic as the English; and this from their total unacquaintance with the science of war. Old wheat and beans blazing for twenty miles round; cart mares shot; sows of Lord Somerville's breed running wild over the country; the minister of the parish wounded sorely in his hinder parts; Mrs. Plymley in fits; all these scenes of war an Austrian or a Russian has seen three or four times over; but it is now three centuries since an English pig has fallen in a fair battle upon English ground, or a farm-house been rifled, or a clergyman's wife been subjected to any other proposals of love than the connubial endearments of her sleek and orthodox mate.'

Against the genius of Bonaparte, what had we to oppose? 'The parliamentary perspirations of the Foreign Secretary?' or the National Anthem? Brother Abraham had declared that 'God Save the King' warmed his heart like the sound of a trumpet. But Peter reminded him that

> ' "God save the King", in these times, too often means God save my pension and my place, God give my sisters an allowance out of the privy purse – make me clerk of the irons, let me survey the meltings, let me live upon the fruits of other men's industry, and fatten upon the plunder of the public.'

It was ill with us if we had to depend on the quips of Canning for our salvation, and Peter Plymley apostrophised Bonaparte: 'Tremble, thou scourge of God, for a pleasant man is come out against thee, and thou shalt be laid low by a joker of jokes.' Worse still if we had to put our faith in Perceval, whose 'Orders in Council' had antagonised neutral countries by prohibiting the exportation of all goods to France which were not carried direct from this country and had not paid an export-duty here, and who had decided that on no terms should the Continent be allowed to have certain drugs, such as rhubarb and quinine, or Jesuit's Bark, as it was called. Could such a man inspire confidence?

'The statesman who would bring the French to reason

by keeping them without rhubarb, and exhibit to mankind the awful spectacle of a nation deprived of neutral salts. This is not the dream of a wild apothecary indulging in his own opium; this is not the distempered fancy of a pounder of drugs, delirious from smallness of profits; but it is the sober, deliberate, and systematic scheme of a man to whom the public safety is intrusted, and whose appointment is considered by many as a masterpiece of political sagacity. What a sublime thought, that no purge can now be taken between the Weser and the Garonne; that the bustling pestle is still, the canorous mortar mute, and the bowels of mankind locked up for fourteen degrees of latitude! When, I should be curious to know, were all the powers of crudity and flatulence fully explained to his Majesty's ministers? At what period was this great plan of conquest and constipation fully developed? In whose mind was the idea of destroying the pride and the plasters of France first engendered? Without castor oil they might for some months, to be sure, have carried on a lingering war; but can they do without bark? Will the people live under a government where antimonial powders cannot be procured? Will they bear the loss of mercury? "There's the rub." Depend upon it, the absence of the *materia medica* will soon bring them to their senses, and the cry of *Bourbon and Bolus* burst forth from the Baltic to the Mediterranean.'

What, then, was to be done with Ireland? Recently the mere mention of Bonaparte had been received with thunderous applause in a Dublin theatre, and 'a politician should not be inattentive to the public feelings expressed in theatres'. There could be no doubt that the Irish loathed us, and with cause: 'Depend upon it, whole nations have always some reason for their hatred.' Would it be possible for us to gain their trust and affection and make them forget the past? Well, to begin with, Peter informed his brother, you must cease to put 'confidence in the little cunning of Bow Street, when you might rest your security upon the eternal basis of the best feelings'. Also he should possess 'one of the most beautiful and important consequences of a religious mind – an inviolable charity to all the honest varieties of human opinion'. Everything else would follow as a natural course – even to state payment of the Catholic priests. Yes, that might be a pretty big pill for Abraham to swallow, but the whole problem of peace and goodwill hinged upon it.

'My plan is very simple; I would have 300 Catholic parishes at £100 per ann., 300 at £200 per ann., and 400 at £300 per ann.: this, for the whole thousand parishes, would amount to £190,000. To the prelacy I would allot £20,000 in unequal proportions, from £1,000 to £500; and I would appropriate £40,000 more for the support of the Catholic schools, and the repairs of Catholic churches; the whole amount of which sum is £250,000, about the expense of three days of one of our genuine, good, English *just and necessary wars*. The clergy should all receive their salaries at the Bank of Ireland, and I would place the whole patronage in the hands of the Crown. Now, I appeal to any human being, except Spencer Perceval Esq., of the parish of Hampstead, what the disaffection of a clergy would amount to, gaping after this graduated bounty of the Crown, and whether Ignatius Loyola himself, if he were a living blockhead instead of a dead saint, could withstand the temptation of bouncing from £100 a year at Sligo, to £300 in Tipperary? This is the miserable sum of money for which the merchants and landowners and nobility of England are exposing themselves to the tremendous peril of losing Ireland.'

As for the Test Act, Peter would willingly pander to Protestant prejudice in order to gain his end. The Act need not be repealed, except that part of it which compelled Catholics to take the oath of supremacy and to make the declaration against transubstantiation.

'They would then come into Parliament as all other

Dissenters are allowed to do, and the penal laws to which they were exposed for taking office would be suspended every year, as they have been for this half century past towards Protestant Dissenters. Perhaps, after all, this is the best method – to continue the persecuting law, and to suspend it every year – a method which, while it effectually destroys the persecution itself, leaves to the great mass of mankind the exquisite gratification of supposing that they are enjoying some advantage from which a particular class of their fellow creatures are excluded. We manage the Corporation and Test Acts at present much in the same manner as if we were to persuade parish boys who had been in the habit of beating an ass to spare the animal, and beat the skin of an ass stuffed with straw; this would preserve the semblance of tormenting without the reality, and keep boy and beast in good humour.'

Finally, Peter Plymley advised the politicians for their own sakes to emancipate the Catholics. If they wanted to keep their jobs, to enjoy their reversions, and to grow fat on their sinecures, they would have to change the hostility of Ireland into friendship: 'The vigour of the ministry is like the vigour of a grave-digger – the tomb becomes more ready and more wide for every effort which they make.'

But Peter was now tired of the subject:

'The only difficulty in discussing it is a want of resistance, a want of something difficult to unravel, and something dark to illumine. To agitate such a question is to beat the air with a club, and cut down gnats with a scimitar; it is a prostitution of industry, and a waste of strength.'

The pen that Peter Plymley laid down was taken up by Sydney Smith again and again. Articles on Catholics appeared in the *Edinburgh Review* in 1807 and 1808, and he returned to the subject in 1813, in 1820, and in 1827 – the last essay he ever wrote for the *Review*. Characteristic Plymley-isms abound in every article. Referring to the promises of politicians, he said: 'Toleration never had a present tense, nor taxation a future one.' And: 'Profligacy in taking office is so extreme, that we have no doubt public men may be found who, for half a century, would postpone all remedies for a *pestilence*, if the preservation of their places depended upon the propagation of the virus.' The English misgovernment of Ireland drew this from him:

> 'Such jobbing, such profligacy – so much direct tyranny and oppression – such an abuse of God's gifts – such a profanation of God's name for the purposes of bigotry and party spirit, cannot be exceeded in the history of civilised Europe, and will long remain a monument of infamy and shame to England.'

Some of the benefits of the Reformation he described in these terms: 'A few potatoes and a shed of turf are all that Luther has left for the Romanist; and, when the latter gets these, he instantly begins upon the great Irish manufacture of children.'

He looked a century ahead and wrote:

> 'Ireland, in short, till her wrongs are redressed, and a more liberal policy is adopted towards her, will always be a cause of anxiety and suspicion to this country; and, in some moment of our weakness and depression, will forcibly extort what she would now receive with gratitude and exultation.'

Also:

> 'What will be said of all the intolerable trash which is issued forth at public meetings of No Popery? The follies of one century are scarcely credible in that which succeeds it. A grandmamma of 1827 is as wise as a very wise man of 1727. If the world lasts till 1927, the grandmammas of that period will be far wiser than the tiptop No Popery men of this day.'

Another evil did not escape him: 'The absent proprietor looks only to revenue, and cares nothing for the disorder and degradation of a country which he never means to visit.' He praised the patriotism of Grattan: 'Great men hallow a whole people, and lift up all who live in their time.' He appealed to the self-interest of the Tory Lords:

> 'I wonder that mere fear does not make you give up the Catholic question! Do you mean to put this fine place in danger – the venison – the pictures – the pheasants – the cellars – the hot-house and the grapery? Should you like to see six or seven thousand French or Americans landed in Ireland, and aided by a universal insurrection of the Catholics? Is it worth your while to run the risk of their success? What evil from the possible encroachment of Catholics, by civil exertions, can equal the danger of such a position as this? How can a man of your carriages and horses and hounds think of putting your high fortune in such a predicament, and crying out, like a schoolboy or a chaplain, "Oh, we shall beat them! we shall put the rascals down!" No Popery, I admit to your Lordship, is a very convenient cry at an election, and has answered your end; but do not push the matter too far: to bring on a civil war for No Popery is a very foolish proceeding in a man who has two courses and a remove! As you value your side-board of plate, your broad riband, your pier glasses – if obsequious domestics and large rooms are dear to you – if you love ease and flattery, titles and coats of arms – if the labour of the French cook, the dedication of the expecting poet, can move you – if you hope for a long life of side-dishes – if you are not insensible to the periodical arrival of the turtle-fleets – emancipate the Catholics! Do it for your ease, do it for your indolence, do it for your safety – emancipate and eat, emancipate and drink – emancipate, and preserve the rent-roll and the family estate!'

He expressed his astonishment that 'the brains of rich

Englishmen do not fall down into their bellies in talking of the Catholic question – that they do not reason through the cardia and the pylorus – that all the organs of digestion do not become intellectual'. He believed that 'the mild and the long-suffering may suffer for ever in this world' and that 'as long as the patient will suffer, the cruel will kick'. Yet, while we could not spare a penny for the Irish priesthood, we could waste thousands on Empire-building:

> 'Every rock in the ocean where a cormorant can perch is occupied by our troops, has a governor, deputy-governor, storekeeper, and deputy-storekeeper – and will soon have an archdeacon and a bishop. Military colleges, with thirty-four professors, educating seventeen ensigns per annum, being half an ensign for each professor, with every species of nonsense, athletic, sartorial and plumigerous. A just and necessary war costs this country about one hundred pounds a minute; whipcord fifteen thousand pounds; red tape seven thousand pounds; lace for drummers and fifers nineteen thousand pounds; a pension to one man who has broken his head at the Pole; to another who has shattered his leg at the Equator; subsidies to Persia; secret-service money to Thibet; an annuity to Lady Henry Somebody and her seven daughters – the husband being shot at some place where we never ought to have had any soldiers at all; and the elder brother returning four members to Parliament. Such a scene of extravagance, corruption, and expense as must paralyse the industry, and mar the fortunes, of the most industrious, spirited people that ever existed.'

He pictured the war of sects: 'There are twenty fettered men in a gaol, and every one is employed in loosening his own fetters with one hand, and riveting those of his neighbour with the other.' A generation before Dickens wrote *Bleak House*, Sydney described a typical humanitarian: 'How wise, and how humane and affecting are our efforts throughout

Europe to put an end to the Slave Trade! Wherever three or four negotiators are gathered together, a British diplomat appears among them, with some article of kindness and pity for the poor negro. All is mercy and compassion except when wretched Ireland is concerned. The saint who swoons at the lashes of the Indian slave is the encourager of No Popery Meetings, and the hard, bigoted, domineering tyrant of Ireland.'

Did the English really imagine that Ireland could be converted by the sword?

> 'Is the best blood of the land to be flung away in a war of hassocks and surplices? Are cities to be summoned for the Thirty-nine Articles, and men to be led on to the charge by professors of divinity? The expense of *keeping* such a country must be added to all other enormous expenses. What is really possessed of a country so subdued? four or five yards round a sentry-box, and no more. And in twenty years' time it is all to do over again – another war – another rebellion, and another enormous and ruinously expensive contest, with the same dreadful uncertainty of the issue!'

Noting the fact that we had been at war 35 minutes out of every hour since the peace of Utrecht, he came to the conclusion that 'the state of war seems more natural to man than the state of peace', and that it was 'at all times a better speculation to make ploughshares into swords than swords into ploughshares'. It was nonsense to talk of the exclusive disposition of the Catholics to persecute: 'The Protestants have murdered, and tortured, and laid waste as much as the Catholics. Each party, as it gained the upper hand, tried death as the remedy for heresy – both parties have tried it in vain.' A number of loyal people had said, after the death of George III, that we should not pass measures for Catholic relief because his late Majesty had disapproved of them.

Sydney dealt with this objection: 'Of all human nonsense, it is surely the greatest to talk of respect to the late king – by not voting for the Catholic question. Bad enough to burn widows when the husband dies – bad enough to burn horses, dogs, butlers, footmen, and coachmen, on the funeral pile of a Scythian warrior – but to offer up the happiness of seven millions of people to the memory of the dead, is certainly the most insane sepulchral oblation of which history makes mention.'

It had been argued that the Irish were quiet under the severe code of Queen Anne –

> 'So the half-murdered man left on the ground bleeding by thieves is quiet; and he only moans and cries for help as he recovers. There was a method which would have made the Irish still more quiet, and effectually have put an end to all further solicitation respecting the Catholic question. It was adopted in the case of the wolves.'

The last sentence that Sydney wrote for the *Edinburgh Review* ran: 'All great alterations in human affairs are produced by compromise.'

In addition to several speeches on the subject, which made him extremely unpopular with his Christian brethren, he issued *A Letter to the Electors upon the Catholic Question*, from which we may take the following:

> 'Mr. Murphy lives in Limerick, and Mr. Murphy and his son are subjected to a thousand inconveniences and disadvantages, because they are Catholics. Murphy is a wealthy, honourable, excellent man; he ought to be in the corporation; he cannot get in because he is a Catholic. His son ought to be King's Counsel for his talents, and his standing at the bar; he is prevented from reaching this dignity because he is a Catholic. Why, what reasons do you hear for all this? Because Queen Mary, three hundred years before the natal day of Mr. Murphy, murdered

Protestants in Smithfield; because Louis XIV dragooned his Protestant subjects, when the predecessor of Murphy's predecessor was not in being; because men are confined in prison, in Madrid, twelve degrees more south than Murphy has ever been in his life; all ages, all climates are ransacked to perpetuate the slavery of Murphy, the ill-fated victim of political anachronisms. . . . When are mercy and justice, in fact, ever to return upon the earth, if the sins of the elders are to be for ever visited on these who are not even their children?'

England was now at peace, Napoleon was dead, and Sydney was forced to make a different sort of appeal from that which had served the turn of Peter Plymley: 'If you think the thing must be done at some time or another, do it when you are calm and powerful, and when you need not do it.' Again he urged the necessity of paying the Catholic clergy: 'All men gradually yield to the comforts of a good income.' Briefly his advice to the electors was: 'Vote for a free altar, an open road to heaven.'

After Sydney's death an unrevised fragment on the Irish Roman Catholic Church was found among his papers, proving that the subject of his first book was also the subject of his last thoughts. Once more his theme was the payment of priests. Once more he prophesied trouble in Ireland when next there was trouble in Europe: 'And then comes an immense twenty per cent income-tax war, a universal insurrection in Ireland, and a crisis of misery and distress in which life will hardly be worth having.' Why was England not represented at the Vatican? 'It turns out that there is no law to prevent entering into diplomatic engagements with the Pope. The sooner we become acquainted with a gentleman who has so much to say to eight million of our subjects the better!'

The condition of the Irish clergy was a scandal:

'I maintain that it is shocking and wicked to leave the

religious guides of six millions of people in such a state of destitution! – to bestow no more thought upon them than upon the clergy of the Sandwich Islands! If I were a member of the Cabinet, and met my colleagues once a week to eat birds and beasts, and to talk over the state of the world, I should begin upon Ireland before the soup was finished, go on through fish, turkey, and saddle of mutton, and never end till the last thimbleful of claret had passed down the throat of the incredulous Haddington: but there they sit, week after week; there they come, week after week – and think no more of paying the Catholic clergy, than a man of real fashion does of paying his tailor! . . . If I were a Bishop, living beautifully in a state of serene plenitude, I don't think I could endure the thought of so many honest, pious, and laborious clergymen of another faith, placed in such disgraceful circumstances! I could not get into my carriage with jelly-springs, or see my two courses every day, without remembering the buggy and the bacon of some poor old Catholic Bishop, ten times as laborious, and with much more, perhaps, of theological learning than myself, often distressed for a few pounds! and burdened with duties utterly disproportioned to his age and strength. I think, if the extreme comfort of my own condition did not extinguish all feeling for others, I should sharply commiserate such a church, and attempt with ardour and perseverance to apply the proper remedy.'

Quite apart from justice and humanity, there was the commonsense view of the case: 'I am fully convinced that a State payment to the Catholic clergy, by leaving to that laborious and useful body of men the exercise of their free judgment, would be the severest blow that Irish agitation could receive.'

Alas! we had no bishops who were capable of allaying the hatreds of contending sects:

'Scarcely any Bishop is sufficiently a man of the world to

deal with fanatics. The way is not to reason with them, but to ask them to dinner. They are armed against logic and remonstrance, but they are puzzled in a labyrinth of wines, disarmed by facilities and concessions and, introduced to a new world, come away thinking more of hot and cold, and dry and sweet, than of Newman, Keble and Pusey. So mouldered away Hannibal's army at Capua! So the primitive and perpendicular prig of Puseyism is softened into practical wisdom, and coaxed into commonsense!'

For advancing such opinions Sydney said that he would be called an atheist, a deist, a democrat, a smuggler, a poacher, a highwayman, and various other things, but –

'I write for three reasons: first, because I really wish to do good; secondly, because if I don't write, I know nobody else will; and thirdly, because it is the nature of the animal to write, and I cannot help it. Still, in looking back I see no reason to repent. What I have said *ought* to be done, generally *has* been done, but always twenty or thirty years too late; done, not of course because I have said it, but because it was no longer *possible* to avoid doing it. Human beings cling to their delicious tyrannies, and to their exquisite nonsense, like a drunkard to his bottle, and go on till death stares them in the face.'

If his advice had been taken, and the Catholic clergy had been paid, another century's hatred and bloodshed would have been avoided, and Ireland would never have become a republic.

CHAPTER VII

RUSTICATION

THE administration of 'All the Talents' justified its existence in one respect if in no other. It had, on the whole, a Whiggish tinge, and the great Whig leaders influenced its policy. Lady Holland quickly took advantage of this and asked Erskine, the Lord Chancellor, to give Sydney Smith a living. In the year 1806 Sydney was presented with the living of Foston-le-Clay in Yorkshire, and went to thank the Chancellor. 'Oh, don't thank *me*, Mr. Smith,' said Erskine: 'I gave you the living because Lady Holland insisted on my doing so; and if she had desired me to give it to the devil, *he* must have had it.' It did not apparently occur to him that the devil's exposition of the scriptures might have been unorthodox.

In those days people were less openly scrupulous in such matters than they are to-day. There was an honest expression of private opinion among public men with which we are totally unfamiliar. Sydney himself, in letters and speeches and conversations, referred to the famous people and events of his time in a manner that would not be reported in a modern newspaper. To take an example. Lord Grenville had once been a Tory and had held several important posts in Tory governments; but when he was leader of 'All the Talents' he came under the influence of Fox, Grey and the Hollands, and at the close of the administration was a lukewarm Whig. Two years later he wished to become Chancellor of Oxford University and Lord Holland begged Sydney to use whatever influence he had at Oxford in favour of Grenville's candidature. Sydney promised to do all he could, but wrote to Lady Holland that he did not want to see Grenville as Chancellor, since it would connect him personally with high Tories and Churchmen and check the growth of his liberal opinions; and as he hankered after his old courses, he should be kept out of bad company. Sydney reported that eight bishops were going to vote for Grenville ('It seems quite unnatural – like a murrain among the cattle') and later, in a large gathering at Holland House, remarked: 'The Whig canvass for Lord Grenville at Oxford is like the trustees of the Magdalen [1] applying to place a reclaimed prostitute at a bawdy house.'

The Act compelling the clergy to reside in their parishes was passed in 1803. Five years later a new Archbishop was enthroned at York and began to put the Act into operation. Sydney had appointed a neighbouring curate to take his duties at Foston until his residence should be enforced, and remained in the south until the summer of 1809, contenting himself with one visit to his parish, when he had a long talk with the Parish clerk, who certified him as 'no fool'. In the last whirl of social engagements before his departure for the north, he put in two days at Sheridan's country house during the Christmas festivities of 1808. Brougham was there, too, and it is doubtful whether four walls ever enclosed three such diverse and remarkable characters. *A chiel amang them takin' notes* would have placed us in his lasting debt. Sydney and Sheridan are two of the most amusing conversational wits in the social records of England, but their styles were widely dissimilar. Sheridan's wit was dry, Sydney's wit sparkled; Sheridan never laughed, Sydney was always laughing; Sheridan prepared his *bon mots* and adroitly led up to their delivery, Sydney's were spontaneous and arose naturally in the course of conversation; Sheridan's wit was savage and saturnine, Sydney's was jovial and kindly. Add to this entertaining contrast the buffoonery and vitality and versatility of Brougham, and we may take Sydney's word for it that the details of that brief visit were 'not uncomical'.

[1] An asylum for 'penitent women'.

Sydney was now to become a country parson. We have already seen what he thought of the country; but what did he think of himself? We can draw a partial portrait of him from the incidental confessions scattered about his correspondence, and complete the picture from other sources.

He had not an atom of shyness in his nature; he was equally at ease with dukes and cobblers, landowners and horse-owners, Whigs and Tories, women and men. He was not conscious of social inferiority in the presence of a prince, nor of social superiority in the presence of a parlour-maid; he was neither self-assertive nor condescending. He adored children, loved to be surrounded by jolly, noisy people, and hated solitude and silence. When alone he was liable to acute attacks of depression. There was a streak of laziness in him which he fought by employing himself with a score of things over the same period of time. He flung himself whole-heartedly into the employment of the moment, forgot all about it the instant he left it, and absorbed himself utterly in the work that came next to his hand. He wrote as he talked, in the midst of domestic noise and chatter, with scarcely a pause for thought between paragraphs, never troubling to re-read or correct what he had written, and leaving his wife to dot the i's and cross the t's and his editor to make good his lamentable lack of punctuation. His writing was often quite illegible; it was, in his own words, 'as if a swarm of ants, escaping from an ink-bottle, had walked over a sheet of paper without wiping their legs'.

Naturally disposed to like everybody who was cheerful, he hated suffering and believed happiness to be the main object of existence. He shrank from hurting people, yet would not lie to spare their feelings; though once, when he wrote a non-committal review of a book which Jeffrey thought he ought to have slated, he excused himself thus: 'I think the book very ill-done; still, it is done by an honest worthy man who has neither bread nor butter. How can I be true under such circumstances?' Inhumanity and callousness in any shape or form brought him to boiling-point. Tolerance and benevolence were to him the chief virtues of mankind. In an age when corruption was rife among the professional classes, including the clergy, and when men sold their beliefs for promotion, he remained incorruptible. 'I believe that it is out of the power of lawn and velvet, and the crisp hair of dead men fashioned into a wig, to make me a dishonest man,' he told Lady Holland. Intensely ambitious at the outset of his career, he became less and less so with the advance of years, and the more he saw of 'the *rattery* and scoundrelism of public life', the less did he desire to participate in the spoils of place. He was, too, a born family man, who loved his home, his wife and children, and who was never happier than when he was making everyone around him happy. Macaulay, who stayed with him at Foston, said that Sydney was not a show-talker who reserved all his good things for special occasions; it appeared to be his greatest luxury to keep his wife and daughters laughing for two or three hours every day.

He was fond of talking nonsense and had an irrepressible gaiety of disposition, which sometimes expressed itself with a humorous coarseness that shocked conventional folk. Much of his life was spent in a state of tearing high spirits, and his speech was punctuated with volleys of laughter. But he could quickly turn from gay to grave and there were times when he behaved in a somewhat alarming and magisterial manner, and when the lighthearted joker became a dominant and forceful personality, imposing his will on individuals and assuming command in social gatherings.

Generally modest as well as merry, he attached such little importance to his own opinions that he gave them freely on any and every subject; and, like many modest people, he did not hesitate to praise himself when he felt he had deserved it. He would roar with laughter over his own articles if he read them in print, and when he considered that he had sung a song particularly well he would say so and *encore* himself. He had no reservations, declaring that he lived with open windows and doors and could be seen, by those who thought it worth while to look at him, as well in five minutes as in five years. His free and open nature (in a country whose inhabitants, since the rise of puritanism, have been mentally imprisoned) was not appreciated by the dispensers of place, and while they were unable to withstand his humour they were careful to overlook his deserts. Referring to his corpulence at a late period of life, he confessed: 'I am, you know, of the family of Falstaff.' Mentally, too, he was of that giant breed; and just as Falstaff was exiled by Henry V, so was Sydney kept in exile by the politicians, who feared his freedom of thought and tongue as greatly as Henry feared Sir John's. And with as much cause.

Such was the man who, at the age of 38, was forced by the Clergy Residence Act to quit the delights of civilisation and bury himself and his family in an outlandish district 200 miles from London. Of course he did not go without a struggle. He made many attempts, then and thereafter, to exchange his Yorkshire living for one nearer the Great Parallelogram ('I believe,' said he, 'the parallelogram between Oxford Street, Piccadilly, Regent Street and Hyde Park, encloses more intelligence and human ability, to say nothing of wealth and beauty, than the world has ever collected in such a space before'), but for reasons we may guess he was never successful. At one time the Hollands thought they had captured the living of St. Paul's, Covent Garden, for him, at another St. George's, Bloomsbury, but somehow both eluded their grasp. Realising that there was no hope of reprieve, Sydney faced the prospect of life-long rustication with equanimity and determined to make the best of it. Not having sought the country for pleasure, he made a better use of his exile than Rousseau, whose passion for Nature and solitude was dealt with by Sydney in a review of Madame d'Epinay's memoirs. This lady, wrote Sydney, admired Rousseau's genius

> 'and provided him with hats and coats; and, at last, was so far deluded by his declamations about the country, as to fit him up a little hermit cottage, where there were a great many

> birds, and a great many plants and flowers – and where Rousseau was, as might have been expected, supremely miserable. His friends from Paris did not come to see him. The postman, the butcher and the baker hate romantic scenery – duchesses and marchionesses were no longer found to scramble for him. Among the real inhabitants of the country, the reputation of reading and thinking is fatal to character; and Jean Jacques cursed his own successful eloquence which had sent him from the suppers and flattery of Paris to smell daffodils, watch sparrows, or project idle saliva into the passing stream.'

The cost of removal was considerable, so Sydney published his sermons in two volumes and with the proceeds (£200) transported his family to Heslington, a village near York, where he lived for five years, driving the dozen miles to Foston with his wife every Sunday. He described his arrival at Heslington:

> 'A diner-out, a wit, and a popular preacher, I was suddenly caught up by the Archbishop of York, and transported to my living in Yorkshire, where there had not been a resident clergyman for a hundred and fifty years. Fresh from London, not knowing a turnip from a carrot, I was compelled to farm three hundred acres, and without capital to build a parsonage house. I asked and obtained three years' leave from the Archbishop, in order to effect an exchange if possible; and fixed myself meantime at a small village two miles from York, in which was a fine old house of the time of Queen Elizabeth, where resided the last of the squires with his lady, who looked as if she had walked straight out of the Ark, or had been the wife of Enoch. He was a perfect specimen of the Trullibers of old; he smoked, hunted, drank beer at his door with his grooms and dogs, and spelt over the county paper on Sundays. At first he heard I was a Jacobin and a dangerous fellow, and turned aside as I passed: but at length, when he found the peace of the village undisturbed, harvests much as usual, Juno and Ponto uninjured, he first bowed, then called, and at last reached such a pitch of confidence that he used to bring the papers, that I might explain the difficult words to him; actually discovered that I had made a joke, laughed till I thought he would have died of convulsions, and ended by inviting me to see his dogs.'

Naturally Sydney's friends wondered how he would be able to settle down to a life for which they believed him unfitted. He soon proved his adaptability:

> 'Instead of being unamused by trifles, I am, as I well knew I should be, amused by them a great deal too much; I feel an ungovernable interest about my horses or my pigs or my plants; I am forced, and always was forced, to task myself up into an interest for any higher objects.'

To Lady Holland he wrote:

> 'I have laid down two rules for the country: first, not to smite the partridge; for if I fed the poor, and comforted the sick, and instructed the ignorant, yet I should be nothing worth if I smote the partridge. If anything ever endangers the Church, it will be the strong propensity to shooting for which the clergy are remarkable. Ten thousand good shots dispersed over the country do more harm to the cause of religion than the arguments of Voltaire and Rousseau. The squire never reads, but it is not possible he can believe that religion to be genuine whose ministers destroy his game.'

His second rule for the country was to visit London once a year; for though there was great happiness in the country, it required a visit to London every year to reassure oneself of the fact. Lady Holland could not picture him in his new role. He helped her to do so:

> 'I hear you laugh at me for being happy in the country, and upon this I have a few words to say. In the first place, whether one lives or dies, I hold, and always have held, to be of infinitely less moment than is generally supposed; but if life is the choice, then it is commonsense to amuse yourself with the best you can find where you happen to be placed. I am not leading precisely the life I should choose, but that which (all things considered, as well as I could consider them) appeared to be the most eligible. I am resolved, therefore, to like it, and to reconcile myself to it; which is more manly than to feign myself above it, and to send up complaints by the post of being thrown away, and being desolate, and such like trash. I am prepared, therefore, either way. If the chances of life ever enable me to emerge, I will show you

that I have not been wholly occupied by small and sordid pursuits. If (as the greater probability is) I am come to the end of my career, I give myself quietly up to horticulture, and the annual augmentation of my family. In short, if my lot be to crawl, I will crawl contentedly; if to fly, I will fly with alacrity; but, as long as I can possibly avoid it, I will never be unhappy. If, with a pleasant wife, three children, a good house and farm, many books, and many friends, who wish me well, I cannot be happy, I am a very silly, foolish fellow, and what becomes of me is of very little consequence. I have at least this chance of doing well in Yorkshire, that I am heartily tired of London. I beg pardon for saying so much of myself, but I say it upon this subject once for all.'

Gradually he became absorbed in the mysteries of gardening, ploughing, baking, brewing, churning, drilling beans and fattening poultry, and he wrote to a female acquaintance:

> 'I have been following the plough. My talk has been of oxen, and I have gloried in the goad. Your letter operated as a charm. I remembered that there were better things than these – that there was a metropolis; that there were wits, chemists, poets, splendid feasts, and captivating women. Why remind a Yorkshire resident clergyman of these things, and put him to recollect human beings at Rome when he is fattening beasts at Ephesus?'

Farming did not take up the whole of his time. He taught his eldest child, doctored his family and the poor of the parish, became a Justice of the Peace (and annoyed his fellow-magistrates by always taking the side of poachers against their enemies the squires), started allotments and Dutch gardens for the poor, experimented with smoking chimneys, tried his hand at candle-making, and made friends with the farmers and labourers. Some of his experiments were less useful than curious. Once he fed his pigs on fermented grain and reported that they were quite happy in their sty grunting the National Anthem. He appointed himself head-cook of the village, and fed the hungry alternately on broth, rice and porridge, in order to find out what was the cheapest diet in a time of scarcity. The villagers were sometimes alarmed by the novelty of his experiments, sometimes amused by his extraordinary conversation, always pleased by his interest in their concerns.

The years went by; every attempt to change his living failed; and at last, feeling that he was likely to remain where he was, he determined to build a rectory. There had been no resident incumbent since the time of Charles II and the parsonage-house was a mere hovel. The Archbishop of York, with whom he was very friendly, had not compelled him to build, and the fact that he would have to sacrifice his entire savings had prevented him from doing so; but now there was no option. 'I may see as many crosiers in the clouds as I please,' he said, 'but when I sit down seriously to consider what I shall do upon important occasions, I must presume myself rector of Foston for life.'

Having made the decision he acted with his usual promptitude. Early in 1813 he sent for an architect, who produced plans that would have ruined him. 'You build for glory, sir; I, for use,' said Sydney, returning the plans and a solatium of £25. Then he and his wife sat down and with rule and compass worked out a plan. They hired a carpenter and mason and work was begun in June. There was difficulty over the bricks. An expert from Leeds advised Sydney to make his own from the clay on the glebe. A hundred and fifty thousand bricks were burnt, but when the kiln was opened they were found to be useless. Off went Sydney and in 24 hours had bought thousands of bricks and tons of timber. The old parsonage furnished enough material for the foundations, but how to transport the bricks and mortar for the house? Sydney was advised by neighbours to employ oxen. He bought four, christening them Tug and Lug, Hawl and Crawl. But the roads were in a shocking condition, there was a mile of deep sand near the village, and the oxen were not equal to the strain. Tug and Lug took to fainting and required buckets of sal volatile to keep them going; Hawl and Crawl just lay down in the mud and roared.

He sold them and bought a team of horses. Throughout

the autumn (during which his second son, Wyndham, was born) he could think of nothing but building. 'I live trowel in hand,' he said, and 'my whole soul is filled up by lath and plaster.' In the winter an eight-weeks frost stopped all work and caused him some anxiety, as he had to be out of his house at Heslington by March 25th. When the weather permitted he redoubled his exertions and the rectory was completed, except for the absence of doors to most of the rooms, by the third week in March. Everyone had prophesied that they would all die from the damp, but Sydney was only afraid of *cold* damp and had kept fires blazing in every room night and day for two months. The furniture was moved by degrees and their last night at Heslington was spent in a house that was empty except for a table, two chairs, and the necessary bedding on the floor – the bedsteads having been taken away the previous day.

On the 20th March, 1814, the family rose at five, the bedding was instantly sent off, and Mrs. Smith followed later in a closed carriage with her three children, a servant, and the baby, now six months old and never before out of the house. They reached Foston without mishap, but there was no road up to the parsonage, which stood in the middle of a field that had been cut up by the constant passage of carts. In this field their carriage stuck fast; Mrs. Smith jumped out, baby in arms, lost her shoe in the clay, and went on without it. Sydney welcomed his family to their new home with becoming pride, took them from room to room, and told them not to mind the fact that the bare plaster walls were running with wet. There were no carpets, no chairs; nothing was unpacked; but under Sydney's direction things were gradually straightened out and at last they sat down on packages before the blazing drawing-room fire – all very happy and joyful – and had tea off a box. Late that night Sydney issued forth with a lantern to meet the last cart, which had of course stuck in the mud. This contained the cook and the cat, and the establishment of Foston Rectory was now complete.

In a few days all was ship-shape and Sydney was writing:

> 'We ought to be ill, I believe, according to rule, and many people seem to be disappointed that we are not – but, be that as it may, we have suffered no evil . . . I am very much pleased with my house. I aimed at making it a snug parsonage and I think I have succeeded. . . . After finishing it I would not pay sixpence to alter it; but the expense of it will keep me a very poor man, a close prisoner here for my life, and render the education of my children a difficult exertion for me.'

In order to build the house he had been forced to draw on the Society for Queen Anne's Bounty. Altogether he spent above £4,000 on the rectory and farm-buildings, on laying out the grounds and road-making. His income from the living was £600 per annum, £130 of which had to be returned to the Society. For years he could hardly make both ends meet, had to practise a most rigid economy, and suffered many sleepless nights of anxiety concerning the future provision for his children. When the house had been furnished and decorated, the gardens laid out and the road made, he approved his handiwork, named his residence the Rector's Head, and thought it 'equal to any inn on the North Road'.

It was, above all, a commodious and comfortable house. All the rooms were large, light and cheerful, with wall-paper of bright colours and flowery patterns. The furniture in the drawing-room was partly Indian; books and papers were strewed upon the tables; the walls were covered with prints, mounted but not framed. In the other rooms the furniture was plain and appropriate. The house was built for use, not ornament, and every room had the furniture and fittings exactly suited to its requirements; simplicity was the keynote, convenience the object. There were no cornices; instead the paper borders encroached upon the ceilings. High walls were also a useless expense, so the whole space of the roof was added to the bedrooms and the ceilings were coved and papered. Marble was too dear and the chimney-pieces were made of Portland stone. Everywhere the wall-paper was bright and all the rooms and corridors were decorated with mounted prints.

What chiefly struck the curious visitor was the number of practical contrivances that Sydney had fitted up. For example, his fires were kept bright by air-tubes, which pierced the outer wall and opened into the centre of the grate, and his fire-irons were secured from falling. Close to his front door was an enormous speaking-trumpet, through which he could shout directions to his labourers in the fields, and a telescope, with which he could keep them under observation. In the middle of a large field stood a strange skeleton-like object: this was his Universal Scratcher, against which every animal from a lamb to a bullock could rub and scratch itself luxuriously, instead of destroying gates and hedges in the performance of that operation. The store-room contained an extraordinary assortment of medicines and pretty well everything else that might be needful to the household and the village. Sydney never used his study for work, since he read and wrote in the midst of the music and argument and bustle of his family, but he kept a quantity of medical appliances there, including his rheumatic armour. This almost amounted to a diver's costume: there were narrow buckets for the legs, which he called jack-boots, a hollow tin collar for the throat, large tin objects like legs of mutton for the shoulders, a hollow tin helmet for the head – each receptacle, when in use, filled with hot water.

The household was as much Sydney's creation as the house. The more notable members may be mentioned. First, there was Annie Kay, who entered his service at Heslington as a girl of nineteen, became nurse to the children, lady's maid, housekeeper, apothecary's assistant, factotum, family consultant and friend, and finally nurse to her old master on his deathbed. Then there was Molly Mills, who looked after the cows, pigs, poultry and garden, acted as postwoman, and was considered the wit of the village. Then there was Bunch, the butler. A man-servant was too expensive, said Sydney, 'so I caught up a little garden-girl, made like a milestone, christened her Bunch, put a napkin in her hand, and made her my butler. The girls taught her to read,

Mrs. Sydney to wait, and I undertook her morals; Bunch became the best butler in the county.' He took great pains over Bunch and at length even trained her to answer questions promptly. 'Bunch, do you like roast duck or boiled chicken?' he asked her suddenly one day. 'Roast duck, please, sir,' she replied, without an instant's hesitation, and went on her way. 'You may laugh,' he said to a friend who was standing by, 'but you have no idea of the labour it has cost me to give her that decision of character.' Her chief crimes, which he made her repeat every day, were plate-snatching, gravy-spilling, door-slamming, blue-bottle fly-catching (which meant standing with her mouth open and not attending), and curtsey-bobbing. Bunch eventually became cook. Finally, there was Jack Robinson, the carpenter, who had a face like a full moon. He made most of the furniture for the house and on state occasions waited at table, when, according to Sydney, he would sometimes stick a gimlet into the bread instead of a fork.

No account of the Foston establishment would be complete without a reference to its means of conveyance.

> 'After diligent research,' Sydney recorded, 'I discovered in the back settlements of a York coachmaker an ancient green chariot, supposed to have been the earliest invention of the kind. I brought it home in triumph to my admiring family. Being somewhat dilapidated, the village-tailor lined it, the village blacksmith repaired it; nay, but for Mrs. Sydney's earnest entreaties, we believe the village-painter would have exercised his genius upon the exterior; it escaped this danger, however, and the result was wonderful. Each year added to its charms: it grew younger and younger; a new wheel, a new spring; I christened it the *Immortal*; it was known all over the neighbourhood; the village boys cheered it, and the village dogs barked at it; but *Faber meæ fortunæ* was my motto, and we had no false shame.'

The village-tailor, Thomas Johnson, fortunately provided not only the lining of the chariot, but another aspect of Sydney's character. Johnson received his orders from Mrs. Smith, and when he had executed them Sydney inspected the work, was displeased with it and spoke pretty sharply to the tailor. The man retaliated and both of them lost their tempers. At last Johnson said that if Mr. Smith repeated his accusation that the work had not been done according to instructions, he would throw the scissors at his head. Mr. Smith repeated it. The scissors were thrown. The rector dodged them, gave the man a severe dressing-down and marched home in anger. Later he reappeared, explained that they had both been right (Mrs. Smith having misunderstood his directions), gave Johnson half a crown, and they parted amicably.

In wet weather the *Immortal* took them to church, drawn by a cart-horse, with Mrs. Smith and the children inside and Sydney perched behind on the dickey. Sometimes it carried them further afield on visits to friends.

Sydney remained at Foston until July, 1829, and throughout that time, except for occasional absences, including a trip to London every spring, he led a retired life, brightened now and then by the arrival of visitors. He improved his land and helped to improve the roads in the neighbourhood. At first he lost money on farming and came to the conclusion that the first receipt to farm well was to be rich; in later years he did not do so badly, though sometimes the weather nearly spoilt his harvest and he only managed to save his corn 'by injecting large quantities of fermented liquors into the workmen and making them work all night'. Once at least even this method failed and he broke the news to a friend: 'We are told that Man is not to live by bread alone; this is comfortable, for there will be very little of it this year.' He bought some Scotch sheep, but they became homesick, crawled through hedges, and proceeded briskly on their return journey to the north. They were brought back and efforts were made to fatten them. Turnips in winter and clover in summer had no effect on them and he declared that certain sheep were 'only emphatically termed Scotch to signify *ill-fed*, as one says Roman to signify *brave*'.

His time was fully occupied. He was village-doctor as well

as village-parson and his job as a magistrate often took him away from his parish. These journeys he did on a horse, whose name, Calamity, explained why he was forced at length to give up riding. Falls were numerous:

> 'Somehow or other my horse and I had a habit of parting company. On one occasion I found myself suddenly prostrate in the streets of York, much to the delight of the Dissenters. Another time my horse Calamity flung me over his head into a neighbouring parish, as if I had been a shuttlecock, and I felt grateful it was not into a neighbouring planet.'

Later he was able to purchase a gig.

He was exceedingly popular among the poor of his parish, not only because he fed them when they were hungry and doctored them when they were ill, but because he took a keen interest in their affairs, gave them advice whenever it was needed, made them laugh, and attended to the wants of their children. Though devoted to children, he had some quaint ideas of disciplining the young. A little girl who was caught biting one of his fallen peaches was made to stand all day on the lawn with a placard round her neck bearing the word 'Thief' in large letters. A lad who was discovered looking covetously at the rector's fruit-trees had his ears pinched with such vigour that they tingled in old age at the remembrance of the episode. It is true that Sydney made amends for such harshnesses, but they displayed a nature that was not wholly free from the tyranny he so often condemned. Against this it must be said that the village children loved him (when he was not feeling sensitive about his fruit) and that he seldom failed them when they clamoured for sweets.

He spent much of his time educating his boys, first Douglas and then Wyndham. The former made such rapid progress that Sydney was seriously concerned about the boy's scholastic future. A public school was beyond his means and in any case he detested the system. Nevertheless Douglas was so clever, so quick at his lessons, that a school of some sort was desirable. Sydney inspected several and had just picked on a place at Richmond when his elder brother 'Bobus' offered to pay all expenses if he would send Douglas to a public school. He could not allow his personal objections to stand in the way of a possible benefit to his son ('Nothing,' he said, 'can be more unjust and natural than the conduct of parents in placing their children'), accepted the offer, and in the spring of 1818 Douglas went to Westminster, where he passed through the regular ill-treatment of those days, his body being lacerated by a master and an eye almost dislodged by an older boy. His father had serious thoughts of removing him from the school and in a letter to a friend referred to the training as 'an intense system of tyranny of which the English are very fond and think it fits a boy for the world; but the world, bad as it is, has nothing half so bad'.

In the autumn of 1818 Douglas was down with an attack of typhus fever and his mother went south to nurse him, the rest of the family travelling to London later in order to spend Christmas with him. Douglas was delicate and had to be nursed by his mother through another attack of typhus four years later, but he did well at school, became Captain, obtained a scholarship, and went to Christ Church, Oxford. His father wrote to him regularly while he was at Westminster, was delighted when he became passionately fond of books, and gave him a piece of advice:

> 'In the time you can give to English reading you should consider what it is most needful to have, what it is most shameful to want – shirts and stockings before frills and collars. . . . For the English poets, I will let you off at present with Milton, Dryden, Pope and Shakespeare; and remember, always in books, keep the best company. Don't read a line of Ovid till you have mastered Virgil; nor a line of Thomson till you have exhausted Pope; nor of Massinger till you are familiar with Shakespeare.'

Wyndham was also educated by his father, who, for the sake of the child's future, threatened to bring him up a Methodist and a Tory. We do not know what means he took to encourage the boy's progress along those lines, but we do know that Wyndham finished up at Charterhouse and Cambridge, became fond of sport, and preferred gambling and horse-racing to reading and writing.

In the midst of his domestic affairs and the other activities in which he was engaged, Sydney still found time for the *Edinburgh Review*, writing long articles at regular intervals and scarcely ever letting the editor down. 'I never break my word about reviews,' he told Jeffrey, 'except when I am in London.' But he found 'a most alarming good-nature' growing upon him, and could not attack writers merely because their political opinions differed from his. Incidentally, he sometimes criticised the Whigs in the *Review*, candidly admitting that he would always like to reconcile the interests of truth with the feelings of party, but that if it could not be done, party had to give way to truth. He was not really a party man. 'Lay aside your Whiggish delusions of ruin,' he wrote to a wealthy manufacturer; 'learn to look the prosperity of the country in the face, and bear it as well as you can.' And he reported the country as profoundly peaceful and prosperous, 'the reverse of everything we have prophesied in the *Edinburgh Review* for 20 years'. He believed the Whigs would introduce the reforms he had at heart, but he did not think they were always quite right in the head: 'Why do you not scout more that pernicious cant that all men are equal?' he asked Jeffrey: 'As politicians they do not differ – but they differ enough to make you and all worthy men sincerely wish for the elevation of the one and the rejection of the other.'

As early as 1819 he strongly advised Jeffrey to start working for parliamentary reform – 'done it *must* and *will* be,' he declared – but he did not think the world's problems could be solved by a democratic government, and the Tory oligarchy then in power was so bad that it was bound to end in democracy or despotism: 'In which of these two evils it terminates is of no more consequence than from which tube of a double-barrelled pistol I meet my destruction.' He wanted to 'show the government to the people in some other attitude than that of taxing, punishing and restraining', and he considered that 'a politician should be as flexible in little things as he is inflexible in great'. Some politicians seemed to imagine there was nothing so difficult as to bully a whole people – 'in fact, there is nothing so easy,' remarked Sydney, 'as that great artist Lord Castlereagh so well knows. . . . Of all ingenious instruments of despotism, I most commend a popular assembly where the majority are paid and hired, and a few bold and able men, by their brave speeches, make the people believe they are free'.

When the elections took a favourable turn in 1817, Sydney wrote: 'The people are all mad; what can they possibly mean by being so wise and so reasonable?' On one occasion he voted for Wilberforce, 'on account of his good conduct in Africa, a place returning no members to Parliament, but still, from the extraordinary resemblance its inhabitants bear to human creatures, of some consequence'. He was not much impressed by the politicians of either side and gave his opinion of an election – 'each party acting and thinking as if the salvation of several planets depended upon the adoption of Mr. Johnson and the rejection of Mr. Jackson.' Another time he wrote: 'Politics, domestic and foreign, are very discouraging: Jesuits abroad – Turks in Greece – No-Poperists in England. A panting to burn B; B fuming to roast C; C miserable that he cannot reduce D to ashes; and D consigning to eternal perdition the three first letters of the alphabet.' Nor was he impressed by the type of politician who courted unpopularity: 'Lord Lauderdale, with all his good qualities and talents, has an appetite for being hooted and pelted, which is ten times a more foolish passion than the love of being applauded and huzzaed.' Only the basest type of man could hope to succeed in politics:

> 'The Tories here are by no means satisfied with —, who is subjected to vacillations between right and wrong. They want a man steadily base, who may be depended upon for want of principle. I think on these points Mr.— might satisfy any reasonable man; but they are exorbitant in their demands.'

When two or three respectable citizens were given government posts, he reached this dismal conclusion: 'I cannot help looking upon it as a most melancholy proof of the miserable state of this country when men of integrity and ability are employed. If it was possible to have gone on without them, I am sure they would have never been thought of.'

While Napoleon was still at large on the continent, Sydney realised it was useless to talk of peace: 'It is better to bring up our young ones to war than to peace. I burn gunpowder every day under the nostrils of my little boy, and talk to him often of fighting to put him out of conceit with civil sciences and prepare him for the evil times which are coming.' He described war as 'that system of vigour which, when displayed by individuals instead of nations, is usually mitigated by a strait waistcoat and low diet'. In his opinion there was no such thing as a 'just war', or at least as a *wise* war, though he followed this statement with: 'We *must* have a small massacre of magistrates; nothing else will do.' When peace was temporarily restored in 1814, Sydney confessed that he never laughed more heartily than at the idea of Bonaparte retiring on a pension. Later he expressed his admiration of the fallen Emperor for not committing suicide, 'which is, in a soldier, easy, vulgar and commonly foolish; it shows that he has a strong tendency to hope, or that he has a confidence in his own versatility of character, and his means of making himself happy by trifling, or by intellectual exertion'. John Allen wrote from Holland House that the restoration of the Bourbons would mean the final blow to liberty. Sydney replied:

> 'I cannot at all enter into your feelings about the Bourbons, nor can I attend to so remote an evil as the encouragement to superstitious attachment to kings, when the proposed evil of a military ministry, or of thirty years more of war, is before my eyes. I want to get rid of this great disturber of human happiness, and I scarcely know any price too great to effect it. If you were sailing from Alicant to Aleppo in a storm, and, after the sailors had held up the image of a saint and prayed to it, the storm were to abate, you would be more sorry for the encouragement of superstition than rejoiced at the pre-

servation of your life; and so would every other man born and bred in Edinburgh. My views of the matter would be much shorter and coarser: I should be so glad to find myself alive, that I should not care a farthing if the storm had generated a thousand new, and revived as many old saints. How can any man stop in the midst of the stupendous joy of getting rid of Bonaparte, and prophesy a thousand little peddling evils that will result from restoring the Bourbons?'

In 1823 it was the opinion of everyone that England would have to go to war in defence of Spain. Sydney declared: 'I would rather the nascent liberties of Spain were extinguished than go to war to defend them,' and asked 'Why are the English to be the sole vindicators of the human race?' When Lady Grey hinted at the necessity of intervention, he sent an explosive reply:

> 'For God's sake, do not drag me into another war! I am worn down and worn out with crusading and defending Europe and protecting mankind; I *must* think a little of myself. I am sorry for the Spaniards – I am sorry for the Greeks – I deplore the fate of the Jews; the people of the Sandwich Islands are groaning under the most detestable tyranny; Baghdad is oppressed – I do not like the present state of the Delta – Tibet is not comfortable. Am I to fight for all these people? The world is bursting with sin and sorrow. Am I to be champion of the Decalogue and to be eternally raising fleets and armies to make all men good and happy? We have just done saving Europe, and I am afraid the consequence will be that we shall cut each other's throats. No war, dear Lady Grey! no eloquence; but apathy, selfishness, common-sense, arithmetic! I beseech you, secure Lord Grey's sword and pistols, as the housekeeper did Don Quixote's armour. If there is another war, life will not be worth having. I will go to war with the King of Denmark if he is impertinent to you, or does any injury to Howick; but for no other cause. "May the vengeance of Heaven" overtake all the Legitimates of Verona! but, in the present state of rent and taxes, they must be *left* to the vengeance of Heaven. I allow fighting in such a cause to be a luxury; but the business of a prudent, sensible man is to guard against luxury.'

Sydney's letters to friends from Foston contain, as usual,

many of those shrewdly humorous comments on people and events, the charm of which entered and left English literature with him. Here are a few passages from his correspondence with Lady Holland:

'I shall be extremely happy to see Henry, and will leave a note for him at the tavern where the mail stops to say so. Nothing can exceed the dullness of this place and this family: but he has been accustomed to live alone with his grandmother, which, though an highly moral life, is not a very amusing one. There are two Scotch ladies staying here with whom he will get acquainted, and to whom he may safely make love the ensuing winter: for love, though a very acute disorder in Andalusia, puts on a very chronic shape in these high northern latitudes; for first the lover must prove *metapheezically* that he ought to; and then in the fifth or sixth year of courtship, or rather argument, if the summer is tolerably warm, and oatmeal plenty, the fair one yields.'

'You are aware that it is necessary to fumigate Scotch tutors; they are excellent men, but require this little preliminary caution. They are apt also to break church windows, and get behind a hedge and fling stones at the clergyman of the parish, and betray other little symptoms of irreligion; but these you must not mind.'

'I hope you have read, or are reading, Mr. Stewart's book, and are far gone in the philosophy of the mind, a science, as he repeatedly tells us, still in its infancy: I propose myself to wait till it comes to years of discretion. I hear Lord Holland has taken a load of fishing-tackle with him; this is a science which appears to me to be still in its infancy.'

'How very odd, dear Lady Holland, to ask me to dine with you on Sunday, the 9th, when I am coming to stay with you from the 5th to the 12th. It is like giving a gentleman an assignation for Wednesday when you are going to marry him on the Sunday preceding – an attempt to combine the stimulus of gallantry with the security of connubial relations.'

'I am concerned to hear of Lord Holland's gout. I observe that gout loves ancestors and genealogy. It needs five or six generations of gentlemen or noblemen to give it its full vigour.'

'Agar Ellis looks very ill; he has naturally a bad constitution, is ennuied and blasé, and vexed that he cannot procure any progeny. I did not say so – but I thought how absurd to discontinue the use of domestic chaplains in cases where landed property is concerned. I was prepared to set off for

London, when a better account arrived from Dr. Bond. I think you mistake Bond's character in supposing he could be influenced by partridges. He is a man of very independent mind with whom pheasants at least, or perhaps turkeys, are necessary.'

'I have written to Maltby . . . that you have peculiar opinions about the preterpluperfect tense; and this, I know, will bring him directly, for that tense has always occasioned him much uneasiness, though he has appeared to the world cheerful and serene.'

Lord Henry Petty, who became the third Marquis of Lansdowne in 1809, had married a daughter of the Earl of Ilchester in 1808. Naturally they wanted a son and heir, but Lady Lansdowne gave no sign of fruition till the autumn of 1810. Sydney heard the good news and wrote to Lady Holland:

'I am happy to hear that there appears now to be a solid foundation laid for a young Petty. Nothing astonishes the country clergy so much as the difficulty which the nobility experience in making these arrangements.'

Lady Holland had a friend who was about to take a voyage in the *Diana*. Sydney wrote:

'I am looking out daily for the *Diana*. What good can there be in a ship with a chaste name? . . . Venus sprang from the sea. Fish increase their kind in prodigious numbers. All seaports are remarkable for their improprieties. Why go to sea in a ship with a chaste name? We are all well and are about to be overpowered with cousins and aunts, a set of relatives grown rapidly rich within a twelvemonth by legacies, and rushing from behind the counter to the Lakes.'

Mrs. Fry was a famous prison reformer. Sydney once accompanied her on a visit to a prison and was much touched by her humanity and the affection she inspired among the prisoners. But –

'Mrs. Fry,' he wrote, 'is very unpopular with the clergy: examples of living, active virtue disturb our repose, and give birth to distressing comparisons: we long to burn her alive.'

Lady Holland had a footman named Antonio, who caused a crisis at Holland House. Sydney reported the matter to Lady Grey:

> 'Antonio is married to one of the under-cook-maids, which makes the French cook very angry, as an interference with his department and perquisites.'

Two passages from his letters to Lady Mary Bennett may be quoted:

> 'I recommend you to read the first and second volumes of the four volumes of the Abbé Georgel's *Memoirs*. You will suppose, from this advice, that there is something improper in the third and fourth; but, to spare you the trouble of beginning with them, I assure you I only exclude them from my recommendation because they are dull.'
>
> 'Pray send me some treasonable news about the Queen. Will the people rise? Will the greater part of the House of Lords be thrown into the Thames? Will short work be made of the Bishops? If you know, tell me; and don't leave me in this odious state of innocence, when you can give me so much guilty information, and make me as wickedly instructed as yourself. And if you know that the Bishops are to be massacred write by return of post.'

Two selections from letters to Mrs. Meynell:

> 'The usual establishment for an eldest landed baby is: two wet nurses, two dry ditto, two aunts, two physicians, two apothecaries; three female friends of the family, unmarried, advanced in life; and often, in the nursery, one clergyman, six flatterers, and a grandpapa! Less than this would not be decent.'
>
> 'Let me beg of you to take more care of those beautiful geraniums, and not let the pigs in upon them. Geranium-fed bacon is of a beautiful colour; but it takes so many plants to fatten one pig, that such a system can never answer. I cannot conceive who put it into your head.'

The following passages have been carefully culled from the rest of his Foston correspondence:

> 'The steady writing of Lord —'s frank indicates a prolonged existence of ten years. If a stroke to the *t* or a dot to the *i* were wanting, little — might have some chance; but I do

not think a single Jew out of the Twelve Tribes would lend him a farthing upon post-obits, if he had seen my Lord's writing.'

'Gaiety – English gaiety – is seldom come at lawfully; friendship or propriety or principle are sacrificed to obtain it; we cannot produce it without more effort than it is worth; our destination is to look vacant and to sit silent.'

'I mean to make some maxims, like Rochefoucauld, and to preserve them. My first is this: – After having lived half their lives respectably, many men get tired of honesty, and many women of propriety.'

'Very few people in writing to their friends have enough egoism. If Horner were to break fifteen of his ribs, or marry, or resolve to settle in America, he would never mention it to his friends; but would write with the most sincere kindness from Kentucky, to inquire for your welfare, leaving you to marvel as you chose at the post-mark, and to speculate whether it was Kentucky or Kensington.'

'Crabbe is coming out with a poem of 12,000 lines, for which, and the copy of his other works, Murray is to give him £3,000 – a sum which Crabbe has heard mentioned before, but of which he can form no very accurate numerical notion. All sums beyond an hundred pounds must be to him mere indistinct vision – clouds and darkness.'

'I will write to Mr. Bailey on the very interesting subject of venison – a subject which is deemed amongst the clergy a professional one.'

'Lord Tankerville has sent me a whole buck; this necessarily takes up a good deal of my time.'

'The Commissioner will have hard work with the Scotch atheists: they are said to be numerous this season, and in great force from the irregular supply of rain.'

'Lord Liverpool's messenger mistook the way, and instead of bringing the mitre to me, took it to my next-door neighbour, Dr. Carey, who very fraudulently accepted it. Lord Liverpool is extremely angry, and I am to have the next.'

'My friend (a potter), to whom we are all so deeply indebted every night and morning, wishes to place a son at Edinburgh. . . . Pray be so good as to . . . mention some good Presbyterian body who takes pupils at no great salary. . . . All I require is that he should be steady and respectable, and that the young fashioner of vases and basins should have an apartment to himself, in which he may meditate intensely on clay.'

Lastly a letter that Sydney wrote to Lady Morpeth in 1820 must be quoted in full, since it contained his own rules of life:

> 'DEAR LADY GEORGIANA, – Nobody has suffered more from low spirits than I have done – so I feel for you. 1st. Live as well as you dare. 2nd. Go into the shower-bath with a small quantity of water at a temperature low enough to give you a slight sensation of cold, 75°. or 80°. 3rd. Amusing books. 4th. Short views of human life – not further than dinner or tea. 5th. Be as busy as you can. 6th. See as much as you can of those friends who respect and like you. 7th. And of those acquaintances who amuse you. 8th. Make no secret of low spirits to your friends, but talk of them freely – they are always worse for dignified concealment. 9th. Attend to the effects tea and coffee produce upon you. 10th. Compare your lot with that of other people. 11th. Don't expect too much from human life – a sorry business at the best. 12th. Avoid poetry, dramatic representations (except comedy), music, serious novels, melancholy, sentimental people, and everything likely to excite feeling or emotion, not ending in active benevolence. 13th. *Do good*, and endeavour to please everybody of every degree. 14th. Be as much as you can in the open air without fatigue. 15th. Make the room where you commonly sit gay and pleasant. 16th. Struggle by little and little against idleness. 17th. Don't be too severe upon yourself, or underrate yourself, but do yourself justice. 18th. Keep good blazing fires. 19th. Be firm and constant in the exercise of rational religion. 20th. Believe me, dear Lady Georgiana, Very truly yours, – SYDNEY SMITH.'

Certain events in Sydney's later life at Foston have now to be recorded. In 1818 the Earl of Ossory died and left his Bedfordshire estates to his nephew, Lord Holland, who instantly offered the vacant living of Ampthill to Sydney. But as it was not such a good living as Foston, and could not be held with it, Sydney declined the offer with thanks. In 1820 the death of his father's sister left him with a private income of £400 a year, and five years later the Duke of Devonshire (at the request of the Earl of Carlisle) gave Sydney the valuable living of Londesborough, which he held along with Foston for seven years, until the Earl's nephew came of age and stepped into it.

In 1824 he was appointed chaplain to the High Sheriff of Yorkshire and preached two sermons in York Minster before the Judges of Assize. At one of them the Judges were a little astonished by the text: 'Sittest thou here to judge me after the law, and commandest thou me to be smitten contrary to the law?' At the other it was the turn of the barristers, who were startled by the opening words: 'And, behold, a certain lawyer stood up and tempted him.' But as is the manner of sermons, the text was the most alarming part of each discourse, and Sydney was not above making his congregation jump before they went to sleep.

In March, 1825, a meeting of the clergy of Cleveland to petition Parliament against the emancipation of the Catholics was held at the 'Three Tuns', Thirsk. Sydney attended it, making his first appearance on a political platform. He spoke, of course, against the majority petition, proposed one of his own (for which he obtained two supporters) and told his reverend brethren exactly what he thought of them.

A month later the clergy of the East Riding of Yorkshire held a meeting for the same purpose at the 'Tiger Inn', Beverley. Again Sydney spoke, and this time he was in a minority of one. 'My excellent and respectable curate, Mr. Milestones, alarmed at the effect of the Pope upon the East Riding, has come here to oppose me,' Sydney informed the meeting, 'and there he stands, breathing war and vengeance on the Vatican.' As a matter of fact, Mr. Milestones had asked Sydney whether he would resent the public opposition of his own curate, but Sydney was not a man of that sort and had assured him that 'nothing would give me more pain than to think I had prevented, in any man, the free assertion of honest opinions – that such conduct on his part, instead of causing jealousy and animosity between us, could not and would not fail to increase my regard and respect for him'. Sydney delivered a trenchant speech, making it as brief as possible, 'from compassion to my reverend brethren, who have trotted many miles to vote against the Pope, and who will trot back in the dark if I attempt to throw additional light upon the subject'. When he sat down a poor clergyman whispered his complete agreement with every word Sydney had said, but confessed that he was the father of nine children. Sydney begged him to remain a Protestant. Always anxious to discuss everything with everybody, Sydney asked the servants of the inn what they thought of the question, and reported their views to a friend: 'The chambermaid was decidedly for the Church of England. Boots was for the Catholics. The waiter said he had often (God forgive him) wished them both confounded together.'

Sydney was in constant touch with the various members of his family. 'Bobus' had gone out to India as Advocate-General of Bengal and after eight years returned with a wife, a family and a fortune. He visited his brother at Foston and when, later, he fell a victim to typhus, Sydney journeyed to Northampton and looked after him. Eventually he settled at Cheam, entered Parliament, and made his fame as a wit in social circles. Sydney was very fond of him and once wrote: 'Let us contrive to last out for the same or nearly the same time; weary will be the latter half of my pilgrimage if you leave me in the lurch.' 'Bobus' had so much of the same feeling that he died within a fortnight of Sydney.

Another brother, Cecil, left India as a consequence of a quarrel with a high official and died at the Cape in 1814 on his way home. His Winchester brother, Courtenay, made a vast fortune in India, quarrelled with the East India Company, and returned home. 'Truly the Smiths are a stiff-necked generation,' commented Sydney; 'and yet they have all got rich but I. Courtenay, they say, has £150,000, and he keeps only a cat!'

After the death of Sydney's mother in 1802, his sister Maria took care of their father. Sydney thought highly of her and when she died in 1816 wrote that he would have cultivated her as a friend if nature had not given her to him as a relation. After her death Sydney visited his father as often as he could afford the journey and got to like him better: 'My father is one of the very few people I have ever seen improved by age. He is become careless, indulgent, and anacreontic.' The old gentleman actually settled down in one place when he reached the age of eighty, and died at Bishop's Lydiard, near Taunton, in 1827, in his eighty-eighth year.

The family circle at Foston Rectory sustained its first loss on New Year's Day, 1828, when Emily, the younger daughter, was married to Nathaniel Hibbert, a young barrister, whose father owned an estate in Hertfordshire and lived at Munden House, Watford. The Archbishop of York performed the ceremony at Foston Church, and after it was over Sydney felt as if he had 'lost a limb and were walking about with one leg'.

Young people were indeed necessary to his existence in the country: 'There is more happiness in a multitude of children than safety in a multitude of counsellors,' he once wrote; 'and if I was a rich man, I should like to have and would have 20 children.' In 1814, when he was financially embarrassed, had no prospects, and was surrounded by a young and increasing family, he had written to Jeffrey: 'The haunts of Happiness are varied and rather unaccountable; but I have more often seen her among little children, and home firesides, and in country houses, than anywhere else – at least, I think so.'

CHAPTER VIII

PEOPLE AND PLACES

AMONG Sydney's early callers following his occupation of Foston Rectory were Lord and Lady Carlisle, who lived nearby at Castle Howard. Their coach was bogged in the field and the Earl, a capricious and haughty old gentleman, did not arrive in a gracious frame of mind; but Sydney soon laughed him into a good temper and from that moment the doors of Castle Howard were open to the new rector and his wife, both of whom frequently stayed there for a few days at a time. Their life at Foston was, in fact, not a little brightened by the family of Howard, and Sydney remained on affectionate terms with its members to the end of his days. Another great house in the north where he was always welcomed was Howick, the residence of Lord and Lady Grey.

It has been said that he was a little too fond of the aristocracy, and it cannot be denied that he was partial to fine company and good dinners, but there was not an atom of servility in his attitude towards his noble hosts, who had to take him on his own terms and who were liable at any moment to find themselves the victims of his raillery. The fact is that he amused them, shook them out of themselves, acted upon them as a mental tonic. It must have been a new sensation for them to see the gravity of their servants completely upset and to be able to dispense for a time with their own dignity.

An extensive search through the chronicles and correspondence of the period has failed to reveal a single instance of obsequiousness in Sydney's attitude to titled people. On the contrary, his public and private utterances showed far less respect for names of distinction than did those of Dr. Johnson, who could scarcely be accused of sycophancy. He expressed such admirations as he felt quite honestly, whether the subject were Mrs. Fry or Lord Grey; but, as Professor Saintsbury pointed out, he was more destitute of romance and reverence than any man who ever lived. He did occasionally use phrases of exaggerated self-abasement which may have been misunderstood by certain people. The most extreme example of this appeared in a note to Lord Grey:

> 'It is not very necessary that a fly should announce to an Elephant the precise hour at which he means to perch upon him – but I may as well say that I shall (if I can) be at Howick on Wednesday next instead of Thursday – but as I am a traveller in stage coaches, I depend upon accident.'

The recipient was scarcely likely to take that for the language of flattery.

Sydney's friends did not forsake him during his long exile in Yorkshire. Most of them stayed with him at one time or another. Jeffrey, Horner, Brougham, Dugald Stewart and John Playfair came south, while Samuel Rogers, Sir James Mackintosh, John Whishaw and Henry Luttrell went north to visit him. Some of these friends now claim a little space in his biography.

Samuel Rogers was one of the three chief wits in the Holland House circle, Sydney and Luttrell being the others. He started life as a banker, but when still fairly young had forsaken the profession of coining money and embraced the profession of coining words. He became a poet, and was highly thought of in that capacity by Byron, though not so highly by Sydney Smith.

'How is Rogers?' asked someone.
'He is not very well,' replied Sydney.
'Why, what is the matter?'
'Oh, don't you know he has produced a couplet? When he is

delivered of a couplet, with infinite labour and pain, he takes to his bed, has straw laid down, the knocker tied up, expects his friends to call and make enquiries, and the answer at the door invariably is "Mr. Rogers and his little couplet are as well as can be expected." When he produces an Alexandrine he keeps his bed a day longer.'

Rogers gained a great reputation as a host. Nearly every writer and artist of note in the first half of the nineteenth century went to one or more of those famous 'breakfasts' at his house in St. James's Place, overlooking the Green Park. He was generous with his money but churlish with his tongue. Finicky, fastidious and old-maidish in his habits, he was waspish in speech and chilling in manner. He enjoyed saying ill-natured things about his acquaintances, excusing himself on the ground that as he had a weak voice no one would listen to him unless he spoke badly of people. He had a corpse-like face and Sydney once said that he never thought of death in London except when he met Rogers. Sydney also advised him, when he was about to have his portrait painted, to adopt the decorous attitude usual with parsons when they entered a pulpit, and cover his face with his hands.

In spite of his cadaverous appearance he was much admired by women and had the reputation of a Don Juan. There was considerable rivalry between the two men in social gatherings, but Sydney's wit was so good-natured and spontaneous that he completely outshone Rogers as a talker whenever they were together. 'As for me,' he once said, 'I like a little noise and nature, and Rogers much chagrined, and a large party very merry and happy.' They were, nevertheless, very fond of one another. Rogers was kind to Sydney from his earliest days in London, and when Rogers was ill Sydney sat for hours by his bedside making him laugh so much that he forgot the nature of his complaint. Rogers suffered from bad health all his life, and, as so often happens with chronic invalids, outlived all his healthy contemporaries. At the age of eighty-seven, on the death of Wordsworth, he was offered the Laureateship, but he declined it, and Poetry lost nothing by his modesty.

Sir James Mackintosh was a philosopher whose well-nigh incredible knowledge of history, law and politics inspired his friends, with the exception of Sydney Smith, to write of him in a manner little short of idolatrous. Sydney never lost his head and his essay on Mackintosh, incomparably better than Macaulay's, is one of the best pen-portraits in the language. The most obvious aspect of Mackintosh's character was a complete absence of envy, hatred, malice and uncharitableness.

> 'He could not hate,' said Sydney; 'he did not know how to set about it. The gall-bladder was omitted in his composition, and if he could have been persuaded into any scheme of revenging himself upon an enemy . . . it would have ended in proclaiming the good qualities and promoting the interests of his adversary. Truth had so much more power over him than anger, that (whatever might be the provocation) he could not misrepresent, nor exaggerate.'

As a talker he had one serious fault. He wrapped up the most insignificant matter in a garment of elaborate prose. Sydney parodied his style to perfection in a letter dated August the 8th, 1826, to Lord Holland:

> 'It struck me last night as I was lying in bed that Mackintosh, if he were to write on pepper, would thus describe it :
>
> > 'Pepper may philosophically be described as the adust and highly-pulverized seed of an oriental fruit, an article rather of condiment than diet, which, dispersed lightly over the surface of food with no other rule than the caprice of the consumer, communicates pleasure rather than affords nutrition, and by adding a tropical flavour to the gross and succulent viands of the North approximates the different regions of the earth, explains the objects of commerce, and justifies the industry of man.'
>
> 'Pray remember me kindly to S. Rogers. Tell him that his Christian name only is a substantive, that his surname is a verb, and that both together form a proposition and assert a fact which makes him the envy of *one* and the favourite of the *other* sex. Mustard and salt in my next.'

A serious weakness in Mackintosh was an absurd good-nature, which prevented him from drawing any distinction between good and bad in people or books. He habitually eulogised everybody and everything, and consequently his praise and commendation were valueless. With this weakness went an inability to look after his own interests, and if his friends had not looked after them for him he would have finished his days in a garret or a workhouse. Lord Holland said that Mackintosh was the only Scot he ever knew who felt the delight of lounging. Add to this a passion for reading and talking. He would travel round the country with so many books that it was often impossible to pull up or let down the windows of his carriage; and, when he left a house, he frequently left his hat behind him.

As a speaker in the House of Commons he was a complete failure. His voice was bad and nasal and while he droned on the benches were gradually emptied; then, as now, members did not wish for instruction but for oratorical platitudes. His conversation lacked spontaneity; he always seemed to be recollecting, not creating, producing facts from the storehouse of his memory, not seeing things suddenly in a new light. There was about him a lack of heartiness and cordiality; his handshake, according to Sydney, came under the genus 'mortmain'; and he had more affection for mankind than for individual men and women; but whenever his philanthropic spirit was aroused he could 'like a great ship of war, cut his cable, and spread his enormous canvas, and launch into a wide sea of reasoning eloquence'.

In 1818 Lady Holland managed to get him a professorship at Haileybury. There had been several outbreaks of insubordination among the students there and on one occasion the professors, subjected to a hail of stones, had been forced to take refuge in the College buildings. Sydney heard of this and made a suggestion: 'Might it not be advisable for the professors to learn the use of the sling (*balearis habena*)? – it would give them a great advantage over the students.' When the news of Mackintosh's appointment reached Foston, Sydney wrote to Lady Holland, described Sir James as a very great and a very delightful man, who 'with a few bad qualities added to his character would have acted a most conspicuous part in life', and went on: 'A professorship at Hertford is well imagined, and if he can keep clear of contusions at the annual peltings, all will be well. The season for lapidating the professors is now at hand; keep him quiet at Holland House till all is over.'

Another of Sydney's Foston visitors was John Whishaw, who was known as 'the Pope of Holland House' because his literary opinions were heard with a deference almost equal to that formerly paid to Dr. Johnson's. His reputation was largely due to the fact that, while other people were busy exchanging views on the book of the moment, he contented himself with looking wise and remaining silent. His behaviour was in marked contrast with Sydney's, who never hesitated a second in proclaiming his likes and dislikes. Once, when all the highbrow world was damning Scott's *The Heart of Midlothian*, Sydney incautiously praised it, thought it 'as good as any except the one in which Claverhouse is introduced and of which I forget the name,' asked 'who can read it without laughing and crying twenty times?' and adduced the final proof: 'My test of a book written to amuse is amusement.' Then he wondered whether he ought to have given such free rein to his feelings and admitted that Whishaw's was the best plan: he gave no opinion for the first week, but confined himself merely to chuckling and elevating his chin; in the meantime he drove diligently about to the fixed critical stations, breakfasted in Mark Lane with Ricardo, heard from Malthus of Hertford College, and by Saturday night was as bold as a lion and as decisive as a court of justice. Nevertheless Sydney considered that Whishaw had 'character enough to make him well received if he were dull, and wit enough to make him popular if he were a rogue'; which was certainly not the effect he produced on Thomas Carlyle, who described him as 'a puffy, thickset, vulgar little dump of an old man,' who waddled into the room where Thomas was sitting and whose manners and talk were far from admirable. 'Nothing real in him but the stomach and the effrontery to fill it', was Carlyle's summary of 'the Pope'. We need not attempt to reconcile the two verdicts, for it is hardly likely that Sydney and Carlyle would have agreed on anything or anybody under the sun; the one had a good digestion, the other had not.

All that remains to be said of Whishaw is that he was Commissioner of Public Accounts from 1806 to 1835, and that he began life with an accident and ended it in the same way. He was to have taken Holy Orders, but lost a leg while at Trinity College, Cambridge, which made him 'canonically ineligible to the service of the altar' and sent him to the Bar instead. The second accident was less painful but more effective. Sydney communicated the news of Lord Holland's death to him so abruptly that the shock gave him a slight stroke, and he died shortly afterwards.

The third wit of the Holland House circle, Henry Luttrell, was a man after Sydney's own heart, partly because he made 'all the country smell like Piccadilly'. A natural son of the second Lord Carhampton (better known as the Colonel Luttrell who contested Middlesex against Wilkes), Henry soon commuted an appointment he had received in the Irish Government for a pension and lived comfortably on it for the remainder of his life, mapping out his holidays with the care of a general about to open a campaign, and spending them at those country mansions of the titled rich where (1) he was not likely to be bored, and (2) there was was a first-rate chef. He was a man of very independent character, with a supreme contempt for riches and rank unless they were accompanied by charm, wit, agreeableness, a talent for providing excellent dinners, and genius in the choice of side-dishes. He was popular wherever he went, being an extremely tactful, amusing person, anxious to please and to be pleased, graceful in manner, conciliating in gesture and tone, interested in a wide range of topics and able to talk on them in a fresh, light, entertaining way. He declined invitations to Holland House until Lady Holland had suppressed an aggressive cat which mauled Rogers and was warded off by Brougham with pinches of snuff; and when he did at last go, he was not altogether pleased with the dining arrangements. Lady Holland loved to see her guests squeezed together and once sixteen people sat down at a table for nine. 'Luttrell, make room,' commanded Lady Holland. 'It will certainly have to be made, for it does not exist,' replied Luttrell.

He wrote a certain amount of satirical poetry, which was liked by the people for whom it was written, but his life was chiefly made up of dinners, of journeys to and from dinners, of talks about past dinners, and of speculations upon future dinners. He was an expert on salads as well as side-dishes and would discuss the art of salad-making with the utmost frankness, even laying down certain basic laws on the subject, but he was not an authority on any meal except dinner. 'Luttrell, before I taught him better, imagined muffins grew,' Sydney had to confess sadly: 'He was wholly ignorant of all the intermediate processes of sowing, reaping, grinding, kneading, and baking.' In spite of such grave gaps in his knowledge, he was an exceptionally delightful companion, pleased with the world, the flesh, the devil and himself, and only drawing the line at monkeys because they reminded him so much of poor relations. 'Luttrell talks more sweetly than birds can sing,' said Sydney, and who could desire a better epitaph?

The two famous professors of Edinburgh University, Dugald Stewart and John Playfair, stayed at Foston and Sydney managed to extract a certain amount of fun out of their gravity and reserve. Dugald Stewart brought his family and the chief topic of conversation was the weather.

> 'He became however once a little overpowered with wine, and in the gaiety of his soul let out some opinions which will doubtless make him writhe with remorse; he went so far as to say that he considered the King's recovery as very problematical.'

This terrible revelation of a man's inmost thoughts was probably obtained at the price of one glass of port. Sydney, however, had a real admiration for Stewart, and when, at a dinner-party many years later, the announcement of his death was received with levity by a lady of rank, Sydney turned on her and said: 'Madam, when we are told of the death of so great a man as Mr. Dugald Stewart, it is usual, in civilised society, to look grave for at least the space of five seconds.'

John Playfair happened to be at Foston at the same time as Mrs. Apreece, whose vivacity had made her the toast of Edinburgh and won the admiration of Madame de Staël. The contrast between them was too much for Sydney, who instantly pretended that she had succumbed to the charms of the mathematical professor and wrote to Lady Holland:

> 'It was wrong at her time of life to be circumvented by Playfair's diagrams; but there is some excuse in the novelty of the attack, as I believe she is the first woman that ever fell a victim to algebra, or that was geometrically led from the paths of virtue.'

At about this time, by the way, Sydney was writing an article on Female Education for the *Edinburgh Review*, in the course of which he attacked the common belief that the acquisition of knowledge would lessen a woman's natural interests and duties, and said it was highly improbable that any mother 'would desert an infant for a quadratic equation'.

Mrs. Apreece had come from Edinburgh with letters of introduction to Sydney, who took to her at once. Jeffrey had warned him that she had been accustomed to flattery, which had slightly turned her head. Sydney replied: 'Your critique on Mrs. Apreece is just, but she seems a friendly, good-hearted, rational woman, and as much under the uterine dominion as is graceful and pleasing. I hate a woman who seems to be hermetically sealed in the lower regions.' Later he begged her not to get married, as she would be lost to her male friends and become a neutral salt instead of an alkali or an acid. Within a year she was married to Sir Humphry Davy, but managed to retain the quality of acidity, for they started quarrelling almost at once. They went abroad and

Sydney wrote: 'I am astonished that a woman of your sense should yield to such an imposture as the Augsburg Alps – surely you have found out by this time that God has made nothing so curious as human creatures.'

In expecting her to admire mountain scenery, Sir Humphry was certainly an optimist. She was jealous of the homage paid to the Jungfrau and vented her temper on her husband. Sydney found a plausible explanation for their constant rows and separations: 'Perhaps he vaunted above truth the powers of chemistry, and persuaded her it had secrets which it does not possess – hence her disappointment and fury.' The fact is that she was not a suitable partner for an earnest and serious scientist. She lived on the adulation of admirers, of whom there was never a dearth. Indeed, we have it on the authority of Sydney that whenever she appeared at a place, though there was no garrison within twelve miles, the horizon was immediately clouded with majors.

Brief mention must be made of another friend, Sir George Philips, a Manchester cotton manufacturer, at whose home, Sedgeley Hall, Prestwich, Sydney's family sometimes stayed. He was of course immensely wealthy, and Sydney usually referred to him as the discoverer of cotton. 'In spite of all his little absurdities, I have an affection for Philips,' Sydney told Lady Holland: 'I never think I am bound to ask myself why I like people.' One can think of several reasons why the manufacturer appealed to him. Philips was a plain, blunt man, and Sydney liked plain, blunt men. Philips knew how to feed well, and Sydney liked being fed well. Philips rode a horse with even less skill than Sydney, and this made him irresistible. Further, the friendship brought Sydney into contact with a section of society of which he would otherwise have remained in ignorance. 'I am going to preach a charity sermon next Sunday,' he wrote from Sedgeley Hall; 'I desire to make three or four hundred weavers cry, which it is impossible to do since the late rise in cottons.'

Philips had one failing which Sydney was not slow to point out: 'Let me warn you against the melancholy effects of temperance. You will do me the justice to remember how often I have entered my protest against it: depend upon it, the wretchedness of human life is only to be encountered upon the basis of meat and wine.' This good advice took root and a little later he was able to congratulate Philips on his improved health as a result of making 'very laudable resolutions of intemperance'. The Cotton King wanted to improve his mind also and showed a disposition to encourage the arts, but the method he adopted did not appeal to his clerical friend: 'Philips . . . has lately returned from Italy, and purchased some pictures which were sent out from Piccadilly on purpose to intercept him.'

Sydney was a lover of tittle-tattle – or, as he would have described it, nonsense and good-nature – and when it was spiced with scandal he could not resist it. He was vastly intrigued by the runaway match between Brougham and Mrs. Spalding in 1819, and wrote to Jeffrey: 'What do you think of Mrs. Brougham – should you covet her as a concubine – or as a wife if you were not already provided? What is the meaning of all the mystery about his marriage? Whence comes it that the curious (I speak only from rumour) cannot find the date of his marriage?' He even expected details from Lord Grey, and when that decorous Earl failed to supply them he probed again: 'On the subject of Brougham's marriage you are too prudent to write, but I long to know all the scandal. If I raise up my tombstone and go to London in the spring I shall of course hear it all; at present it seems very black and unaccountable.' With the discovery that a marriage had actually taken place at Coldstream his interest naturally subsided.

This excitement was followed by another in which Brougham also figured – the scandal of George IV and Queen Caroline. Sydney had no illusions about George IV, whom he described on different occasions as a profligate prince and a rascal who had lost no time in occasioning 'the dilapidation of kingly power', but he had too good a nose for gossip to assume the Queen's innocence: 'Luckily for the Queen,' he told Jeffrey, 'the boatswain who saw the courier and her in full venery is not to be found. I suppose Brougham has given him some medicine.'

Lady Holland, who herself had caused a scandal by living with Lord Holland before they were able to get married and was permanently 'cut' by the more respectable members of society, was Sydney's favourite gossip-monger. Needless to say, she visited Foston, alarmed the village by the gorgeousness of her coach, the number of her outriders and the apparel of her servants, and, if Sydney's report is to be trusted, 'produced the same impression as the march of Alexander or Bacchus over India, and will be as long remembered in the traditions of the innocent natives'.

But quite a different sort of person made Sydney's acquaintance in July, 1826 – the outstanding figure among the rising generation of writers on the *Edinburgh Review*, a young man who took himself and the world about him very seriously, the most characteristic specimen of the new age then dawning: Thomas Babington Macaulay.

Staying in York for the Assizes, Macaulay was changing his neck-cloth one day when the landlady knocked at the door of his bedroom and told him that Mr. Smith wished to see him and was waiting in the room below. The name was not sufficient to label the visitor; Macaulay thought hard of all the Smiths he had ever known, but there were so many that he gave it up. Having finished the wrestle with his neck-cloth, he went downstairs, and beheld, to his amazement, 'the Smith of Smiths'. He had forgotten Sydney's very existence; but the queer contrast between the snow-white head and the black coat, between the clerical amplitude of the body and the most unclerical expression of the eye, quickly convinced him that he stood in the presence of the one and only 'Peter Plymley', and almost before they had done shaking hands they were discussing the Catholic question. Sydney pressed him to stay a week-end at Foston, and Macaulay jumped at the prospect of closer acquaintance with 'the greatest master of ridicule who has appeared in England since Swift'.

Macaulay enjoyed every minute of that week-end. The rectory was the neatest, most commodious, and most appropriate he had ever seen. The rector's wit, humour and shrewdness kept his family in fits of laughter for hours on end. On Sunday the church (a miserable little hovel with a wooden belfry) was well filled with decent people who seemed to take very much to their pastor. Sydney's sermon, though not without some ingenuity of thought and expression, was in part too familiar and in part too florid. But the parson was also an apothecary and most liberal of his skill, his medicine, his soup and his wine, among the sick. Clearly his misfortune was to have chosen a profession at once above him and below him, and Macaulay wrote: 'Zeal would have made him a prodigy, formality and bigotry would have made him a bishop; but he could neither rise to the duties of his order, nor stoop to its degradations.' Sydney advised his guest to tone down the asperity and contempt that too often crept into his controversial articles, and Macaulay, feeling the justice of the criticism, decided to benefit by it. On Monday morning they drove to York and parted with many expressions of goodwill, having taken a great liking to one another.

A few years later Macaulay was a regular visitor to Holland House and in course of time became the chief talker of that famous circle. But while Sydney talked to entertain, Macaulay talked to instruct. His knowledge was extraordinary, his memory incredible. Sydney said that he could repeat the whole History of the Virtuous Blue-Coat Boy, in three volumes, post octavo, without a slip, and added that he ought to take 'two table-spoonfuls of the water of Lethe every morning to correct his retentive powers'. He was 'a book in breeches'; he 'not only overflowed with learning but stood in the slops'; he was 'laying society waste with his waterspouts of talk; people in his company burst for want of an opportunity of dropping in a word; he confounded soliloquy and colloquy'; and Sydney claimed that 'the great use of the raised centre, revolving on a round table, would be to put Macaulay on it and distribute his talk fairly to the company'. With these and similar expressions did Sydney give vent to his fury, which of course was quite good-humoured and meant to amuse.

Nothing could stop Macaulay, when he had begun to impart information, except the loud rat-a-tat-tat of Lady Holland's fan, and after one of his monologues Sydney reproached him with: 'Now, Macaulay, when I am gone you will be sorry that you never heard me speak.' Nothing short of illness could temporarily dam that deluge of words and Sydney was not slow to take advantage of one such peaceful spell. He called, found Macaulay in bed and 'more agreeable than I have ever seen him. There were some gorgeous flashes of silence'.

This weakness for sermonising did not blind Sydney to the good points of the 'talk-mill'. He knew Macaulay to be absolutely sincere and incorruptible and constantly pressed his claims to a government post on Lord Grey. When, at last, Macaulay got his post and had to forego his social engagements, Sydney mourned him in these words: 'To take Macaulay out of literature and society and put him in the House of Commons is like taking the chief physician out of London during a pestilence.'

Sydney's holidays during the Foston days were spent in various places. Sometimes he took the family to York, sometimes to see his father in Somersetshire, sometimes to Scarborough, where he reported a clear view from his window of the Hague and Amsterdam. When Jeffrey wanted to know why he could not pay regular visits to Edinburgh, he replied: 'A clergyman can by law be absent only 3 months from his living and is liable to be informed against and to heavy penalties if he is so. I should certainly be informed against; I know that I am watched.' Two of those three months he naturally wanted to spend with his wife and children, who were always wretched when he was away from them. The other month was spent every spring in London. But the moment his financial position took a favourable turn he transported his family to Edinburgh, which he found much improved in appearance, staying there with Jeffrey in 1821, and seeing a lot of the Whig leaders of the Scotch Bar,

> 'each possessing thirty-two different sorts of wine. My old friends were glad to see me; some had turned Methodists – some had lost their teeth – some had grown very rich – some very fat – some were dying – and alas! alas! many were dead; but the world is a coarse enough place, so I talked away, comforted some, praised others, kissed some old ladies, and passed a very riotous week.'

Leaving his family at Jeffrey's place, he next went to stay with Lord Lauderdale at Dunbar and then with Mr. Lambton (afterwards Lord Durham) at Lambton Castle. This was one of the first country mansions to be lit with gas and Sydney was ecstatic in his praises. Writing to Lady Mary Bennett he asked:

> 'What use of wealth so luxurious and delightful as to light your house with gas? What folly to have a diamond necklace or a Correggio, and not to light your house with gas! The splendour and glory of Lambton Hall make all other houses mean. How pitiful to submit to a farthing-candle existence, when science puts such intense gratification within your reach! Dear lady, spend all your fortune in a gas-apparatus. Better to eat dry bread by the splendour of gas, than to dine on wild beef with wax-candles.'

In 1819 Sydney took his family to London.[1] 'You cannot conceive the blunders and agony, the dust and distraction, the roaring and raving with which a family like mine is conveyed through three degrees of latitude to its place of destination,' he wrote. The children were surprised and delighted with the crowds. 'It is the first time they have ever seen four people together, except on remarkably fine days at the parish church.' Of course they had to visit all the sights. They spent four hours looking over the British Museum, where he observed that the visitors were principally maid-servants. Then they saw the Custom House, being much struck by the long room and the façade towards the river. They were impressed by the Mint, and Sydney declared that

[1] 47 Hertford Street.

one of the finest things in London was the terrace between Vauxhall and Westminster Bridge. He considered the national monuments in St. Paul's Cathedral, with the exception of Samuel Johnson's monument by Bacon, 'a disgusting heap of trash'. Nash, the architect, took him over Carlton House, and he thought the suites of golden rooms, 450 feet long, were extremely magnificent, but not good enough for a palace. He saw an exhibition of pictures, liking West's contributions and disliking Haydon's, but he steadfastly refused to support the drama: 'I never go to plays, and should not care (except for the amusement of others) if there was no theatre in the whole world; it is an art intended only for amusement, and it never amuses me.' Another form of entertainment was still less to his taste: 'Nothing can be more disgusting than an Oratorio. How absurd to see 500 people fiddling like madmen about the Israelites in the Red Sea!' He detested long musical evenings; they were a menace to conversation:

> 'Music for such a length of time (unless under sentence of a jury) I will not submit to. What pleasure is there in pleasure if quantity is not attended to as well as quality? I know nothing more agreeable than a dinner at Holland House; but it must not begin at ten in the morning and last till 6. I should be incapable for the last four hours of laughing at Lord Holland's jokes, eating Raffaelle's cakes, or repelling Mr. Allen's attacks upon the Church.'

His annual visits to London were spent in a ceaseless round of social functions. The moment it became known that he was coming, invitations began to pour in, and he was engaged for pretty well every meal of every day some weeks before his arrival. He usually stayed with brother 'Bobus', first at No. 81 Jermyn Street and afterwards at No. 20 Saville Row. During one of these visits he tried the experiment of drinking water instead of wine, and found it agreed with him so well that his chief difficulty was to control the additional flow of animal spirits brought on by abstinence, which threatened to break all bounds.

According to his own version London made a different man of him: 'I have got into all my London feelings, which come on the moment I pass Hyde Park Corner. I am languid, unfriendly, heartless, selfish, sarcastic, and insolent.' His friends would not have recognised him from that description. Wherever he went, laughter went with him. One could trace him round 'the parallelogram' by that laugh of his. In the country his neck-cloth always looked like a pudding tied round his throat and the arrangement of his clothes seemed more the result of accident than design, but in London he contrived to look at least clerical, and the contrast between his garments and his gaiety drew the stares of street and salon. Some people were shocked by his hilarity, or pretended to be, and held aloof from him at first; but, unless they were exceptionally stupid, they could not resist him for long. The actor, Macready, thought him outrageous, probably because, for once, the actor did not hold the centre of the stage and was merely one of the crowd. Sarah Siddons was more honest, and after a preliminary struggle caught the infection. Thomas Moore, the poet, fought hard to keep his self-control, but one April day in 1823 he surrendered completely to a description by Sydney of an imaginary duel between two doctors, who, with oil of croton on the tips of their fingers, were trying to touch each other's lips.

After that Moore never missed an opportunity of meeting Sydney. They went to a phrenologist's with Lord Lansdowne and had their characters revealed by their bumps. The phrenologist informed Sydney that he was a naturalist and was seldom happy when away from his collections of birds and fishes. 'Sir,' said Sydney solemnly, 'I don't know a fish from a bird.' The visit was a complete failure, though Moore was reduced to tears by Sydney's inextinguishable and contagious laughter. A week later they were breakfasting with Rogers, where Sydney sent the company into hysterics with a description of dram-drinkers catching fire, pursuing the idea in every possible shape – the inconvenience of a man coming too near the candle when he was speaking ('Sir, your observation has caught fire') – a parson breaking into a blaze in the pulpit; the engines called to put him out; no water to be had, the man at the waterworks being an Unitarian or an Atheist.

There was always an atmosphere of rivalry between Rogers and Sydney. The former still lived in luxury on the family's banking business, and Sydney, seeing a large display of royal invitations over the chimney-piece, remarked: 'Does it not look as if the Bank had been accommodating the Duchess of Kent?' Once, when Rogers gave a dinner, he had all the candles placed high up on the walls in order to show off the pictures. Sydney, when asked how he liked the plan, replied: 'Not at all; above there is a blaze of light, and below nothing but darkness and gnashing of teeth.' Another time, when Walter Scott, Campbell, Moore, Wordsworth and Washington Irving were of the company, Sydney declared that himself and Irving, if the only prose-writers, were not the only prosers present. When Rogers ironically praised the good behaviour of Sydney's horse, the latter assured him that it was 'a cross of the rocking-horse'.

The American author, Fenimore Cooper, came to London in the spring of 1828 and Sydney went to see him. It soon appeared that Cooper was more than a little touchy; he began complaining of his treatment in English society; he was indignant with Lord Nugent for having asked him to walk down the street and, on being admitted to a house, leaving him to return alone; he was furious with the Duke of Devonshire for not returning his call; in short, he did not regard the English aristocracy as well-bred and threatened to spread the news. Shortly after this Moore ran across Sydney and said that he was about to visit Cooper. 'Then call him out the first thing you do,' advised Sydney, 'for, as it must come to a duel sooner or later, you may as well begin with it.'

Two years later they were breakfasting with Jeffrey and the talk was about the recent death of Sir Thomas Lawrence, which had apparently been due to the ignorance of his servant in not binding on a bandage that had come off after he had been bled. Moore remarked that Lawrence was to be pitied for the additional ill-luck of falling into the hands of such a biographer as Thomas Campbell. Whereupon Sydney started up and exclaimed theatrically: 'Look to your bandages, all ye that have been blooded; there are biographers abroad!'

Moore was a little disappointed when, quite early one evening and just after he had sung a song, Sydney vanished from the gathering. He wrote expressing his sorrow, adding that his singing had improved later in the evening and that Sydney was one of the few he always wished to do his best for. Sydney, thinking his early disappearance had really hurt Moore, replied as follows:

> 'By the Beard of the prelate of Canterbury, by the Cassock of the prelate of York, by the breakfasts of Rogers, by Luttrell's love of side-dishes, I swear I had rather hear you sing than any person male or female. For what is your singing but beautiful poetry floating in fine music and guided by exquisite feeling? Call me a Dissenter, say that my cassock is ill put on, that I know not the delicacies of decimation, and confound the greater and the smaller Tythes – but do not think or say that I am insensible to your music. The truth is that I took a solemn oath to Mrs. Beauclerc to be there by 10, and set off to prevent perjury at eleven – but was seized with a violent pain in the stomach by the way, and went to bed suffering under a Pergery of another sort.'

The memoirs and diaries of that time make frequent mention of Sydney but are disappointingly barren of Boswelliana. People could not remember what had made them laugh; they merely remembered that they had laughed. 'Sydney walks in while I am writing. Laughter of course stops my pen.' Thus the Earl of Dudley. 'Sydney Smith called on me for a few seconds – I can scarcely say minutes – talked about a thousand things, and went away laughing.' So Thomas Campbell. 'An irresistibly amusing companion,' noted George Ticknor, the American scholar; 'he was in great spirits and amused us excessively by his peculiar humour. I do not know, indeed, that anything can exceed it, so original, so unprepared, so fresh.' The French Ambassador and historian, F. Guizot, wrote home: 'I conversed last evening with Mr. Sydney Smith, who really overflows with wit.' A collection of such references would fill a volume. In a later chapter we shall have an opportunity of judging him as wit and humourist on the strength of such records as we possess. Here it need only be said that he had a comical personality, that people laughed at his manner no less than his matter, that they laughed at what he said and laughed before he said it and sometimes laughed when he was being extremely serious; for once, while he was saying grace before dinner, a young lady had a fit of giggles and exclaimed: 'Oh, Mr. Smith, you are always so amusing!'

All his life Sydney had wanted to see Paris. 'I must not die without seeing Paris. Figure to yourself what a horrid death – to die without seeing Paris.' And at last, in 1826, his ambition was gratified. Whenever away from home he wrote to his wife every day; and as the letters describing his Paris trip were the only ones she kept, we can follow his movements with their help. Perhaps his chief pleasure throughout the holiday was derived from the feeling that one day he would be able to take his wife to the same places. He arrived at the Ship Inn, Dover, on April 14th.

> 'I am much pleased with Dover. They have sunk a deep shaft in the cliff, and made a staircase, by which the top of the cliff is reached with great ease – or at least what they call with great ease, which means the loss of about a pound of liquid flesh, and as much puffing and blowing as would grind a bushel of wheat. The view from the cliff, I need not tell you, is magnificent.'

He crossed to Calais the following day, put up at Dessein's, and was delighted with the place, the food, and the good manners of the people: 'I have not seen a cobbler who is not better bred than an English gentleman.' On the road to Paris he found the inns good, the sheep, cows and pigs miserable. He obtained excellent lodgings at the Hotel Virginie, rue St. Honoré, No. 350, and determined to see as much as he could and eat as well as he could. The only purchase he made for himself while there was a huge seal, containing the arms of a peer of France, which he picked up at a broker's shop for four francs and which he decided should henceforth be the arms of his branch of the Smith family. ('The Smiths,' he once informed an heraldic expert, 'never had any arms and have invariably sealed their letters with their thumbs.')

He found that Paris was not so well lighted at night-time as London, and that the equipages were less splendid and less numerous; on the other hand, Regent Street was a poor affair in comparison with the finest streets in Paris, and the London shops were not so good. The absence of foot-pavements in Paris was a serious inconvenience and the lack of table-cloths in the coffee-houses annoyed him. The fountains delighted him and he was much pleased and affected by the cemetery of Père La Chaise. He saw, and liked, Talma in tragedy and Mademoiselle Mars in comedy. He listened to a debate in the Assembly and said that the Deputies read their speeches like very bad parsons. At the Opera he noticed that 'the house was full of English, who talk loud and seem to care little for other people. This is their characteristic, and a very brutal and barbarous distinction it is'. He admired the profusion of mirrors in French drawing-rooms. Entering a room with glass all round it he saw himself reflected on every side: 'I took it for a meeting of the clergy, and was delighted, of course.' He went through the Louvre, the Luxembourg, the House of Peers; visited St. Cloud, Meudon and the Castle of Vincennes; was not impressed by the pictures in any of these places, preferring the rooms in which there were no pictures. He saw a royal procession to the Place Louis XV, where the King (Charles X) laid the first stone of the statue to Louis XVI:

> 'The procession passed under my window. . . . There were about twelve hundred priests, four cardinals, a piece of the real Cross, and one of the nails, carried under a canopy upon a velvet cushion; the King, the Marshals, the House of Peers, and the House of Commons following. A more absurd,

disgraceful, and ridiculous, or a finer sight, I never saw. The Bourbons are too foolish and too absurd; nothing can keep them on the throne.'

He prophesied another revolution three times in his letters from Paris; it occurred four years later.

The Hollands were staying in Paris, so he was introduced to the best Parisian society. Dining with Lord Holland one day 'there was at table Barras, the ex-Director, in whose countenance I immediately discovered all the signs of blood and cruelty which distinguished his conduct. I found out, however, at the end of dinner, that it was not Barras, but M. de Barante, an historian and man of letters, who, I believe, has never killed anything greater than a flea'. He breakfasted with the Duc de Broglie (no table-cloth), dined at the English Ambassador's, mingled with 'a profusion of French duchesses', attended Granville's ball ('nothing could be more superb'), met Humboldt, the great traveller, 'a lively, pleasant, talkative man', was introduced to Cuvier, and considered Sismondi 'an energetic and sensible old man'. He paid a number of calls and described one of them: 'It is curious to see in what little apartments a French *savant* lives; you find him at his books, covered with snuff, with a little dog that bites your legs.'

His namesake, Sir Sidney Smith, was unpopular in Paris and showed some concern over the arrival of a popular edition of the name; it did not improve matters when the Hero of Acre was told, after listening to a sermon by Sydney, that he ought to be proud of his name. But they met, and Sir Sidney was charmed by the Reverend Sydney, for whose social success in Paris there is independent testimony in the Journal of the Hon. H. E. Fox (afterwards fourth and last Lord Holland): 'He was very witty and amusing, and though not master enough of the language to give full vent to all his pleasantry, he talked it sufficiently to enjoy conversation and to be a prominent person.'

One evening the Duke of Bedford took him to dine with Talleyrand. They had met before at Holland House, but their intercourse had been restricted by Talleyrand's peculiar habits of speech. Sydney explained the difficulty to several friends, amongst whom was Dr. Holland (no relation to the peer of that name):

'Lady Holland laboured incessantly to convince me that Talleyrand was agreeable, and was very angry because his arrival was usually a signal for my departure: but, in the first place, he never spoke at all till he had not only devoured but digested his dinner, and as this was a slow process with him, it did not occur till everybody else was asleep, or ought to have been so; and when he did speak he was so inarticulate I never could understand a word he said.'

'It was otherwise with me,' said Dr. Holland; 'I never found much difficulty in following him.'

'Did you not? Why, my dear Holland, it was an abuse of terms to call it talking at all; for he had no teeth, and, I believe, no roof to his mouth – no uvula – no larynx – no trachea – no epiglottis – no anything. It was not talking, it was gargling; and that, by the by, now I think of it, must be the very reason why Holland understood him so much better than I did.'

Apparently Talleyrand was seen to better advantage at his own table; and as his cook was the best in Paris, Sydney had no grounds for complaint.

Though realising that he had arrived a month too soon to see it in all its glory, Sydney came to the conclusion that 'Paris' was merely an abbreviation of 'Paradise', and made up his mind to return at a later date in order to die there. He took away with him a number of presents for his family, a lot of wallpaper for his house, the new Smith seal for himself, and some knowledge of the French people:

> 'I set off at nine o'clock on Tuesday in the diligence, with a French lady and her father, who has an estate near Calais. I found him a sensible man, with that propensity which the French have for explaining things which do not require

explanation. He explained to me, for instance, what he did when he found coffee too strong; he put water in it. He explained how blind people found their way about Paris – by tapping upon the wall with a stick; what he principally endeavoured to make clear to me was, how they knew when they were come to a crossing – it was when there was no longer a wall to strike against with their stick. I expressed my thorough comprehension of these means used by blind men, and he paid me many compliments upon my quickness.'

CHAPTER IX

PROMOTION

'WITH the politics of so remote a period I do not concern myself,' wrote Sydney Smith after reading Burke's letters, and we need not concern ourselves with the politics of Sydney's period, except in so far as they directly affected him. During his twenty years exile in the north the strength of the Tory party had been gradually undermined by the repeated attacks of the Edinburgh Reviewers and other reformers and the disappearance of their own giants. Perceval had been murdered in 1812 and had been succeeded by Lord Liverpool. Castlereagh had committed suicide in 1822, and early in the year 1827 Lord Liverpool was struck with paralysis, being succeeded by Canning. Lord Eldon retired and Sir John Copley took his place on the Woolsack as Baron Lyndhurst. In August of the same year Canning died and a coalition was formed under Lord Goderich. It lasted about three months and on January the 8th, 1828, the Tories returned to power under the Duke of Wellington.

Just before the arrival of the Duke in Downing Street, however, Lord Lyndhurst nominated Sydney to a vacant stall at Bristol. Lyndhurst was a political opponent and had been attacked by Sydney in the *Edinburgh Review*, so it is probable that the latter owed his appointment partly to the influence in the cabinet of his friend, Lord Lansdowne. All the same Lyndhurst liked him very much personally, and he received the good news towards the end of January, 1828, in a letter of congratulation from Lady Lyndhurst, who had also been solicitous in his behalf, begging Lord Dudley as well as her husband to approach the King on the subject. George IV, when Prince Regent, had met Sydney at Holland House and had been shocked by some of his unclerical jokes, for the vanity of the libertine is touched when the religion against which he has sinned is not taken too seriously by one of its priests. On receiving the requests of Lyndhurst and Dudley, he remarked that he had never met a more profligate parson than Sydney Smith, and gave his consent – thereby justifying Sydney's reference to him as a profligate prince.

By the middle of February the new canon was comfortably lodged in his prebendal house at Bristol, with a view of the masts of West-Indiamen from his windows, and pleased with the novelty of the place. Back at Foston in July he was enjoying Scott's *Napoleon* and trying to arrange for an exchange of livings. With his prebend he had received the small living of Halberton, near Tiverton, but he was now anxious to come south and exchange Foston for something equally good within a reasonable distance of Bristol.

In August of that year Brougham maintained that the Catholic question was as good as carried, upon which Sydney commented: 'I never think myself as good as carried till my horse brings me to my stable-door.' For this reason he continued to spur the horse. It so happened that he was chosen to deliver the Gunpowder Plot anniversary sermon in Bristol Cathedral before the Mayor and Corporation. Little did the authorities realise what they were doing. The usual pulpit utterances on such an occasion were reactionary and patriotic, that is to say, anti-Catholic and idiotic. The clergy dined at the Mansion House and drank a number of absurd toasts, and the civic authorities went to the Cathedral service and heard a number of ridiculous sentiments. Sydney had no intention of drinking the usual toasts or talking the usual nonsense. Instead he preached a carefully reasoned sermon on Toleration, in which the most Protestant Corporation in England was informed that 'to do wrong, and to gain nothing by it, is surely to add folly to fault', that 'other sects may be right', and that every religion was as fallible as human judgment could make it. The sermon caused great offence. The Mayor and Corporation glared at the preacher. 'Several of them,' he said, 'could not keep the turtle on their stomachs.' Whether from indigestion or indignation the city fathers discontinued their official attendance at the 5th of November service from that date, and the new canon was assailed in pamphlet and pulpit for several weeks. But Sydney had become hardened to abuse and generously helped to increase it by publishing his sermon.

Having fluttered the eagles of intolerance, the dove of conciliation returned to Foston. The winter of 1828–9 was passed in the usual way. 'Nothing can make the country agreeable to me,' he once wrote; 'it is bad enough in summer, but in winter is a fit residence only for beings doomed to such misery for misdeeds in another state of existence.' Yet, had he known it, that winter was to be the last he would ever spend without a pang of irreparable grief. For up to now, it must be admitted, his life had been singularly free from misfortune. He had felt the death of his mother and sister; he had felt the death of Francis Horner; but time had done its work; no sorrow had cut him deeply enough to leave a pain after the wound had healed. He was now about to face the only real tragedy of his life.

Douglas, his eldest son, had never been robust, and the hardships he had endured at Westminster, followed by the strain of working for the law while at Oxford, had gravely impaired his health. He became seriously ill and his father went to London to watch over him. He died, after a long and painful illness, on April the 14th, at the age of 24. 'The first great misfortune of my life and one which I shall never forget,' wrote Sydney in his diary. 'I never suspected how children weave themselves about the heart,' he confessed to a friend, and, to another, 'the habit of providing for human beings, and watching over them for so many years, generates a fund of affection of the magnitude of which I was unaware.' He never completely recovered from the shock, though many years later he characteristically did his best to view the tragedy from a different angle: 'It was terrible at the time, but it has been best for me since; it has been bad enough in life to have been ambitious for myself; it would have been dreadful to have been ambitious for another.'

Two days before the death of Douglas, while watching with alternate hope and despair at his bedside, Sydney heard that the Catholic Emancipation Bill had been passed, and when the tumult and the shouting had died down he wrote to a Catholic friend: 'I rejoice in the temple which has been reared to Toleration; and I am proud that I worked as a bricklayer's labourer at it – without pay, and with the enmity and abuse of those who were unfavourable to its construction.'

He had now an additional reason for leaving Foston, where every stick and stone reminded him painfully of his lost boy, and fortunately for him Lord Lyndhurst, who was still Chancellor, managed to obtain a most satisfactory exchange of livings. In the summer of 1829 he bade farewell to Foston and removed his family to Combe Florey, a pretty village in beautiful country about seven miles from Taunton, on the Minehead road. A few of their old servants went with them. It was a charming rectory, owning a wood of four acres close by and a glebe of sixty acres, but the house was in a dilapidated state and Sydney had to start re-building at once. At a cost of £2000 he turned it into an ideal residence, his early building experiences in Yorkshire serving him well. But the 28 workmen he employed were not altogether satisfactory:

> 'Nothing so vile as the artificers of this country. A straight line in Somersetshire is that which includes the greatest possible distance between the extreme points. . . . Every day's absence from home costs me £10 in the villainy of carpenters and bricklayers; for as I am my own architect and clerk of the works, you may easily imagine what is done when I am absent.' The climate was partly responsible for this: 'What with the long torpor of the cider, and the heated air of the west, they all become boozy; the squires grow blind, the

labourers come drunk to work, and the maids pin their mistresses' gowns awry.'

One of the principal features in the restored rectory was a library, 28 feet long and 8 feet high, ending in a bay window which looked on to the garden. Sydney now had the means to buy what he wanted, and it was not long before the walls of the library were covered with books, all of them bound in the most vivid blues and reds. Their exterior was all-important, and though it would not be true to say that he was indifferent to their subject-matter, he liked them chiefly for their decorative value and revelled in their colours rather than their contents. 'What makes fire so pleasant is that it is a live thing in a dead room,' he once said, and the primary object of the books was to liven up the room. Another feature was the apothecary's shop, filled with drugs and groceries for the benefit of everyone in the parish. He was really fond of doctoring people. At Foston he had nursed his own children through an attack of typhoid, and was delighted when half the village of Combe Florey was down with influenza, as it improved his medical practice. On the other hand, an epidemic of scarlet-fever, which resulted in 15 deaths, was not quite in his line: 'You will naturally suppose that I have killed all these people by doctoring them; but scarlet-fever awes me and is above my aim. I leave it to the professional and graduated homicides.'

He was provoked, now and then, to look into the claims of these graduated homicides and was not always impressed by their achievements. He disposed of fashionable doctors in this manner: 'There is always some man of whom the human viscera stand in greater dread than of any other person, who is supposed, for the time being, to be the only person who can dart his pill into their inmost recesses, and bind them over, in medical recognisance, to assimilate and digest.' And his final summary of the profession was delivered in one trenchant phrase: 'The Sixth Commandment is suspended by one medical diploma from the North of England to the South.'

The villagers liked being doctored by him because he never mixed the Thirty-nine Articles in his prescriptions for their health, and even when he felt bound to read them moral lectures he did it with so much common sense and humour that they were amused and edified (or scared) simultaneously. He did not tell them it was wicked to steal; he emphasised the discomforts of life in Botany Bay as a result of stealing. He did not tell them it was wrong to be disrespectful to the gentry; he explained that politeness was invariably rewarded by gifts and jobs. He did not say it was sinful to get drunk; he pointed out that to drink more than they could afford ended in the break-up of home life and the wretchedness of the workhouse. He did not pretend that poaching was a crime; he merely remarked that it led to pauperism. He advised the girls not to yield to the seductive flatteries of their swains, however pleasant the evening, because they had everything to lose while the boys had nothing, and told them how to reply to such proposals: 'When I am axed in the church, and the parson has read the service, and all about it is written down in a book, then I will listen to your nonsense, and not before.' Even his orders were given in a reasonable manner. A guest drew his attention to the fact that the gardener was tearing off too many leaves of a vine. Sydney told the gardener to stop; but the man, a Scot, looked unconvinced. 'Now understand me,' said Sydney, 'you are probably right, but in this instance I don't wish you to do what is right; and as it is my vine, and there are no moral laws for pruning, you may as well do as I wish.'

Observers noted the singular mixture of grin and reverence with which he was greeted by his rustic friends. The grin was not caused solely by his friendly and jocular way with them. His actions must often have seemed to them a trifle freakish. When a lady hinted that his paddock would be improved by deer, he promptly fitted his two donkeys with antlers. The effect, enhanced by the puzzled looks of the animals, was ludicrous, though he was careful to explain that the length of their ears and the curious quality of their voices were peculiarities of parsonic deer. These braying stags were to be seen at frequent intervals throughout one summer and the villagers must have thought him a curious priest. On being asked the following year to repeat the exhibition, he declined on the ground that donkeys with horns had been regarded as typical of the neighbouring squires.

The warmth and softness of the climate was a constant theme of his, and he even claimed that oranges grew wild in his garden. To prove this assertion he had oranges tied to the shrubs and trees, and these looked so natural that people believed him – until he told them to pick a few, when they discovered the growth a little too tenacious to be true. Again the villagers scratched their heads and wondered whether the parson was quite right in his.

But they revered him, too. When they were seriously ill he would drive in to Taunton and bring out a doctor. Whenever they were in trouble they would come to him for help and advice and never in vain. He had a horror of debts, encouraged his parishioners to save every penny they could, and always drove round to their cottages before visiting Taunton in order to collect their monthly deposits for the Savings Bank. He was at their beck and call, and nothing would delay him a moment when they wanted him. An instance of his prompt and practical behaviour may be given. He was sitting at breakfast one morning when a poor woman came, begging him to christen a new-born infant without loss of time as she thought it was dying. Sydney left his breakfast at once and went off to the cottage. On his return he was questioned about the infant. 'Why,' said he, 'I first gave it a dose of castor-oil, and then I christened it; so now the poor child is ready for either world.' Apart from the patent armour for rheumatism already described he was proud of his stomach-pump, with which he saved the life of a footman who had swallowed a lot of arsenic. In fact, he thought very highly of his *materia medica:* 'Everybody who comes is expected to take a little something; I consider it a delicate compliment when my guests have a slight illness here.'

The improvement in the scenery brought about by the exchange of livings did not increase his love of the country. Indeed he never expressed his real dislike of rural life so strongly as at Combe Florey. 'In the country I hybernate and lick my paws. . . . The charm of London is that you are never glad or sorry for ten minutes together; in the country you are the one and the other for weeks.' It may seem curious that he should have been bored by protracted gladness in the country; but he was a man who liked rapid changes; he could not remain on one note for more than half an hour at a time; his conversation was a bewildering alternation of sense and nonsense, gravity and frivolity; he liked a constant flow of guests at his own house; he never stayed longer than three days at anyone else's house, if he could help it, unless the other visitors came and went with a pleasing celerity; he was easily bored and easily amused.

> 'You say I have many comic ideas rising in my mind,' he wrote to Philips; 'this may be true, but the champagne bottle is no better for holding the champagne. . . . I don't mean to say I am prone to melancholy; but I acknowledge my weakness enough to confess that I want the aid of society and dislike a solitary life.'

He candidly admitted that he was not one of those mortals who have infinite resources in themselves, but was fitted up with the commonest materials and had to be amused.

He found life unendurable in the country without children, and when his eldest daughter married in 1834 he was perfectly miserable. 'I shall advertise for a daughter; I cannot possibly get on without a daughter.' Saba Smith married Dr. Holland, who was afterwards knighted and became physician-in-ordinary to Queen Victoria and the Prince Consort. Fortunately Dr. Holland was already the father of several children and Sydney had them to stay at Combe Florey, telling his daughter, 'your children are my children'. At one time he had seven grandchildren staying with him, 'all in a dreadful state of perspiration and screaming'. He liked girls better than boys – 'all little boys ought to be put to death' – and often declared his intention of adopting a daughter.

It was impossible to deny that the country around Combe Florey was extremely pretty, and his parsonage the prettiest place in it; yet he found 'the neighbourhood much the same as all other neighbourhoods. Red wine and white, soup and fish, bad wit and good nature.' He did his level best to enjoy a rural existence, but in vain: 'It always seems in the country as if Joshua were at work and had stopped the sun.' He described the country as 'a kind of healthy grave', referred to 'the serious apoplexy of a country life', and spoke of 'the delusions of flowers, green turf, and birds; they all afford slight gratification, but not worth an hour of rational conversation: and rational conversation in sufficient quantities is only to be had from the congregation of a million people in one spot'. The real use of the country was to find food for cities, its only advantage was that 'a joke once established is good for ever'. As for living in it – 'You may depend upon it, all lives out of London are mistakes, more or less grievous – but mistakes.' He endeavoured to believe the poetical lies which he read in Samuel Rogers and others on the wonders of the country – 'which said deviations from the truth were, by Rogers, all written in St. James's Place'. But it was no good. 'Of all the saints, I hate La Trappe the most.'

One of the joys of a good and steady income was that he could now keep a carriage and pair for his wife and take her for holidays to the seaside and abroad. They went to Lynton and Lynmouth, which he thought 'the finest thing in England', though early in life he had been quite as much struck by Malvern. His father had occupied Bromesberrow Place, Ledbury, for some years, and Sydney was familiar with all that district: 'The double view from the top of the hill is one of the finest things I know.' They also stayed at Sidmouth and Dover and paid several visits to Brighton, which pleased him so much that he said he would like to live there for the three months, November, December and January, every year. Writing from No. 52 Marine Parade in

1840 he referred to the Chain Pier as a great luxury – 'and I think all rich and rational people living in London should take small doses of Brighton from time to time.'

In the autumn of 1835 they went with their daughter Emily and her husband to Paris. They reached Dover in a hurricane, 'and we were kept awake by thinking of the different fish by which we should be devoured on the following day. I thought I should fall to the lot of some female porpoise, who, mistaking me for a porpoise but finding me only a parson, would make a dinner of me'. The weather was so bad the next day that the captain wondered whether he ought to sail. 'The passage was tremendous. . . . I lay along the deck, wrapped in a cloak, shut my eyes, and as to danger reflected that it was much more apparent than real, and that as I had so little life to lose it was of little consequence whether I was drowned, or died, like a resident clergyman, from indigestion.'

They stayed at Rouen on the way and were delighted with it:

> 'The churches far exceed anything in England in richness of architectural ornament. The old buildings of Rouen are most interesting. All that I refuse to see is, where particular things were done to particular persons – the square where Joan of Arc was burnt – the house where Corneille was born. The events I admit to be important; but from long experience I have found that the square where Joan of Arc was burnt and the room where Corneille was born have such a wonderful resemblance to other rooms and squares that I have ceased to interest myself about them.'

In Paris they put up at the Hôtel de Londres, Place Vendôme, and did the usual things. 'The opera by Bellini, *I Puritani*, was dreadfully tiresome and unintelligible in its plan. I hope it is the last opera I shall ever go to.' He compared the excellent French dishes with 'the barbarian Stonehenge masses of meat with which we feed ourselves', and again thought he would like to die in Paris:

> 'I suspect the fifth act of life should be in great cities; it is

there, in the long death of old age, that a man most forgets himself and his infirmities, receives the greatest consolation from the attentions of friends, and the greatest diversion from external circumstances.'

On further acquaintance he thought the French very ugly – 'I have not seen one pretty French woman' – but their cooking was superb: 'I shall not easily forget a *matelote* at the Rochers de Cancale, an almond tart at Montreuil, or a *poulet à la Tartare* at Grignon's. These are impressions which no changes in future life can obliterate.'

On their return journey they 'vomited as usual into the channel which divides Albion from Gallia. Rivers are said to run blood after an engagement; the Channel is discoloured, I am sure, in a less elegant and less pernicious way by English tourists going and coming'. His wife went straight back to Combe Florey. He followed her later, writing a description of his journey down to his daughter, Saba:

'Few are the adventures of a Canon travelling gently over good roads to his benefice. In my way to Reading I had for my companion the Mayor of Bristol when I preached that sermon in favour of the Catholics. He recognised me and we did very well together. I was terribly afraid that he would stop at the same inn and that I should have the delight of his society for the evening; but he (thank God!) stopped at the Crown, as a loyal man, and I, as a rude one, went on to the Bear. Civil waiters, wax candles, and off again the next morning, with my friend and Sir W. W—, a very shrewd, clever, coarse, entertaining man, with whom I skirmished *à l'amiable* all the way to Bath. At Bath, candles still more waxen, and waiters still more profound. Being, since my travels, very much gallicized in my character, I ordered a pint of claret; I found it incomparably the best wine I ever tasted; it disappeared with a rapidity which surprises me even at this distance of time. The next morning, in the coach by eight, with a handsome valetudinarian lady, upon whom the coach produced the same effect as a steam-packet would do. I proposed weak warm brandy and water; she thought, at first, it would produce inflammation of the stomach, but presently requested to have it warm and *not* weak, and she took it to the last drop, as I did the claret.'

In the spring of 1837 they went to Holland, via Dunkirk, Ypres and Bruges. Sydney thought it a hideous country, populated by hideous people, and advised his friends never to go near it, though he was much struck with the 'commercial grandeur' of Amsterdam. Then they went to Brussels, which he declared was the only city, of all he had seen, that he could live in. Here they dined with the English Ambassador, and Sydney had an interview with King Leopold, afterwards dining with him at Laeken. He returned with an overpowering sense of England's superiority to the rest of the world, and wrote from Combe Florey: 'I am getting innocent as fast as I can, and have already begun to purge my parishioners, which, as I do not shoot or hunt, is my only rural amusement.'

His country solitude during these later years was frequently relieved by the visits of friends. Jeffrey came to stay while the house was still being rebuilt, and they sat on the lawn in the midst of rafters and tiles discussing everything, from women to politics. Sydney stopped writing for the *Edinburgh Review* when he became a canon, feeling that a dignitary of the Church should write nothing that he did not sign. Luttrell came for a day to test Mrs. Sydney's side-dishes, approved them, and decided to spend a week there later on. Sydney described him during that flying visit:

> 'He had not his usual soup-and-pattie look; there was a forced smile upon his countenance which seemed to indicate plain roast and boiled, and a sort of apple-pudding depression as if he had been staying with a clergyman. . . . He was very agreeable, but spoke too lightly, I thought, of veal soup. I took him aside, and reasoned the matter with him, but in vain; to speak the truth Luttrell is not steady in his judgments on dishes. Individual failures with him soon degenerate into generic objections, till, by some fortunate accident, he eats himself into better opinions. A person of more calm reflection thinks not only of what he is consuming at that moment, but of the soups of the same kind he has met with in a long course of dining, and which have gradually and justly elevated the species. I am perhaps making too much of this, but the failures of a man of sense are always painful.'

Sydney's conversation and Mrs. Sydney's side-dishes drew Luttrell to Combe Florey on several occasions. 'I have given notice to the fishmongers and poulterers and fruit-women,' wrote Sydney before one of these visits, later reporting the curious fact that Luttrell was 'remarkably well, considering that he has been remarkably well for so many years'.

Another visitor was the Rev. Thomas Robert Malthus, whose *Essay on the Principle of Population* had made him famous, or infamous. 'Philosopher Malthus came here last week. I got an agreeable party for him of unmarried people. There was only one lady who had a child; but he is a good-natured man, and, if there are no appearances of approaching fertility, is civil to every lady.' Staying with Sydney in the autumn of 1833 was a woman who had previously suffered a miscarriage and was now hopefully pregnant again. 'I was forced to decline seeing Malthus, who came this way,' the canon wrote regretfully; 'I am convinced her last accident was entirely owing to his visit.' Sydney thought highly of Malthus, and urged Lord Grey to give him a prebend, but in 1834 he died, and Sydney spoke of him as 'one of the most practically wise men I ever met, shamefully mistaken and unjustly calumniated and receiving no mark of favour from a Liberal Government, who ought to have interested themselves in the fortunes of such a virtuous martyr to truth'.

The canon's new friends included George Grote, historian of Greece, and his wife; a curious pair, who seem to have been rather like the traditional middle-aged married couple of late Victorian farce – an insignificant, quiet, hen-pecked husband; a domineering, loud-voiced, talkative wife. 'I like them, I like them,' said Sydney; 'I like him, he is so ladylike; and I like her, she's such a perfect gentleman.' At a party one day Mrs. Grote made a sensational entrance, wearing a rose-coloured turban on her head. Resorting to a form of humour he rather despised, but which on this occasion was possibly justified, Sydney remarked: 'Now I know the meaning of the word grotesque.' A tireless person, Mrs. Grote liked to have a finger in every pie. 'Go where you will, do what you please,' Sydney told her, 'I have the most perfect confidence in your indiscretion.' She had innumerable hobbies, among them horticulture and democracy, defined by Sydney as 'the most approved methods of growing cabbages and destroying kings'.

Always more interested in the future than the past, he was quick to appreciate fresh talent and got to know most of the promising young writers of the rising generation. Among these special mention must be made of Richard Monckton Milnes, afterwards Lord Houghton, who left some valuable memorials of Sydney. Milnes was what would now be called 'a gate-crasher'. He made it a point of duty to know everyone of note to whom, by whatever means in his power, he could obtain an introduction. He was present at a party in the Temple when someone, a perfect stranger to him, announced that he was about to call on Lady Blessington. 'Oh!' exclaimed Milnes, 'then you can take me with you; I want very much to know her, and you can introduce me.' While the other was standing aghast at the impudence of the proposal and muttering something about having only a slight acquaintance with Lady Blessington himself, Sydney broke in: 'Pray oblige our young friend; you can do it easily enough by introducing him in a capacity very desirable at this close season of the year – say you are bringing with you the *cool* of the evening.'

From that moment Milnes was known as 'the cool of the evening' and he made a social position for himself by living up to the phrase. He was a conceited, self-satisfied young man with a Boswellian talent for surviving snubs. When he complained of the insolence of some fashionable woman, Sydney comforted him with: 'You should remember that they are poodles, fed upon cream and muffins, and the wonder is that they retain either temper or digestion.' In order to increase his prestige Milnes imitated Rogers and started giving breakfasts, getting as many literary and political lions at his table as he could. Sydney found something to like in him and a good deal to laugh at. Perhaps he laughed a little too freely;

at any rate Milnes heard rumours to that effect, and wrote an angry letter to the canon, who replied: 'Never lose your temper, which is one of your best qualities, and which has carried you hitherto safely through your startling eccentricities. If you turn cross and touchy, you are a lost man. No man can combine the defects of opposite characters.' Milnes was as fond of Sydney as he could be of anybody except himself, and often asked the older man's advice. In response to one urgent inquiry, Sydney wrote: 'If you want to get a place for a relation, you must not delay it till he is born, but make an application for him *in utero*, about the fifth or sixth month. The same with any smaller accommodation.'

It must not be supposed that Sydney Smith was altogether content with his Bristol prebend. Before Lord Lyndhurst had made him a canon, he had written to several of the leading Whigs in the Goderich coalition, reminding them of his existence and asserting his claim to promotion. He had told Brougham that he only wanted a prebend or a better living, anything higher being good neither for the party nor for himself, and Brougham had replied that he showed his usual good sense in preferring the snugnesses to the fastnesses of the Church. However, nothing had come of it; the Whigs were more frightened of him than the Tories; and it was left to a Tory to repay his services to the Whigs.

In June, 1830, 'that rascal' George IV died, and a cry for parliamentary reform was heard in the land. Wellington's administration collapsed in the autumn, the Whigs came to power under Lord Grey, and early in 1831 Lord John Russell introduced the Reform Bill. With the coming of the Whigs the Edinburgh Reviewers – Jeffrey, Murray, Brougham and Co. – stepped up in the world. 'The *Review* began in high places (garrets) and ends in them,' wrote Sydney: 'It will seem very odd to me to pass into Downing Street and to see all my old friends turned into official dignities (*sic*).' Brougham was made Lord Chancellor and Sydney lost no time in drawing attention to his own deserts:

> 'I want another living instead of this and as good – about £700 a year clear; and I want a prebend of about a thousand per annum. . . . These are my objects in the Church. These points obtained, I give you and fortune a *receipt in full of all demands*, and I think I shall have obtained fully as much as I merit, and more than before this latter period I ever expected. Now nature, time and chance have made you one of the greatest men in the country, and it will be very much in your power from time to time to forward my views. I appeal therefore to your justice, in consideration of the bold and honest part I have acted in the Church – and next to your kindness, from a long acquaintance and friendship – to lend your assistance at convenient seasons, and to aid me with your voice and just authority.'

Brougham did not quite know how to deal with this. Such candour and honesty were alien to a born politician. He immediately offered Sydney an exchange of livings; but the offer was declined with thanks. He showed the letter to Lord Grey, who liked and admired Sydney and realised that he had been of incalculable service to the party. But neither Brougham nor Grey could visualise Sydney as a bishop; they were afraid he might suddenly shock the Church with some farcical outburst, or horrify the House of Lords with some unseemly jest. While they were pondering over the difficulty, the object of their fears was betting on his chances of preferment. He followed the health of the deans with the greatest anxiety: 'Westminster was better this morning, but Durham has had a wretched night.' Writing to John Murray from No. 8 Gloucester Place, Clifton, he outlined the situation:

> 'I think Lord Grey will give me some preferment if he stays in long enough; but the upper parsons live vindictively, and evince their aversion to a Whig ministry by an improved health. The Bishop of — has the rancour to recover after three paralytic strokes, and the Dean of — to be vigorous at eighty-two. And yet these are men who are called Christians!'

Grey had an opportunity to acknowledge services that had been so disinterestedly rendered when the Bishop of Worcester died on the 5th of September, 1831, but he gave the vacant mitre to a Tory. It is a pity that no one recorded

Sydney's comments. On the 10th of September Grey offered him a Residentiary Canonry of St. Paul's Cathedral – 'a snug thing, let me tell you, being worth full £2,000 a year,' said the Prime Minister. He accepted the offer and was installed on the 27th of September, writing that day to a friend: 'It puts me at my ease for life. I asked for nothing – never did anything shabby to procure preferment. These are pleasing recollections.' It is true that he did not ask Grey for preferment, and it is true that he never did anything shabby to procure it; indeed a large part of his life was spent in attacking the abuses that led to preferment.

Shortly afterwards he was presented at Court, but went

> 'horrible to relate! with strings to my shoes instead of buckles – not from Jacobinism, but ignorance. . . . I found to my surprise people looking down at my feet; I could not think what they were at. At first I thought they had discovered the beauty of my legs, but at last the truth burst on me . . . and gathering my sacerdotal petticoats about me (like a lady conscious of thick ankles) I escaped further observation.'

Much to his joy he was now compelled to be in London for three months every year for duty at St. Paul's. He did not wish to live in the house that was provided for him in Amen Corner, partly because it was 'an awkward name on a card, and an awkward annunciation to the coachman on leaving any fashionable mansion', but chiefly because of its distance from 'the parallelogram'. So for a time he contented himself with ready-furnished houses during his periods of residence. At first he stayed at 3 Weymouth Street; later he occupied 18 Stratford Place, from which Saba was married; but at last he decided to have a house of his own, and in 1835 bought No. 33 Charles Street, Berkeley Square, which was quite close to the chapel in John Street where he had preached in his early London days. He obtained a fourteen-years' lease for a lump sum of £1,400 and paid £10 per annum ground rent. In January, 1836, the negotiations were almost concluded: 'The lawyers discovered some flaw in the title about the time of the Norman Conquest; but, thinking the parties must have disappeared in the quarrels of York and Lancaster, I waived the objection.' In the autumn of 1839 he bought a larger house, No. 56 Green Street, Grosvenor Square, which was his London residence until his death.

Meanwhile, both before and after his succession to a stall at St. Paul's Cathedral, he had been busy writing and speaking in favour of the Reform Bill then before Parliament. On the 9th of March, 1831, shortly after the introduction of the Bill in the Commons, he addressed a meeting at Taunton. His main theme was the rotten boroughs. The Tories argued that as the nation had grown rich and powerful while these boroughs had been represented in Parliament, it would be madness to destroy them. Sydney illustrated their argument:

> 'There happens, gentlemen, to live near my parsonage a labouring man, of very superior character and understanding to his fellow-labourers; and who has made such good use of that superiority, that he has saved what is (for his station in life) a very considerable sum of money, and if his existence be extended to the common period, he will die rich. It happens, however, that he is (and long has been) troubled with violent stomachic pains, for which he has hitherto obtained no relief, and which really are the bane and torment of his life. Now, if my excellent labourer were to send for a physician, and to consult him respecting this malady, would it not be very singular language if our doctor were to say to him "My good friend, you surely will not be so rash as to attempt to get rid of these pains in your stomach. Have you not grown rich with these pains in your stomach? have you not risen under them from poverty to prosperity? has not your situation, since you were first attacked, been improving every year? You surely will not be so foolish and so indiscreet as to part with the pains in your stomach?" – Why, what would be the answer of the rustic to this nonsensical monition? "Monster of Rhubarb!" he would say, "I am not rich in consequence of the pains in my stomach, but in spite of the pains in my stomach; and I should have been ten times richer, and fifty times happier, if I had never had any pains in my stomach at all." Gentlemen, these rotten boroughs are your pains in the stomach – and you would have been a much richer and greater people if you had never had them at all.'

It had even been hinted that, should these boroughs be disfranchised, their owners ought to be compensated. Sydney was equal to the hint:

> 'When I was a young man, the place in England I remember as most notorious for highwaymen and their exploits was Finchley Common, near the metropolis; but Finchley Common, gentlemen, in the progress of improvement, came to be enclosed, and the highwaymen lost by these means the opportunity of exercising their gallant vocation. I remember a friend of mine proposed to draw up for them a petition to the House of Commons for compensation, which ran in this manner– "We, your loyal highwaymen of Finchley Common and its neighbourhood, having, at great expense, laid in a stock of blunderbusses, pistols, and other instruments for plundering the public, and finding ourselves impeded in the exercise of our calling by the said enclosure of the said Common of Finchley, humbly petition your Honourable House will be pleased to assign to us such compensation as your Honourable House in its wisdom and justice may think fit." Gentlemen, I must leave the application to you.'

The Second Reading of the Reform Bill was passed on the 22nd of March, but the government was defeated on an amendment in Committee, and Parliament was dissolved on the 23rd of April. Lord John Russell, who had introduced the Bill, was the hero of the hour. He contested Devonshire at the General Election, and Sydney met him at Exeter: 'The people all along the road were very much disappointed by his smallness. I told them he was much larger before the Bill was thrown out, but was reduced by excessive anxiety about the people. This brought tears into their eyes.' A few months later Russell and his family went to stay at Combe Florey and there was great excitement in the village.

During the election Sydney published a Speech to the Freeholders on Reform, in which he made the remarkable statement that 'if a man does not vote for the Bill, he is unclean – the plague-spot is upon him – push him into the lazaretto of the last century – purify the air before you approach him – bathe your hands in Chloride of Lime if you have been contaminated by his touch'. He showed how offices were obtained under the system of rotten boroughs: 'A neighbouring country gentleman, Mr. Plumpkin, hunts with my Lord – opens him a gate or two, while the hounds are running – dines with my Lord – agrees with my Lord – wishes he could rival the South-Down sheep of my Lord – and upon Plumpkin is conferred a portion of the government.' In the meantime nothing was ever done for the poor, who were at the mercy of such antiquated enormities as the Game Laws: 'For every ten pheasants which fluttered in the wood, one English peasant was rotting in jail.' He spoke highly of the honesty of Lord Grey and prophesied that in two thousand years his name would be a legend, like the fable of Perseus and Andromeda:

> 'Britannia chained to a mountain – two hundred rotten animals menacing her destruction, till a tall Earl, armed with Schedule A., and followed by his page Russell, drives them into the deep, and delivers over Britannia in safety to crowds of ten-pound renters, who deafen the air with their acclamations. Forthwith, Latin verses upon this – school exercises – boys whipt, and all the usual absurdities of education.'

He warned his readers not to expect Utopia the moment the Bill was passed:

> 'There will be mistakes at first, as there are in all changes. All young Ladies will imagine (as soon as this Bill is carried) that they will be instantly married. Schoolboys believe that Gerunds and Supines will be abolished, and that Currant Tarts must ultimately come down in price; the Corporal and Sergeant are sure of double pay; bad Poets will expect a demand for their Epics; Fools will be disappointed, as they always are; reasonable men, who know what to expect, will find that a very serious good has been obtained.'

Opponents of the Bill deprecated all the pother that had been raised by the reformers, and asserted that no change of government could make the least difference to the condition of the people – 'They want to keep the bees from buzzing and stinging, in order that they may rob the hive in peace.'

A leading Tory had declared that there was no eagerness among the people for reform: 'Five minutes before Moses struck the rock, this gentleman would have said that there was no eagerness for water.' If this necessary reform were postponed, the result would be the breeding of conspiracies and wholesale concessions at a later date, when no gratitude would be felt for what had been extorted by fear: 'In this way peace was concluded with America, and Emancipation granted to the Catholics; and in this way the war of complexion will be finished in the West Indies.' He concluded with the statement that the rotten boroughs were only useful to the Anglophagi – the jobbers and place-seekers and time-servers.

When the new Parliament assembled it contained a large majority of reformers. A fresh Bill was introduced, passed the Second Reading on the 8th of July, and was sent up to the Lords. In the summer Sydney warned Lord Grey that any attempt of the Lords to throw out the Bill would cause serious trouble in the country, and in September he addressed another meeting on the subject at Taunton. On October the 7th Sydney was in London and told Lord Dudley that if the House of Lords rejected the Reform Bill 'not one single house belonging to any peer that voted against it would have one stone standing upon another at the end of six months'. The following day the Lords took the risk and flung out the Bill.

Instantly there was an outbreak of disorder and violence in the great unrepresented industrial centres. The whole country shook with excitement. Meetings were held everywhere. Speakers deluged their districts with oratory. Anyone who possessed a paper containing the latest news was mobbed. But high above the babel of tongues came one clear and comical note from Taunton, where a meeting was held on the 11th of October. The crowd was enormous and the place of meeting had to be changed at the last moment from the Guildhall to the Castle Hall – where Jeffreys had held his Bloody Assize, where Henry Fielding had addressed a country jury, and where William Pitt had first displayed his powers of oratory. The hall was packed, the atmosphere tense, when Sydney Smith rose from his seat on the platform. He proceeded to ridicule the notion that the House of Lords could kill the Reform Bill, in words that were shortly to be repeated up and down the country and illustrated by prints which sold in thousands:

> 'I do not mean to be disrespectful, but the attempt of the Lords to stop the progress of reform reminds me very forcibly of the great storm of Sidmouth, and of the conduct of the excellent Mrs. Partington on that occasion. In the winter of 1824 there set in a great flood upon that town – the tide rose to an incredible height – the waves rushed in upon the houses, and everything was threatened with destruction. In the midst of this sublime and terrible storm, Dame Partington, who lived upon the beach, was seen at the door of her house with mop and pattens, trundling her mop, squeezing out the sea-water, and vigorously pushing away the Atlantic Ocean. The Atlantic was roused. Mrs. Partington's spirit was up. But I need not tell you that the contest was unequal. The Atlantic Ocean beat Mrs. Partington. She was excellent at a slop, or a puddle, but she should not have meddled with a tempest. Gentlemen, be at your ease – be quiet and steady. You will beat Mrs. Partington.'

Half a century later an eye-witness described the scene:

> 'The introduction of the Partington storm was startling and unexpected, but as he recounted in felicitous terms the adventures of the excellent dame, suiting the action to the word with great dramatic skill, he commenced trundling his imaginary mop, and sweeping back the intrusive waves of the Atlantic, with an air of resolute determination, and an appearance of increasing temper. The scene was realistic in the extreme, and was too much for the gravity of the most serious; and even the staid brethren in drab were convulsed with uncontrollable mirth. The house rose, the people cheered, and tears of superabundant laughter trickled down the cheeks of fair women and veteran Reformers.'

On the 12th of December the Reform Bill was brought in a third time; again it passed the Commons, and again it was in danger from the Lords. Sydney was in constant communication with Grey and urged upon him the necessity of creating peers if the Bill could not otherwise be carried. Grey was a conscientious man, apprehensive of disaster, and easily worried by people and events. Sydney took him to task: 'Do your best with a gay and careless heart. What is it all but the scratching of pismires upon a heap of earth? Rogues are careless and gay, why not honest men? Think of the Bill in the morning, and take your claret in the evening, totally forgetting the Bill.'

He went to hear Grey speak in the House and advised him to stand more upright, raising his arm from the shoulder, not the elbow – a thing that foreigners always did, Englishmen never. Again and again Sydney sent words of encouragement to the Whig leader, now advising him to make forty peers, now advising resignation if the King refused to make them: 'If you wish to be happy three months hence, create Peers. If you wish to avoid an old age of sorrow and reproach, create Peers.' The essence of his frequent admonitions was expressed in the phrase: 'You are just in that predicament in which the greatest boldness is the greatest prudence.' Grey took his advice and obtained the King's written consent to the creation of as many peers as were necessary to get the Bill through the Upper House. The moment this became known, the opposition collapsed, and the Bill received the Royal Assent on the 7th of June, 1832.

Thereafter Sydney's political zeal began to cool, though he went on urging Lord Grey to pay the Irish priests. He had fought harder, longer, more whole-heartedly and with more effect than anyone else for the great reforms of his period, and now he left the applause, the profits and the popularity to others. When we consider that he had projected and established the *Edinburgh Review*, the first great independent periodical in this country, the influence of which among the educated classes of that time has no modern parallel; when we remember that he had spent his life in attacking the bigotry and inhumanity of the ruling classes of his day, that he had exposed the cupidity of the clergy, the avarice of politicians, the selfishness of the aristocracy, and the stupidity of the squirearchy – at a period, too, when the only hope of reward lay in continued lip-service to these dispensers of place and power – it must remain a permanent stain on the reputation of the Whig leaders that he was not offered a bishopric; a very slight gesture of gratitude to the man who had largely helped to place them in a position to make it.

It goes without saying that Sydney's behaviour from the beginning was entirely disinterested; his actions were dictated solely by a love of justice and truth; but he would have been more than human had he not felt indignant at the cowardice of the Whig politicians, who showered honours upon innumerable eleventh-hour reformers and neglected the claims of the one man who had borne the heat and burden of the day, though restricted by a profession that made such service both dangerous and invidious. 'In the Church,' he once said, 'if you are not well born, you must be very base or very foolish, or both.'

One or two of the prominent Whigs had the decency to feel ashamed of themselves. In reviewing his past career, Lord Melbourne said that he regretted nothing so much as his failure to make Sydney Smith a bishop. Lord John Russell declared that, if it had rested entirely with him, Sydney should have had the offer of the mitre. Lord Grey's first thought when he became Prime Minister was that he would be able to do something for Sydney; but his enthusiasm cooled in the atmosphere of Downing Street, and the most notable clergyman of the day was fobbed off with a canonry. On the whole, Sydney took a lenient view of their timidity; he probably knew what to expect of politicians; and so, towards the end of his life, strolling with a friend in the garden at Combe Florey, he spoke without bitterness:

> 'They showed a want of moral courage in not making me a bishop, but I must own that it required a good deal. *They* know, *you* know, all who have lived or talked much with me must know, that I should have devoted myself heart and soul to my duties, and that the episcopal dignity would have sustained no loss in my keeping. But I have only myself to blame if I have been misunderstood.'

He certainly would not have been happy as a bishop: 'I dread the pomp, trifles, garments, and ruinous expense of the episcopal life; and this is lucky, as I have not the smallest reason for believing that anyone has the most remote intention of putting the mitre on my head.' While there was yet a chance that he would receive the distinction, he was 'decidedly of opinion that it would be the greatest act of folly and absurdity to accept it – to live with foolish people, to do foolish and formal things all day, to hold my tongue, or to twist it into conversation unnatural to me'.

The moment he realised that he was not even going to be given the chance of refusing a bishopric, he smothered the pang of thwarted ambition with a sigh of relief, and, behaving quite like a dignitary of the Church, confined himself to digestion. The older he grew the more convinced he became that 'digestion is the great secret of life, and that character, talents, virtues and qualities, are powerfully affected by beef, mutton, pie-crust, and rich soups'. All the miseries of body and mind proceeded from indigestion, and young people should be taught the moral, intellectual and physical evils of it. He believed that old friendships could be destroyed by toasted cheese, that lobster followed by tart could bring on an abnormal state of depression, that suicide had been caused by hard salted meat, and that a morsel of indigestible food was enough to produce a pessimistic outlook on life. To keep healthy and therefore happy, one must follow the common rules: exercise without fatigue, generous living without excess, early rising and moderation in sleeping. Then, too, wealthy people drank more wine than was good for them, and he sent a word of advice to Lady Holland:

> 'I find that I have been very ill all my life without knowing it. Let me state some of the goods arising from abstaining from all fermented liquors. 1st, sweet sleep; having never known what sleep was, I sleep like a baby or a ploughboy. If I wake, no needless terror, no black views of life, but pleasing hope and pleasing recollection: Holland House, past and to come. If I dream, it is not of lions and tigers, but of Love – and Tithes. 2ndly, I can take longer walks and make greater

exertions without fatigue. My understanding is improved, and I comprehend Political Economy. I see better without wine and spectacles than when I use both. Only one evil ensues from it: I am in such extravagant spirits that I must lose blood, or look out for some one who will bore and depress me. Pray leave off wine – the stomach quite at rest; no heartburn, no pain, nor distension.'

The alternative had to be bravely faced: it was London water with a million insects in every drop. 'He who drinks a tumbler of London water has literally in his stomach more animated beings than there are men, women and children on the face of the globe.' He did not forget that some people were only happy when ill, and he mentioned that a certain neighbour 'having lost his disease has also lost his topics of conversation; has no heart to talk about, and is silent from want of suffering'.

In the spring of 1830 Sydney had his first twinge of gout, which, however, improved his eyesight. Lumbago was another enemy – 'equally severe, as it seems, upon priest and anti-priests' – but his most serious trouble was hay-fever in the summer months. This was nothing new. He had suffered from it nearly all his life and had written to Allen in 1819:

'I have never a cold in winter by any accident or any carelessness; in summer no attention can preserve me from them; and they come upon me with a violence which is extremely distressing – no cough, merely catarrh, but catarrh which prevents me from hearing, seeing, smelling or speaking for weeks together, indeed all the summer.'

In a letter to his son-in-law, Dr. Holland, written in June 1835, he returned to the subject, spoke of Holland's forthcoming visit to Combe Florey, and had a word to say on one of his aristocratic patients and one of his professional rivals:

'We shall have the greatest pleasure in receiving you and yours; and if you were twice as numerous, it would be so much the better.

'Illness must be peculiarly disagreeable to the Duchess of Sutherland, as I take it all Duchesses descend when they die, and there are some peculiar circumstances in the life of that lady that will certainly not occasion any exemption in her favour. The defunct Duke must by this time be well informed of her infidelities and their first meeting in Tartarus will not therefore be of the most agreeable description.

'. . . I shall be in town on Tuesday, the 23rd, and, I hope, under better auspices than last year. I have followed your directions, and therefore deserve a better fortune than fell to my lot on that occasion. Sir Henry Halford is the Mahomet of rhubarb and magnesia – the greatest medical impostor I know.

'I am suffering from my old complaint, the hay-fever (as it is called). My fear is of perishing by deliquescence – I melt away in nasal and lachrymal profluvia. My remedies are warm pediluvium, cathartics, topical application of a watery solution of opium to eyes, ears, and the interior of the nostrils. The membrane is so irritable, that light, dust, contradiction, an absurd remark, the sight of a dissenter – anything, sets me a sneezing, and if I begin sneezing at 12, I don't leave off till two o'clock – and am heard distinctly in Taunton when the wind sets that way, at a distance of six miles. Turn your mind to this little curse. If consumption is too powerful for physicians, at least they should not suffer themselves to be outwitted by such little upstart disorders as the hay-fever.

'I am very glad you married my daughter, for I am sure you are both very happy ; and I assure you I am proud of my son-in-law.

'I have ordered a Brass Knocker against you come and we have a case of chronic bronchitis next door – some advanced cases of dyspepsia not far off – and a considerable promise of acute rheumatism at no great distance – a neighbouring squire has water forming on the chest, so that I hope things will be comfortable and your visit not unpleasant.

'I did not think Copplestone, with all his nonsense, could have got down to tar-water. I have as much belief in it as I have in holy water – it is the water has done the business, not the tar. They could not induce the sensual prelate to drink water but by mixing it up with nonsense and disguising the simplicity of the receipt. You must have a pitch battle with him about his tar-water, and teach him what he has never learnt – the rudiments of common sense. Kindest love to dear Saba. Ever your affectionate father, SYDNEY SMITH.'

Bishop Copleston, the 'sensual prelate' whose belief in tar-water called forth Sydney's scorn, was Dean of St. Paul's from 1827 till 1849. We shall meet him again in the next chapter.

The warm air of the south, the added comforts of a larger income, the increasing discomforts of age and illness, and the improved political outlook, made Sydney more conservative in his attitude and less inclined to exert himself in public matters. 'The whole of my life has passed like a razor – in hot water or a scrape.' Now he confessed: 'I love liberty, but hope it can be so managed that I shall have soft beds, good dinners, fine linen, etc., for the rest of my life. I am too old to fight or to suffer'; and 'we have had important events enough within the last twenty years – may all remaining events be culinary, amorous, literary, or anything but political'.

He had given a lot of sound advice to Lord Lansdowne on the subject of licensing, and the Beer-house Act of 1830, in particular the clause which allowed anyone to retail beer on merely taking out an excise-licence, was largely drawn up on the suggestions he made. But when it became law his enthusiasm waned: 'The New Beer Bill has begun its operations. Everybody is drunk. Those who are not singing are sprawling. The sovereign people are in a beastly state.' His normal attitude to beer and such-like 'sweeteners of existence' for the poor was the same as Dr. Johnson's: 'We cannot help reflecting sometimes that an alehouse is the only place where a poor tired creature, haunted with every species of wretchedness, can purchase three pennyworth of ale, a liquor upon which wine-drinking moralists are always extremely severe.'

There was a note of weariness, too, in his reply to someone who wanted to know how the problem of unemployment could be dealt with: 'I can give you no plan for employing the poor. I took great pains about these matters when I was a magistrate, but have forgotten all my plans. There are too many human beings on the earth: every two men ought to kill a third.' The outlook all over Europe depressed him, and he wrote to his friend, Mrs. Meynell:

> 'Arbitrary governments are giving way everywhere, and will doom us to half a century of revolutions and expensive wars. It must be waded through, but I wish it had all been done before I was born. Wild beasts must be killed in the progress of civilisation, but thank God that my ancestors – that is, not mine, for I have none, but Mr. Meynell's ancestors – did this some centuries ago.'

The martyr's crown was not for him. After one period of riot and insurrection he spoke with the accent of Falstaff: 'I had made up my mind to make an heroic stand till the danger became real and proximate, and then I should have been discreet and capitulating.'

He suffered the disillusionment from which no honest man who pins his faith to a political party can escape:

> 'Never was astonishment equal to that produced by the dismissal of the Whigs,' he wrote in January, 1835. 'I thought it better at first to ascertain whether the common laws of nature were suspended; and to put this to the test, I sowed a little mustard and cress seed, and waited in breathless anxiety the event. It came up. By little and little I perceived that, as far as the outward world was concerned, the dismissal of Lord Melbourne has not produced much effect.'

It really did not seem to matter very much whether the Whigs or the Tories were in power: 'On looking into my own mind, I find an utter inability of fighting for either party.' Having a number of Tory friends he had 'never given way to that puritanical feeling of the Whigs against dining with Tories'. They were all the same. None of them had 'that legion of devils in the interior, without whose aid mankind cannot be ruled'.

Already, in 1836, he was beginning to perceive the danger of giving political power to the people. So long as the country was in a prosperous state, little need be feared, but matters might take a serious turn in a period of bad harvests and checked manufactures. He came to the conclusion that 'it would be an entertaining change in human affairs to determine everything by *minorities*. They are almost always in the right'. No wonder that the finest tribute to his political sagacity should have come from that sound old Tory, Professor Saintsbury: 'He would always and naturally have been on the side opposite to that on which most of the fools were.'

Such vitality as he had in these later years was reserved for his parish and St. Paul's Cathedral. Apparently he expended a good deal of nervous energy on his sermons. 'Do not flatter yourself with the delusive hope of a slumber,' he warned Mrs. Grote; 'I preach violently, and there is a strong smell of sulphur in my sermons.' Lady Davy wanted to hear him, too, but he did his best to put her off: 'Commonplace, delivered in a boisterous manner three miles off; and bad, tedious music. If you choose to expose yourself to this in cold blood, it becomes my duty to afford you the means of doing so.' He tried to frighten another friend:

> 'To go to St. Paul's is certain death. The thermometer is several degrees below zero. My sentences are frozen as they come out of my mouth, and are thawed in the course of the summer, making strange noises and unexpected assertions in various parts of the church; but if you are tired of a world which is not tired of you, and are determined to go to St. Paul's, it becomes my duty to facilitate the desperate scheme. Present the enclosed card to any of the vergers, and you will be well placed.'

But though his political ardour cooled, his humour showed no sign of abatement, and his letters during the decade after his arrival at Combe Florey contain a fair sprinkling of passages that could have been written by no pen but his. Let us now extract from the collection those gems that have not already been exhibited.

The following was written to the Countess of Morley, of whom he once said: 'I have more tenderness for her than it would be ecclesiastical to own':

> 'God send peace to the Empire, and particularly to the Church; and may mankind continue quietly to set forth a tenth of the earth's produce for the support of the clergy;

inasmuch as it is known to draw a blessing on the other nine parts, and is wonderfully comfortable to all ranks and descriptions of persons.'

In January, 1832, he wrote to Lady Grey:

> 'We have had the mildest weather possible. A great part of the vegetable world is deceived and beginning to blossom – not merely foolish young plants without experience, but old plants that have been deceived before by premature springs; and for such, one has no pity. It is as if Lady Glengall were to complain of being seduced and betrayed.'

In August of the same year he comforted her with one of his favourite computations:

> 'The cholera will have killed by the end of the year about one person in every thousand. Therefore it is a thousand to one (supposing the cholera to travel at the same rate) that any person does not die of the cholera in any one year. This calculation is for the mass; but if you are prudent, temperate and rich, your chance is at least five times as good that you do not die of the cholera – in other words, five thousand to one that you do not die of cholera in a year; it is not far from two millions to one that you do not die any one day from cholera. It is only seven hundred and thirty thousand to one that your house is not burnt down any one day. Therefore it is nearly three times as likely that your house should be burnt down any one day, as that you should die of cholera; or, it is as probable that your house should be burnt down three times in any one year, as that you should die of cholera.'

He liked making estimates of this nature. We have already seen his calculation of the amount of food he had eaten in the course of his life, and in the same way he worked out the amount of time he had spent in shaving.

> 'Do you ever reflect how you pass your life?' he once asked a girl: 'If you live to 72, which I hope you may, your life is spent in the following manner: An hour a day is three years; this makes 27 years sleeping, 9 years dressing, 9 years at table, 6 years playing with children, 9 years walking, drawing and visiting, 6 years shopping, and 3 years quarrelling.'

At the close of the Parliamentary session the Greys went home for a holiday, and Sydney wrote:

'You must be sick of the human countenance, and it must be a relief to you to see a cow instead of a christian.'

'Little Aunty', in this letter to Colonel Fox, was Lord Holland's sister:

'If you have ever paid any attention to the habits of animals, you will know that donkeys are remarkably cunning in opening gates. The way to stop them is to have two latches instead of one: a human being has two hands, and lifts up both latches at once; a donkey has only one nose, and latch *a* drops as he quits it to lift up latch *b*. Bobus and I had the grand luck to see little Aunty engaged intensely with this problem. She was taking a walk, and was arrested by a gate with this formidable difficulty: the donkeys were looking on to await the issue. Aunty lifted up the first latch with the most perfect success, but found herself opposed by a second; flushed with victory, she quitted the first latch and rushed at the second: her success was equal, till in the meantime the first dropped. She tried this two or three times, and, to her utter astonishment, with the same results; the donkeys brayed, and Aunty was walking away in great dejection, till Bobus and I recalled her with loud laughter, showed her that she had two hands, and roused her to vindicate her superiority over the donkeys. I mention this to you to request that you will make no allusion to this animal, as she is remarkably touchy on the subject.'

The following refers to the meetings of the British Association at Bristol in the summer of 1836:

'I thought you had been paying a visit to the wise men of Bristol. Their occupations appear to be of the greatest importance. On Monday they dissected a frog; on Tuesday they galvanized a goose; on Wednesday they dissected a little pig, and showed that wonderful arrangement of the muscles of the throat by which that animal is enabled to squeak or grunt at pleasure. On Thursday they tried to go up in a balloon; but the balloon would not stir. The causes of the failure were, however, pointed out in a most satisfactory manner. On Friday a new and philosophical mode of making butter was brought forward, and several pats of butter exhibited. On

Saturday they all set off on the outside of coaches, believing they had conferred the utmost benefits on the human race. You and I know better.'

Other correspondents were treated to these passages:

'What is real piety? What is true attachment to the Church? How are these fine feelings best evinced? The answer is plain: by sending strawberries to a clergyman. Many thanks.'

'You have met, I hear, with an agreeable clergyman: the existence of such a being has been hitherto denied by the naturalists; measure him, and put down on paper what he eats.'

'Before I form any opinion on Establishments, I should like to know the effects they produce on vegetables. Many of our clergy suppose that if there was no Church of England, cucumbers and celery would not grow; that mustard and cress could not be raised. If Establishments are connected so much with the great laws of nature, this makes all the difference; but I cannot believe it.'

'Very high and very low temperature extinguishes all human sympathy and relations. It is impossible to feel affection beyond 78° or below 20° of Fahrenheit; human nature is too solid or too liquid beyond these limits. Man only lives to shiver or to perspire. God send that the glass may fall, and restore me to my regard for you, which in the temperate zone is invariable.'

'If any man asks, why am I to do what is generally useful? he should not be reasoned with, but called rogue, rascal, etc., and the mob should be excited to break his windows.'

'When a man is a fool, in England we only trust him with the immortal concerns of human beings.'

'The departure of the Wise Men from the East seems to have been on a more extensive scale than is generally supposed, for no one of that description seems to have been left behind.'

'The complete—has returned from Italy a greater bore than ever; he bores on architecture, painting, statuary and music.

'I quite agree with you as to the horrors of correspondence. Correspondences are like small-clothes before the invention of suspenders; it is impossible to keep them up.'

Lastly, two letters to children:

'Lucy, Lucy, my dear child, don't tear your frock; tearing frocks is not of itself a proof of genius; but write as your mother writes, act as your mother acts; be frank, loyal, affectionate, simple, honest; and then integrity or laceration of frock is of little import. And Lucy, dear child, mind your arithmetic. You know, in the first sum of yours I ever saw, there was a mistake. You had carried two (as a cab is licensed to do) and you ought, dear Lucy, to have carried but one. Is this a trifle? What would life be without arithmetic but a scene of horrors? You are going to Boulogne, the city of debts, peopled by men who never understood arithmetic; by the time you return, I shall probably have received my first paralytic stroke, and shall have lost all recollection of you; therefore I now give you my parting advice. Don't marry anybody who has not a tolerable understanding and a thousand a year, and God bless you, dear child.'

And this to his grandchild, who had sent him a letter overweight:

'Oh, you little wretch! your letter cost me fourpence. I will pull all the plums out of your puddings; I will undress your dolls and steal their under petticoats; you shall have no currant-jelly to your rice; I will kiss you till you cannot see out of your eyes; when nobody else whips you, I will do so; I will fill you so full of sugar-plums that they shall run out of your nose and ears; lastly, your frocks shall be so short that they shall not come below your knees. Your loving grandfather.'

CHAPTER X

A BRANCH OF THE CIVIL SERVICE

WE have now to consider Sydney Smith as a clergyman. No one was ever less of a fanatic than he. He believed that Christianity was made for man, not man for Christianity; and so, whenever he detected an attitude of superstitious reverence towards any institution, he promptly attacked it as idolatrous. Christianity was for him a moral code, not a dogma, and he thought the Church of England its best exponent. Jesus Christ was for him a perfect type of man, not a god, whose teachings were the acme of common sense and common humanity. This is not to say that he questioned the divinity of Christ; it was a subject he never discussed, and he certainly thought Jesus more godlike than any other son of man; but if he had been asked what he thought of the doctrine of the Immaculate Conception, his reply would have lacked reverence.

He disliked theological questions. Christianity was simply a practical code of behaviour. When it ceased to be reasonable and useful, it became dangerous and harmful. We have read his attacks on the Methodists and his defence of the Catholics. In each case his attitude was founded on common sense. He satirised the Methodists because they lived in a world of unreality; he came to the rescue of the Catholics because their opponents lived in a world of unreality. The Methodists hated his common sense because it made them look foolish; the Catholics liked his common sense because it made their oppressors look foolish, though they never felt quite at ease over some aspects of his championship. Towards the end of his life another variation of Christianity arose in the shape of Puseyism. Had he been younger an entertaining version of *Tracts for the Times* would have alarmed the victims of 'Newmania' (as he called it) and produced a panic secession of Puseyites to Rome. A materialist and a rationalist in his general outlook, he grounded a belief in the immortality of the soul on sense and reason:

> 'We count over the pious spirits of the world, the beautiful writers, the great statesmen, all who have invented subtly, who have thought deeply, who have executed wisely:—all these are proofs that we are destined for a second life; and it is not possible to believe that this redundant vigour, this lavish and excessive power, was given for the mere gathering of meat and drink. If the only object is present existence, such faculties are cruel, are misplaced, are useless. They all show us that there is something great awaiting us – that the soul is now young and infantine, springing up into a more perfect life when the body falls into dust.'

He saw the good and the bad in every creed, but believed the Church of England taught the soundest, because the sanest, doctrine. There was no enthusiasm in the Church of England, therefore less probability of error. It was a native growth, admirably adapted to the temperament of the race, catholic in its allowance for diversity of opinion, humanly tolerant, theologically incomprehensible. It was, like the British polity, a representative and national institution, a necessary prop to the state – a Branch of the Civil Service. Also it happened to be his profession.

For these reasons he defended it whenever it was attacked, from within by the pretensions of its priests, from without by the arrogance of atheists. He seriously complained of an essay in the *Edinburgh Review* which in his opinion encouraged 'infidel' principles and threatened to withdraw his support unless Jeffrey promised to mend his ways. (Jeffrey promised.) He wrote to a firm of booksellers, which had sent him an advertisement of some 'infidel' work, advising them in their own interests not to publish irreligious books: 'I hate the insolence, persecution and intolerance which so often pass under the name of religion, and (as you know) I have fought against them, but I have an unaffected horror of irreligion and impiety, and every principle of suspicion and fear would be excited in me by a man who professed himself an infidel.'

This expressed one very important feature of his character, but it was only a feature. Many of his friends were 'infidels' and their views did not excite suspicion and fear in him. The fact is that he suffered from violent twinges of conscience; there were moments when, in the gallop of his spirits, he forgot that he was a clergyman, and was shaken by remorse when the reaction set in. In this respect he went further than Falstaff, who revelled luxuriously in thoughts of future repentance (the future being always at a comfortable distance), while Sydney was seriously disturbed by moods of immediate repentance, when his dejection was as deep as his previous elation had been exalted. Thomas Moore was so impressed by these sudden changes from gay to grave that he believed the solemn, austere Sydney to be the natural man, and the uproarious humour a mere excrescence. Lord Dudley described one of these spectacular transitions:

> 'Sydney is in prodigious glory. By the way, I must tell you a trait of him which is truly characteristic of him. You remember of old what a source of amusement I used to be to him. Well, it is just the same now. He looks at me till he thinks of a joke, and then away he goes for half an hour, but so good-humouredly and inoffensively, as well as with so much drollery, that it is impossible even for the object of his attack not to laugh and be pleased. We had a scene of this sort the other day at a dinner with Luttrell, Lord Cowper, Lord Aberdeen, etc, etc. I laughed myself almost to death, answered as well as I could, when laughter would allow me utterance, and we passed a delightful evening. You may imagine that all this by no means prepared me for a grave epistle which I received from him the next day, in which he complained formally "that we had got into a habit of *rowing* each other", candidly owned that "he was as much to blame as I, but that the whole thing was wrong, and might lead to an interruption of the good humour with which he hoped always to meet me."

Then came something about his *clerical character*, prudence, gravity, discretion, and the Lord knows what besides – and all this not ironical, but in sober good earnest. I wrote him an answer, half joke, half earnest, merely to remind him that I was not the row-er but the row-ee, and had been so for many years – laughed at him when we met, and we go on just as usual. The history of all this is, that he is subject to ebbs as well as flows of spirits, and that when the tide is out he takes a gloomy view of things, reproaches himself for the extravagancies of his own conversation, and seeks comfort by laying the blame upon somebody else.'

Perhaps he felt, too, that his excessive merriment reflected in some way upon the Church. At any rate, we are faced here with a dual nature, embracing creative excitement and morbid exhaustion. There can be very little doubt as to which was the normal and natural man: he was a clergyman from necessity, not choice. Nevertheless he recognised certain conventional obligations; he disliked dining out on a Sunday, and was observed leaving a party before midnight because the next day was Good Friday. Also he lived in constant fear of being misunderstood: 'You must not mistake my afternoon nonsense for my serious and morning opinions,' he told Lord John Russell. Frequently he defended religion from the attacks of agnostics. A French *savant* at Holland House spoke scathingly of the Supreme Being. After listening for some time in silence, Sydney suddenly addressed him: 'Very good soup, this.' The Frenchman agreed: '*Oui, monsieur, c'est excellente.*' Said Sydney: 'Pray, sir, do you believe in a cook?' He did not allow anyone except himself to attack the cloth. After a heated argument with a country squire, the latter became abusive: 'If I had a son who was an idiot, by Jove, I'd make him a parson!' 'Very probably,' returned Sydney, 'but I see that your father was of a different mind.' It was not only religion that forced gravity upon him. Whenever a subject upon which he felt strongly, such as the Slave Trade, was brought into the conversation, he instantly became serious, and the feeling he evinced contrasted strangely with the fun that had led up to it.

Assured that religion was made for the greater comfort and happiness of mankind, he disliked Methodists who made a burden of it and priests who made a hobby of it. After visiting a puritanical family, he wrote:

> 'I endeavour in vain to give them more cheerful ideas of religion, to teach them that God is not a jealous, childish, merciless tyrant; that he is best served by a regular tenour of good actions – not by bad singing, ill-composed prayers and eternal apprehensions. But the luxury of false religion is to be unhappy.'

As for those bishops who were more concerned over the teaching of the Church than with the spirit of Christ, he honestly believed them to be enemies of true religion and attacked them without mercy. When the Bishop of Lincoln, in a Charge delivered to his clergy, assailed the Catholics and gave reasons for continuing their disabilities, Sydney commenced an article in the *Edinburgh Review* with these words:

> 'It is a melancholy thing to see a man, clothed in soft raiment, lodged in a public palace, endowed with a rich portion of the product of other men's industry, using all the influence of his splendid situation, however conscientiously, to deepen the ignorance, and inflame the fury, of his fellow creatures.'

The Bishop had said that the moment Catholics were emancipated they would begin to conspire against the Church of England because it would be to their interest to become the paramount creed in the State. Quite so, agreed Sydney –

> 'but is it not also the decided interest of his Lordship's butler that he should be Bishop, and the Bishop his butler? That the crozier and the corkscrew should change hands – and the washer of the bottles which they had emptied become the diocesan of learned divines? What has prevented this change, so beneficial to the upper domestic, but the extreme improbability of success, if the attempt were made; an improbability so great, that we will venture to say the very notion of it has scarcely once entered into the understanding of the good man. Why, then, is the Reverend Prelate, who lives on so safely and contentedly with *John*, so dreadfully alarmed at the

Catholics? And why does he so completely forget, in their instance alone, that men do not merely strive to obtain a thing because it is good, but always mingle with the excellence of the object a consideration of the chance of gaining it.'

Another prelate who came under the lash of Sydney's scorn was the Bishop of Peterborough, who suddenly decided to put eighty-seven questions on points of doctrine to all the clergy in his diocese, in order to detect the slightest taint of Calvinism in their creed. Exclusion from livings would follow failure to answer these questions to his satisfaction.

'The longer we live,' wrote Sydney, 'the more we are convinced of the justice of the old saying that *an ounce of mother wit is worth a pound of clergy;* that discretion, gentle manners, common sense, and good nature, are, in men of high ecclesiastical station, of far greater importance than the greatest skill in discriminating between sublapsarian and supralapsarian doctrines. Bishop Marsh should remember that all men wearing the mitre work by character as well as doctrine; that a tender regard to men's rights and feelings, a desire to avoid sacred squabbles, a fondness for quiet, and an ardent wish to makeevery body happy, would be of far more value to the Church of England than all his learning and vigilance of inquisition. . . . The Bishop not only puts the questions, but he actually assigns the limits within which they are to be answered. Spaces are left in the paper of interrogations, to which limits the answer is to be confined; – two inches to original sin, an inch and a half to justification, three quarters to predestination, and to free will only a quarter of an inch. But if his Lordship gives them an inch, they will take an ell. His Lordship is himself a theological writer, and by no means remarkable for his conciseness. To deny space to his brother theologians, who are writing on the most difficult subjects, not from choice, but necessity; not for fame, but for bread; and to award rejection as the penalty of prolixity, does appear to us no slight deviation from Christian gentleness.'

When criticised for drawing up this list of questions, the Bishop had said that only two curates had been excluded. Sydney quickly availed himself of this opening:

'So the Emperor of Hayti boasted that he had only cut off two persons' heads for disagreeable behaviour at his table.

In spite of the paucity of the visitors executed, the example operated as a considerable impediment to conversation; and the intensity of the punishment was found to be a full compensation for its rarity.'

The Bishop, to assert his noble disinterestedness, had spoken of the drudgery of wading through all the answers to his eighty-seven questions.

'But to be intolerably strict and harsh to a poor curate, who is trying to earn a morsel of hard bread, and then to complain of the drudgery of reading his answers, is much like knocking a man down with a bludgeon, and then abusing him for splashing you with his blood, and pestering you with his groans.'

A memory of days on Salisbury Plain stirred Sydney as he wrote, and he pictured the existence of a typical curate:

'There is something which excites compassion in the very name of a Curate!!! How any man of Purple, Palaces, and Preferment, can let himself loose against this poor working man of God, we are at a loss to conceive – a learned man in an hovel, with sermons and saucepans, lexicons and bacon, Hebrew books and ragged children – good and patient – a comforter and a preacher – the first and purest pauper in the hamlet, and yet showing that in the midst of his worldly misery he has the heart of a gentleman and the spirit of a Christian and the kindness of a pastor; and this man, though he has exercised the duties of a clergyman for twenty years – though he has most ample testimonies of conduct from clergymen as respectable as any bishop – though an Archbishop add his name to the list of witnesses, is not good enough for Bishop Marsh; but is pushed out in the street, with his wife and children, and his little furniture, to surrender his honour, his faith, his conscience, and his learning – or to starve!'

The Bishop, however, was quite satisfied with himself, and declared that he had a *right* to do what he had done –

'just as if a man's character with his fellow creatures depended upon legal rights alone and not upon a discreet exercise of those rights. A man may persevere in doing what he has a right to do, till the Chancellor shuts him up in Bedlam, or till the mob pelt him as he passes. It must be presumed, that all men whom the law has invested with rights, Nature has invested with common sense to use those rights. For these reasons, children have no rights till they have gained some common sense, and old men have no rights after they lose their common sense. All men are at all times accountable to their fellow creatures for the discreet exercise of every right they possess.'

In conclusion, his Lordship was reminded that 'men of very small incomes . . . have very often very acute feelings, and a Curate trod on feels a pang as great as when a Bishop is refuted.'

On the subject of bishops generally, Sydney had this to say:

> 'It is in vain to talk of the good character of bishops. Bishops are men; not always the wisest of men; not always preferred for eminent virtues and talents or for any good reason whatever known to the public. They are almost always devoid of striking and indecorous vices; but a man may be very shallow, very arrogant, and very vindictive, though a bishop; and pursue with unrelenting hatred a subordinate clergyman whose principles he dislikes and whose genius he fears. Bishops besides, are subject to the infirmities of old age, like other men; and in the decay of strength and understanding, will be governed as other men are, by daughters and wives, and whoever ministers to their daily comforts. We have no doubt that such cases sometimes occur, and produce, wherever they do occur, a very capricious administration of ecclesiastical affairs. I have seen in the course of my life, as the mind of the prelate decayed, wife bishops, daughter bishops, butler bishops, and even cook and housekeeper bishops.'
>
> 'I never remember in my time a real Bishop,' wrote Sydney on another occasion; 'a grave elderly man, full of Greek, with sound views of the middle voice and preterperfect tense, gentle and kind to his poor clergy, of powerful and commanding eloquence; in Parliament never to be put down when the great interests of mankind were concerned; leaning to the Government when *it* was right, leaning to the People when *they* were right; feeling that if the Spirit of God had called him to that high office, he was called for no mean purpose, but rather that, seeing clearly, and acting boldly, and intending purely, he might confer lasting benefits upon mankind.'

Never in his early days did he dream that he might become a bishop. 'Political independence,' he said in 1809, 'discouraged enough in these times among all classes of men, is sure, in the timid profession of the Church, to doom a man to eternal poverty and obscurity.' A year later he wrote: 'As for being a bishop, that I shall never be; but I shall, I believe, be quite as happy a man as any bishop.' Ten years passed by, leaving him unembittered: 'My constitutional gaiety comes to my aid in all the difficulties of life; and the recollection that, having embraced the character of an honest man and a friend to rational liberty, I have no business to repine at that mediocrity of fortune which I *knew* to be its consequence.'

We cannot feel surprise that he was never made a bishop. His impulsive candour and incurable honesty, his lack of interest in the finer shades of doctrine, were sufficient to mark him as dangerous. Add to these his truly shocking exhibitions of wit and high spirits, which scandalised many good men and true, to say nothing of many proper women. Some of the latter, after hearing him talk, thought him an atheist. Harriet Martineau and Fanny Kemble, though they could not help liking him and enjoying his society, were respectively 'pained' and 'disturbed' by his freedom of speech; and we must remember that in those days, before the gloom of Victorian respectability had set in, speech in mixed assemblies was decently free. It is the business of his biographer to exhibit him at his recorded worst, though it is probable that even the most godly modern reader will remain calm during this revelation of a parson's improprieties.

Quite early in life he wrote from Edinburgh to the mother of his pupil: 'In England I maintain that (except amongst ladies in the middle class of life) there is no religion at all.' When she expostulated, he went further:

> 'Religion (I am sorry to say) is much like heraldry – an antiquated concern – a few people attend to the one and the other – but the world laugh at them for engaging in such a superannuated pursuit. In 50 years more the whole art of going to church – how the squire's lady put on her best hat

and cloak – and how the squire bowed to the parson after church – and how the parson dined with the squire – and all these ceremonies of worship will be in the hands of the antiquarian, will be elucidated by laborious investigation, and explained by appropriate drawings.'

A month later he was writing:

> 'We are just going to church. The wind is outrageous – to the infinite joy of those ladies who can boast of good ankles, who will not fail this day to be punctually attentive to the public duties of religion – while those of more clumsy fabric will no doubt discover that prayers read at home are quite as efficacious.'

When one of Nelson's victories was announced, he observed:

> 'I can compare the joy visible on the public countenance to nothing so much as the faces of an audience just as the *Discourse* is over and they are coming out of church – a spectacle truly delightful to those who are fond of seeing a great number of people happy at once.'

In this manner did Sydney display his early feelings concerning the Church; they were scarcely those of a devout man with a 'call' to the office of priesthood. An episode in his life at Foston does not cancel the impression left on us by those letters. He was preaching away from home and spending Saturday night with the rector whose pulpit he was to occupy on Sunday. The squire, a Mr. Kershaw, dined with them, and the evening was passed in great hilarity. A funny clergyman was a new thing to the squire, and he nearly laughed himself into an apoplexy. 'You must not laugh at my sermon to-morrow,' Sydney warned him when the squire rose to go. 'I hope I know the difference between being here or at church,' answered Kershaw rather severely. 'I'm not so sure of that,' returned Sydney. 'I'll bet you a guinea on it,' said Kershaw. 'Take you,' replied Sydney. The next morning he went into the pulpit apparently suffering from a severe cold and making his sneezes sound exactly like 'Ker-shaw', which he repeated several times in various intonations. A loud guffaw burst from the squire, the congregation (not being in the joke) were scandalised, the preacher gave him a look of stern reproach – and collected a guinea from him after the service.

Here are some of Sydney's scattered sayings, which, however true, were perhaps a little unexpected in the mouth of a clergyman: –

'The observances of the Church concerning feasts and fasts are tolerably well kept upon the whole, since the rich keep the feasts and the poor the fasts.'

'The Church attempting to be useful is much as if Sheridan were to take to keeping accounts – but it cannot last.'

'Church and King in moderation are very good things, but we have too much of both.'

'I must believe in the Apostolic Succession, there being no other way of accounting for the descent of the Bishop of Exeter from Judas Iscariot.'

'Benevolence is a natural instinct of the human mind. When A sees B in grevious distress, his conscience always urges him to entreat C to help him.'

'Lady Cork was once so moved by a charity sermon that she begged me to lend her a guinea for her contribution. I did so. She never repaid me, and spent it on herself.'

'His idea of heaven is, eating *pâtés de foie gras* to the sound of trumpets.'

'What a mystery is the folly and stupidity of the good!'

'There is not the least use in preaching to anyone unless you chance to catch them ill.'

'What a pity it is that we have no amusements in England but vice and religion!'

'England is almost the only country in the world (even at present) where there is not some favourite religious spot, where absurd lies, little bits of cloth, feathers, rusty nails, splinters and other invaluable relics, are treasured up, and in defence of which the whole population are willing to turn out and perish as one man.'

'That most solemn and terrible duty of a bishop, the entertainment of the clergy.'

Speaking of Milman's *History of Christianity*: 'No man should write on such subjects unless he is prepared to go the whole *lamb*.'

He once begged another canon to take a service for him, saying that he was so rheumatic in his *professional* joints.

A Puseyite dated a letter to him with some Saint's Day. He dated his reply: 'Washing-Day.'

Puseyism he described as 'inflexion and genuflexion, posture and imposture, bowing to the east and curtseying to the west'.

Imploring him to be present at a large party, someone used the expression: 'We shall be on our knees to you if you come.' He replied: 'I'm glad to hear it. I like to see you in that attitude, as it brings me in several hundreds a year.'

Of attorneys he said: 'You have no right to assume that any other class of men is damned.'

Of Dr. Arnold he said: 'He seems to have been a learned, pious, virtuous person, without five grains of common sense.'

During a period of bad health he said that he felt so ill and confused that he could not remember whether there were nine articles and thirty-nine muses or the contrary.

There was a proposal in his time that St Paul's Cathedral should be surrounded by a wooden pavement. He strongly favoured the proposal: 'Let the Dean and Canons lay their heads together and the thing will be done.'

Writing to congratulate Lord Grey on the birth of an infant: 'If Lady Grey wishes to see a child gracefully held, and to receive proper compliments upon its beauty, and to witness the consummation of all ecclesiastical observances, she will invite me to perform the ceremony.'

He frequently visited the Kinglake family at Taunton, and mention was made one afternoon of a neighbouring clergyman who had refused to read the burial service over a Dissenter. 'Would you object, Mr. Smith, to bury a Dissenter?'

asked old Mrs. Kinglake. 'Not bury Dissenters!' exclaimed Sydney; 'I should like to be burying them all day.'

Preaching in London on a special occasion he noticed that the congregation consisted almost entirely of women, and altered his text to: 'Oh, that *men* would therefore praise the Lord!'

In the course of a charity sermon he said that the English were distinguished for generosity and a love of their species. The collection was disappointing and he announced that he wished to correct a remark he had made from the pulpit; he should have said that the English were distinguished for a love of their *specie*.

He advised a sculptor to present his statue of Satan to the Reform Club, because 'the devil was the first Reformer and came to grief in Heaven for the too great zeal, indiscretion and untimeliness with which he agitated the Reform question'.

Advice to a clergyman who had witnessed the massacre of Peterloo and wished to write an account of it for publication: 'A true and candid narrative of what you saw would for ever put an end to your chances of preferment.'

Concerning the matrimonial troubles of George IV, when there was a probability that the Queen would defeat the King and throw out the administration, he wrote: 'The majority of the bishops with the Archbishop of York at their head are against the divorce. . . . Whence this profusion of honesty and principle in churchmen, I know not; do the rogues smell a change?'

At times he appeared to be very strict upon the forms and ceremonies of the Church and once reproved an unorthodox person in these words: 'It is a vile heresy and you deserve to be burnt for it – with green faggots.' At other times he adopted a broader view. When he performed the ceremony of marriage for his brother 'Bobus' in 1797, he wrote to Mrs. Hicks-Beach that he was about to read 'a little form of service (such are the prejudices of mankind) to constitute a legal marriage'. That his views did not narrow with age is proved by a letter he wrote to Lord Denman in 1841.

Denman was Lord Chief Justice; he is chiefly remembered to-day for the phrase, 'A delusion, a mockery and a snare'. Sydney had asked him and his wife to dinner and then had suddenly remembered that Lady Denman might object to meeting another guest, whose early life had not been pure in the eyes of the Church, though closely modelled on that of certain excellent biblical characters. So he wrote:

> 'Dear Lord Denman, Mrs. Smith and I have made a blunder, which I am sure you will have the goodness to excuse, and the more especially as it proceeded from our desire to secure Lady Denman's company in conjunction with yours. Lady Holland dines with us on the 17th. Does Lady Denman know Lady Holland? and, if not, will that deprive us of the pleasure of Lady Denman's company? Lady Holland sinned early in life, with Methuselah and Enoch, but still is out of the pale of the regular ladies, and the case ought to have been put. Pray tell me if this will make any difference. Your answer will be received by me in the strictest confidence.'

This short catalogue of unspiritual anecdotes and sayings may aptly be terminated with a passage from the diary of Thomas Moore (April 6, 1832):

> 'Turned back with Sydney to call at the Duke of Northumberland's – left our cards. Told me that he had been knocked down by a coach the other day in crossing the street, and was nearly run over; and that, knowing how much of Lord Grey's patronage had accrued from accidents happening to clergymen, he found himself saying as he came down, "There's a vacancy".'

There may be doubts as to whether Sydney Smith was a sound Churchman; there can be no doubt that he was a sound Christian. 'True, modest, unobtrusive religion – charitable, forgiving, indulgent Christianity, is the greatest ornament and the greatest blessing that can dwell in the mind of man.' So he wrote in the *Edinburgh Review*. This was his creed and he lived up to it. 'Not only is religion calm and tranquil, but it has an extensive atmosphere round it, whose calmness and tranquility must be preserved, if you would avoid misrepresentation.' Of that, too, he was convinced, and he taught it by precept and practice. Naturally quick-tempered, he fought against his tendency to explosive speech, and instantly regretted having given way to it, not knowing a moment's ease until he had made peace with the momentary object of his wrath. He was extremely sensitive. 'I never go to tragedies,' he said, 'my heart is too soft; there is too much real misery in life.' Scenes of distress moved him quickly to tears. In 1843, on the death of a fellow-canon, the valuable living of Edmonton fell vacant and by the rules of the Chapter of St. Paul's it lay with Sydney either to take it himself or present it to a friend or relation. He went down to see the family of the deceased clergyman and found them in a dreadful state of dejection at the prospect of being turned out of the house; they had no money and the eldest son, who had acted as his father's curate, would shortly be forced to find work elsewhere. Sydney had already determined to give the living to this eldest son, and when he announced the fact to the assembled family they all burst into tears of relief and gratitude. 'It flung me also into a great agitation of tears,' he told his wife, 'and I wept and groaned for a long time.' A strange scene and highly characteristic of Sydney.

He despised the type of philanthropist who contented himself with high-sounding hopes of world-betterment and never put hand in pocket to help an individual. Reviewing Godwin's principle of Universal Benevolence, excluding particular affection, he wrote: 'It is as much as to say that all the crew ought to have the *general* welfare of the ship so much at heart, that no sailor should ever pull any *particular* rope or hand any *individual* sail.' The knowledge of the good work he had done as a writer and speaker gave him not half so much pleasure at the end of his life as the reflection that he had lived on good terms with his fellow-men. In spite of his belief that Catholics were human beings and that bishops were all-too-human beings, he was popular with his professional brethren, because of his cheerfulness, his simplicity of demeanour, his active interest in parochial matters, and the thousand and one remedies for everything, from smoking chimneys to mental depression, that were always at their disposal. He had an exhilarating effect on everyone he met and he made people who were naturally shy and modest have a better opinion of themselves. 'Reverence and stand in awe of yourself,' was his advice to the humble and meek.

There was not an atom of arrogance in his nature; he was always willing to listen to the opinions of others and learn from them. Henry Fothergill Chorley, afterwards famous as a musical critic, witnessed to his forbearance and gentleness. Chorley, when an 'obscure penny-a-liner' (his own description), met Sydney at some reception. At that time Lady Blessington ran a rival establishment to Lady Holland's and the latter told many tales to the discredit of the former; among others, that Lady Blessington, at the instance of d'Orsay, lured foolish youths of cash and quality to Gore House. Sydney was retailing this with much mirth when Chorley told him it was untrue and put him in possession of the facts. Sydney immediately said 'Thank you for setting me right' and thereafter treated Chorley with great kindness.

Though Sydney was liked by nearly everyone who met him, there were several bishops who longed to revive the torture-chamber for his benefit. One of them directly charged him with irreligion, which annoyed him so much that in a letter to Lord John Russell (April 3, 1837) he really let fly:

> 'I defy him to quote a single passage of my writing contrary to the doctrines of the Church of England; for I have always avoided speculative, and preached practical, religion. I defy him to mention a single action in my life which he can call immoral. The only thing he could charge me with would be high spirits and much innocent nonsense. I am distinguished as a preacher and sedulous as a parochial clergyman. His real charge is that I am a high-spirited, honest, uncompromising man, whom all the bench of Bishops could not turn, and who would set them all at defiance upon great and vital questions. This is the reason why (as far as depends upon others) I am not a bishop; but I am thoroughly sincere in saying I would not take any bishopric whatever, and to this I pledge my honour and character as a gentleman.'

We have impartial evidence, as well as his own, that he was distinguished as a preacher. George Ticknor went to St. Paul's in July, 1835 and listened to 'the best sermon I ever heard in Great Britain'. It was written, said the Harvard professor, with great condensation of thought and purity of style, and sometimes with brilliancy of phrase and expression, and it was delivered with great power and emphasis. After the service, as they were going away, Sydney appeared mysteriously through one of the iron gates that led into the body of the Cathedral, took them round the building, placed them under the dome and showed them the effect from the end of the nave. It was all very solemn, though their guide could not refrain from his accustomed humour and severe criticism. Charles Greville, the diarist, heard Sydney preach in St. Paul's and thought him very good; manner impressive, a little familiar but not offensively so; voice sonorous and agreeable; language simple and unadorned; sermon clever and illustrative. From other evidence we gather that he had no difficulty in reducing his congregation to tears whenever the occasion seemed to warrant it.

In his day most sermons were read in a sort of drawling monotone; and though his own sermons were always written, he put a great deal of energy into their delivery: 'When I began to thump the cushion of my pulpit on first coming to Foston, as is my wont when I preach, the accumulated dust of a hundred and fifty years made such a cloud that for some minutes I lost sight of my congregation.' He was contemptuous of the petrified preacher: 'I like to look down upon my congregation – to fire into them. The common people say I am a *bould preacher*, for I like to have my arms free and to thump the pulpit.' People were easily distracted in church and unless one spoke directly at them, their attention was liable to wander: 'A sparrow fluttering about the church is an antagonist which the most profound theologian in Europe is wholly unable to overcome.' On the other hand he was often lazy over the composition of sermons. One Sunday he announced his subject as 'Putting one's hand to the plough and looking back' and calmly informed his congregation that they could find the exact text 'somewhere in the Epistles'. (It is in St. Luke.) Thomas Moore heard him preach at Bowood; a good sermon but obviously written for people living in London (one of his St. Paul's sermons, in fact) and therefore about ninety miles wide of the mark. He confessed to Lady Grey that he had never longed to steal anything except some manuscript sermons from his fellow-clergymen, a temptation he had resisted with difficulty. Early in 1844 he preached a sermon at St. Paul's against war and followed it up with a letter on the subject to Lady Grey:

> 'I think Channing an admirable writer. So much sense and eloquence! such a command of language! Yet admirable as his sermon on war is, I have the vanity to think my own equally good, quite as sensible, quite as eloquent, as full of good principle and fine language; and you will be the more inclined to agree with me in this comparison when I tell you that I preached in St. Paul's the identical sermon which Lord Grey so much admires. I thought I could not write anything half so good, so I preached Channing.'

His appearance in the pulpit was very impressive; the piercing eyes, prominent nose, snow-white hair, swarthy complexion, burly build and upright carriage, added to the deep musical voice, caught and held the attention. People who had known him in society and were a little nervous that he might make them giggle, were soon under the influence of his solemnity and sincerity. The primary features of his sermons, which seldom exceeded twenty minutes in length, were simplicity and directness. He went to hear Irving preach, thought him tiresome and did not quite understand what the sermon was about. No one was ever left in doubt as to the meaning of Sydney's sermons. From the beginning to the end of his life he never attempted to speak above the heads of his congregation. Two extracts will give us a clear conception of his quality as a preacher. The first is from a charity sermon on behalf of the Blind, delivered in Edinburgh at the commencement of his career:

> 'The author of the book of Ecclesiastes has told us "that the light is sweet, that it is a pleasant thing for the eyes to behold the sun." The sense of sight is indeed the highest bodily privilege, the purest physical pleasure, which man has derived from his Creator. To see that wandering fire, after he has finished his journey through the nations, coming back to his eastern heavens, the mountains painted with light, the floating splendour of the sea, the earth waking from deep slumber, the day flowing down the sides of the hills till it reaches the secret valleys, the little insect recalled to life, the bird trying her wings, man going forth to his labour – each created being moving, thinking, acting, contriving, according to the scheme and compass of its nature, by force, by cunning, by reason, by necessity. Is it possible to joy in this animated scene, and feel no pity for the sons of darkness? for the eyes that will never see light? for the poor clouded in everlasting gloom? If you ask me why they are miserable and dejected, I turn you to the plentiful valleys; to the fields now bringing forth their increase; to the freshness and the flowers of the earth; to the endless variety of its colours; to the grace, the symmetry, the shape of all it cherishes and all it bears; these you have forgotten, because you have always enjoyed them; but these are the means by which God Almighty makes man what he is – cheerful, lively, erect, full of enterprise, mutable, glancing from heaven to earth, prone to labour and to act. Why was not the earth left without form and void? Why was not darkness suffered to remain on the face of the deep? Why did God place lights in the firmament, for days, for seasons, for signs, and for years? That He might make man the happiest of created beings; that He might give to this His favourite creation a wider scope, a more permanent duration, a richer diversity of joy. This is the reason why the blind are miserable and dejected – because their soul is mutilated, and dismembered of its best sense – because they are a laughter and a ruin, and the boys of the streets mock at their stumbling feet. Therefore, I implore you, by the Son of David, have mercy on the blind. If there is not pity for all sorrows, turn the full and perfect man to meet the inclemency of fate; let not those who have never tasted the pleasure of existence be assailed by any of its sorrows; the eyes which are never gladdened by light should never stream with tears.'

The second extract is from a sermon delivered in St. Paul's Cathedral towards the close of his career on the accession of

Queen Victoria to the throne. Its subject was 'the Duties of the Queen'. First and foremost, he said, the new Queen should bend her mind to the very serious consideration of educating the people. Then he touched a favourite theme:

> 'A second great object, which I hope will be impressed upon the mind of this Royal Lady, is a rooted horror of war – an earnest and passionate desire to keep her people in a state of profound peace. The greatest curse which can be entailed upon mankind is a state of war. All the atrocious crimes committed in years of peace – all that is spent in peace by the secret corruptions, or by the thoughtless extravagance of nations, are mere trifles compared with the gigantic evils which stalk over the world in a state of war. God is forgotten in war – every principle of Christian charity trampled upon – human labour destroyed – human industry extinguished – you see the son, and the husband, and the brother, dying miserably in distant lands – you see the waste of human affections – you see the breaking of human hearts – you hear the shrieks of widows and children after the battle – and you walk over the mangled bodies of the wounded calling for death. I would say to that Royal child, Worship God by loving peace – it is not *your* humanity to pity a beggar by giving him food or raiment – *I* can do that; that is the charity of the humble and the unknown – widen you your heart for the more expanded miseries of mankind – pity the mothers of the peasantry who see their sons torn away from their families – pity your poor subjects crowded into hospitals, and calling in their last breath upon their distant country and their young Queen – pity the stupid, frantic folly of human beings who are always ready to tear each other to pieces, and to deluge the earth with each other's blood; this is your extended humanity – and this the great field of your compassion. Extinguish in your heart the fiendish love of military glory, from which your sex does not necessarily exempt you, and to which the wickedness of flatterers may urge you. Say upon your death-bed, "I have made few orphans in my reign – I have made few widows – my object has been peace. I have used all the weight of my character, and all the power of my situation, to check the irascible passions of mankind, and to turn them to the arts of honest industry: this has been the Christianity of my throne, and this the gospel of my sceptre; in this way I have striven to worship my Redeemer and my Judge." '

In England more than in any country stupidity is often confused with honesty, cleverness with untrustworthiness. 'I never was asked in all my life to be a trustee or an executor,' said Sydney: 'No one believes that I can be a plodding man of business, as mindful of its dry details as the gravest and most stupid man alive.' As canon of St. Paul's his ability as a plodder was triumphantly manifested. The Chapter clerk, the architect and other officials connected with the Cathedral bore witness to his business capacity and the care with which he entered into the estimates and accounts. He was the first canon for many years who had taken the trouble to master the affairs of the Chapter and he cut down unnecessary expenditure right and left. Naturally his interference in business that had previously been left in less responsible hands was at first resented. C. R. Cockerell, the architect and superintendent of the Cathedral, declared that Sydney investigated with the utmost minuteness all transactions that came within his province, doing so with a severity of discipline neither called for nor agreeable; his early communications with all the officers of the Chapter were therefore extremely unpleasant, but when satisfied by 'a little collision' (as he termed it) that all was right and above-board, his subsequent treatment of them was candid and kind, and their early dislike was converted into confidence and regard.

There were some nasty moments at the outset. Writing to Cockerell from No. 24, Hanover Square in June, 1832, he referred to the painting of the Chapter-house, the replacing of dog-spikes in the stonework, the repairing of the iron staircase in the west tower, and remarked: 'I will also in future sign my name to all the bills that I audit.' Dealing with the golden gallery, the painting of ironwork, the putting in of window panes, of new flags in the churchyard and an iron safe in the Chapter-room, he stated that no work was to be undertaken without his consent and complained that he had not received the accounts for the work then in hand. Cockerell was annoyed over a curt verbal message he had received from Sydney, but the latter explained that the message had been incorrectly delivered, adding: 'If I did not respect you and all other gentlemen too much to leave such a message, you may depend upon it I respect myself too much to do so.'

He insisted on personally inspecting the roof of the Chapter-house, refused to pay any tradesman's account until the job had been completed, and wanted to know why no memorandum of work done had been kept by the deputy-surveyor. 'Your idea of respectability,' he wrote to Cockerell, 'seems to be that no tradesman can be respectable who does not charge high prices.' Cockerell said that a man named Tight could provide a satisfactory estimate for a certain job. 'I am all against Tight,' came Sydney's answer; 'it is impossible a man by the name of Tight can have sense, genius or taste.' In another letter he asked Cockerell to obtain the fabric bills: 'We had better set about it directly, as it takes a considerable time to collect, object and scold.' Punctuality was the only virtue that Sydney made disagreeable, and it was thoughtless of Cockerell, after an acquaintanceship of eight years, to keep the canon waiting. On July 15, 1840, Sydney was still writing in this strain: 'I appeal to your common sense, is this fair play between architect and fabric or between gentleman and gentleman? You neither answer my letter nor appear at the Cathedral at the time I fixed nor give any explanation of your absence.'

The surveyor to the Cathedral testified that there had been no superintendence at all comparable with Sydney's: he had warmed the library and rebound the books; he had insured the fabric against fire and had 'brought the New River into the Cathedral by mains'; he had repaired and cleaned the monuments and set them in order. He did not at first believe that the Cathedral itself could be warmed: 'You might as well try to warm the county of Middlesex.' But the plan succeeded and he gratefully admitted his error. Henry Hart Milman, who succeeded Copleston as Dean of St. Paul's four years after Sydney's death, wrote:

> 'I find traces of him in every particular of Chapter affairs; and on every occasion where his hand appears, I find stronger

> reason for respecting his sound judgment, knowledge of business, and activity of mind; above all, the perfect fidelity of his stewardship. In his care of his own interests as member of the Chapter, there was ever the most honest (rarely, if I may not say singularly honest) regard for the interests of the Chapter and the Church. His management of the affairs of St. Paul's (for at one time he seems to have been *the* manager) only commenced too late, and terminated too soon.

It appears, by the way, that music in the minor key had always had a depressing effect on him, and he forbade its introduction into the services whenever he was in residence.

A shrewd and curious eye was turned upon Sydney at close quarters throughout the whole of his official connection with St. Paul's Cathedral, the eye of a minor canon who was also a literary man of note – the Rev. R. H. Barham, author of *Ingoldsby Legends*. Barham was very friendly with the Dean, Bishop Copleston, and we may therefore assume that he received a certain amount of inside information concerning Sydney straight from the Dean's mouth. Barham was a good-natured, sensible, unpretentious man, a wit and the friend of wits. By nature indolent, he always required some external stimulus before he would settle down to literary work: the *Ingoldsby Legends* were only written to help his old friend Bentley, the publisher. Being an Englishman of a distinctively national type, and a Tory into the bargain, he heard of Sydney's appointment to St. Paul's with misgiving; but no one could withstand Sydney for long, least of all a pleasant person like Barham, and soon they were close friends.

Their friendship, however, did not shut Barham's eyes to the dictatorial and conspiratorial methods of the new canon. By the end of 1834 Sydney was at open feud with the minor canons and scarce cater-cousin with the more exalted dignitaries. He was too anxious to influence the affairs of the Cathedral and closely questioned the lesser clergy as to their grievances. The latter believed that he merely wished to be their spokesman in order to use their discontent as a means of strengthening his own position; they refused to rise to the bait, and he was angry.

It seems pretty certain that Sydney was a man who hated playing second-fiddle to anyone. He was a born leader, organiser and diplomat, with an immense reserve of energy; and here at last he found himself in a position of some importance. He was fully aware of his own powers and could not take a back seat when there was a chance of slipping into a front one. Since he was in the Church, he probably felt that he ought to have been Archbishop of Canterbury. Had he been allowed to follow his own inclinations and to make the law his profession, he would have aimed at the Woolsack and probably got there. Had he been in politics, nothing less than the Premiership would have satisfied him. As things turned out he was a square peg in a round hole (his own position no doubt called forth that famous passage in one of his lectures) and it was only natural that, his energies dammed and thwarted, friction should result from the misfit.

Yet he was always careful not to go too far. The moment he found that he could not get what he wanted, he gave way without complaint. He could back out of a difficult position with a good grace. When, for example, he discovered that he could not nominate a vicar's churchwarden to the living of Halberton which was attached to his stall at Bristol, he wrote to the vestry:

> 'Gentlemen, – It has always been a rule with me through life to be as firm and tenacious in the maintenance of my just rights, as I am willing to sacrifice those to which I am not entitled. I must in candour confess that from all the evidence I can collect – and I have employed two active solicitors in the search – I cannot find that the clergyman of Halberton has been in the habit of nominating a churchwarden. I shall therefore not attempt to exercise that power this year at the ensuing Easter. If, from any fresh evidence I can collect, I should see reason to alter my opinion another year, I reserve to myself the full right of doing so; but, that I may not take the parish by surprise, I engage to give two months' notice of such an intention. . . . If I could have satisfied myself that I possessed the right, I would have contested it at any expense, but I am not so satisfied, and I give it up as I said I would.'

His successor, Canon Girdlestone, was not so sensible; he carried the matter to the Court of Queen's Bench and at a cost of £1,750 to his opponents established the vicar's right in perpetuity to nominate a churchwarden.

Barham believed that Sydney was gradually turning Tory; certainly his language became more and more reactionary, partly from age, partly from position. The contrast between his severity as a man of business and his levity at the dinner-table was neatly hit off at about this period by Lord Lansdowne, who described him as 'an odd mixture of Punch and Cato'. Both those characters are suggested in Barham's letters. 'Be a fool, sir, if you will be a fool!' was Sydney's advice to a man who had asked whether he should marry a certain lady. 'If ever a religious war should arise again,' he told Barham, 'I should certainly take arms against the Dissenters. Fancy me with a bayonet at the heart of an Anabaptist with "Your church-rate or your life!" ' Nothing should ever induce him to go up in a balloon, he declared, unless it would benefit the Established Church. Barham recommended him to make the ascent at once, as there would at least be a chance of it.

He gave Barham the recipe for a salad, with a word of advice: 'As this salad is the result of great experience and reflection, it is hoped young salad-makers will not attempt to make any improvements upon it.' He allowed Barham to occupy his residentiary house. Barham was delighted and sent him a small token of regard, receiving this acknowledgment: 'Many thanks, my dear sir, for your kind present of game. If there is a pure and elevated pleasure in this world, it is roast pheasant and bread sauce. Barn-door fowls for Dissenters, but for the real Churchman, the thirty-nine times articled clerk – the pheasant, the pheasant!' One day Longman, the publisher, showed Barham a note he had just received from Sydney, which ran: 'Dear Longman, I can't accept your invitation, for my house is full of country cousins. I wish they were once removed.'

Sydney did not always get his own way. When an early

service was badly attended, he suggested doing away with it, but met with strong opposition and did not press the suggestion. He posted Barham an order for £20, 'a sum which, with your care and discretion, will soon raise the library at St. Paul's to a level with that of Alexandria in ancient times; I don't mean its level after combustion, but before.'

On October the 28th, 1844, Queen Victoria visited the City in state to open the Royal Exchange. It was Sydney's duty to arrange with the different City companies the seats they were to occupy on the scaffolding erected in the Cathedral yard. The clerk of one of the companies behaved in a very officious manner, loftily objected to the disposition of seats, and finally said: 'Perhaps, Mr. Smith, all these details had better be left to us. We will form a little committee of our own and spare you all further trouble in the arrangement. Too many cooks, you know, spoil the broth.'

'Very true, sir,' replied Sydney; 'but let me set you right in one particular. Here there is but one cook – myself. You are only scullions, and will be good enough to take your directions from me.'

CHAPTER XI

MR. SYDNEY SMITH COMING UPSTAIRS

THERE are certain social conditions in which every man appears at his best. Dr. Johnson was thoroughly at home in a club; Carlyle flowered at his fireside; Gibbon was happiest in his study; Keats preferred the company of a single friend; Shakespeare, we may be sure, loved the freedom of a tavern; Borrow joyed in the society of gypsies; Scott was at the top of his form when playing the host at Abbotsford; Shelley revelled in country solitude and was probably seen at his best by wild animals; and so on. Sydney Smith's kingdom, where he reigned without a rival for more than forty years, was the social world of London; his throne was at the dinner-table; his subjects were of all classes, all ages, and all sexes (of which he said there were three – men, women and clergymen).

It would be impossible to overrate his love of London. He loved its noise, its bustle, its streets, its parks, its mansions, its shops, its squares, its people, its body and soul. What had been made by the hand of man was to him infinitely more wonderful and desirable than Nature. His conception of Paradise was 'the parallelogram' at the height of the season, which he pictured lovingly – an immense square full of trees flowering with flambeaux, with gas for grass, every window illuminated by countless chandeliers, and voices reiterating for ever and for ever *Mr. Sydney Smith coming upstairs*.

When the news spread that he was on the stairs a group would quickly form to greet him and from the time of his arrival to the time of his departure he would not be left alone for an instant. A limitless supply of wit and humour was expected from him and the consciousness of this would sometimes annoy him, but he had a pleasure-loving and pleasure-giving temperament and it was impossible to damp his cheerfulness in a crowd. Towards the end of his life his social popularity was enormous; his presence in any house was an event; and such was his reputation as a wit that people laughed at his most trivial and idiotic sayings.

No doubt he was often oppressed by the weight of his comical obligations and came on the stage like a great actor, forced to exert himself when not in the mood to play his part, but so responsive was he to atmosphere, so full of animal spirits and ludicrous ideas, that he quickly managed to soar without effort. Part of the entertainment must have lain in his own delight in the game. His laugh was frequent and infectious. He laughed when a comic idea came into his mind; he laughed as he put it into words; he joined in the laughter with which it was received. His eyes glistened with merriment, his great belly shook, while his lungs gave forth volley after volley. Someone described his laughter as 'loud but soft', meaning presumably that it had a pleasant ring. It must at least have been a distinctive attribute, since all his friends noticed it, though usually in convulsions themselves. His corpulence, his quick-glancing hazel eyes, his clumsiness of movement and gesture, his massive Roman nose, his large pouting lips, his full cheeks, the comical twitch of his mouth – all these, added to his own contagious enjoyment of the fun he was providing, helped to make his conversation irresistible.

Though he never monopolised the talk, somehow or other it took its hue and tone from him; and though he willingly followed the lead of others, no subject was introduced that he did not irradiate and transform with his own charm. He was a master of every branch of conversational art. His versatility was astonishing. Farce, light comedy, repartee, humour, buffoonery, mimetic drollery; one would follow the other with matchless ease; and then, in an instant, he would become grave and fence with a Macaulay or a Mackintosh on ethics or metaphysics. But no mood was allowed to hold the table for long; variety was everything; all tastes were catered for. In this respect he was unlike any of the great talkers of the past. Some people were irritated with the assertiveness of Dr. Johnson, others were overwhelmed by the discursiveness of Coleridge, a few were depressed by the monologues of Carlyle, a number were bored by the long-windedness of Macaulay, many were annoyed by the affectation of Oscar Wilde; but the only complaint ever made against Sydney Smith was that he was too amusing. This was his crowning gift: he could make people laugh until they cried, until they forgot themselves and their surroundings and surrendered utterly to the music of mirth. Prostration followed his progress through 'the parallelogram'.

With one accord the memoirists of the period state emphatically that no printed report of his conversation could give the least idea of the effect he produced in society. It was not only what he said but how he said it; the electric contact of his fun, his inimitable voice, his comical mannerisms, the expression of his face, the sheer physical vitality, the bubbling spirits, the happiness of the man. He was Falstaff incarnate. He was a great creative artist in speech, entirely spontaneous; he talked because he could not help it, because his spirits were excited and his mind was full.

Subjects grew in his conversation. He would begin with a chance observation on some topic of the moment; this in an instant suggested a ludicrous image, which begat another and another, each following the last with such rapidity that there was scarcely time to laugh. Gradually a conception of such staggering absurdity was formed in the minds of his listeners that they were shaken by paroxysms of helpless, hysterical merriment, and the full imaginative picture, capped by some master-stroke of comedy, left them gasping for breath. The train of ridiculous images and farcical anecdotes thus produced was varied at innumerable points by witty comments and humorous asides and punctuated by the unsophisticated laugh of the speaker, who revelled in the performance every bit as much as the audience.

Lord John Russell, who was intimate with Sydney for many years, emphasised the futility of attempting to repeat or reproduce these amazing exhibitions and merely recorded the effect of one of them: 'Having seen in the newspapers that Sir Aeneas Mackintosh was come to town, he drew such a ludicrous caricature of Sir Aeneas and Lady Dido, for the amusement of their namesake, that Sir James Mackintosh rolled on the floor in fits of laughter, and Sydney Smith, striding across him, exclaimed "*Ruat Justitia!*" This is not very satisfactory, but Lord John gave us a hint of greater value. According to him, two footnotes in *Peter Plymley's Letters* closely resembled the pictures their author raised up in social conversation. It seems that Canning had described the detection of public abuses as fanaticism –

> 'a term,' wrote Sydney, in the first of these footnotes, 'invented by him and adopted by that simious parasite who is always grinning at his heels. Nature descends down to infinite smallness. Mr. Canning has his parasites; and if you take a large buzzing blue-bottle fly, and look at it in a microscope, you may see 20 or 30 little ugly insects crawling about it, which doubtless think their fly to be the bluest, grandest, merriest, most important animal in the universe, and are convinced the world would be at an end if it ceased to buzz.'

The second footnote reads:

> 'In the third year of his present Majesty, and in the 30th of his own age, Mr. Isaac Hawkins Brown, then upon his travels, danced one evening at the Court of Naples. His dress was a volcano silk with lava buttons. Whether (as the Neapolitan wits said) he had studied dancing under St. Vitus, or whether David, dancing in a linen vest, was his model, is not known; but Mr. Brown danced with such inconceivable alacrity and vigour, that he threw the Queen of Naples into convulsions of laughter, which terminated in a miscarriage, and changed the dynasty of the Neapolitan throne.'

Luckily there are fragments of Sydney's recorded talk that give us a better picture of him than either of those footnotes.

Still, we are grateful to Lord John Russell for his evidence and grateful for his description of Sydney's wit, which he likened to that kind of firework which blazes and bursts in every direction, exploding at one moment, shining brightly at another, eccentric in its course, and changing its shape and colour to many forms and many hues; unlike the wit of Sheridan and Talleyrand, which was like a rocket, shooting suddenly into the sky and astonishing because of the previous silence and gloom.

The following flashes of his conversation are amusing enough without the aid of the speaker's personality.

Quakers were being discussed. Sydney joined in:

'Though I am not generally considered an illiberal man, yet I must confess to one little weakness, one secret wish – I should like to roast a Quaker.'

'Good heavens, Mr. Smith!' exclaimed a serious gentleman sitting nearby; 'roast a Quaker?'

'Yes, sir,' replied Sydney, with the utmost gravity; 'roast a Quaker.'

'But do you not consider the terrible torture?'

'Yes, sir, I have considered everything. It may be wrong, as you say; the Quaker would undoubtedly suffer acutely; but everyone has his tastes, and mine would be to roast a Quaker. *One* would satisfy me, only one. I hope you will pardon my weakness, but it is one of those peculiarities I have striven against in vain.'

The gentleman looked so serious that Sydney was at length forced to abandon his roasted Quaker in order to retain the other's good opinion.

Someone mentioned that a young Scot was about to marry an Irish widow, twice his age and more than twice his size.

'Going to marry her!' cried Sydney; 'going to marry her! Impossible! You mean a part of her; he could not marry her all himself. It would be a case, not of bigamy, but trigamy; the neighbourhood or the magistrates should interfere. There is enough of her to furnish wives for a whole parish. One man marry her! – it is monstrous! You might people a colony with her; or give an assembly with her; or perhaps take your morning's walk round her, always provided there were frequent resting-places, and you were in rude health. I once was rash enough to try walking round her before breakfast, but only got half-way and gave it up exhausted. Or you might read the Riot Act and disperse her; in short, you might do anything with her but marry her.'

Once he enumerated and acted the different methods of shaking hands that were in use:

'There is the *high-official* – the body erect, and a rapid, short shake near the chin. There is the *mortmain* – the flat hand introduced into yours and hardly conscious of its contiguity. The *digital* – one finger held out, much used by the higher clergy, and by Brougham, who puts forth his forefinger and says with his strong northern accent "How arrre you?" There is the *shakus rusticus*, where your hand is seized in an iron grasp, betokening rude health, warm heart, and distance from the Metropolis; but producing a strong sense of relief on your part when you find your hand released and your fingers unbroken. The next to this is the *retentive shake* – one which, beginning with vigour, pauses as it were to take breath, but without relinquishing its prey, and before you are aware begins again, till you feel anxious as to the result, and have no shake left in you.'

When General Cleveland was publicly reproved by the Duke of Wellington, Sydney remarked:

'He can't live, you know; his wife and children will be always in tears, his pointers will bite him, the pew-opener won't give him a seat, the butcher won't trust him, his horse will always kick him off, prussic acid will be too good for him.'

Sydney was seriously concerned when Fanny Kemble

broke the news that, during her recent visit to the U.S.A., she had married an American. He said:

'Now do, my dear child, be persuaded to give up this extraordinary delusion; let it, I beg, be recorded of us both that this pleasing and intelligent young lady laboured under the singular and distressingly insane idea that she had contracted a marriage with an American; from which painful hallucination she was eventually delivered by the friendly exhortations of a learned and pious divine, the Rev. Sydney Smith.'

'Oh, but the baby!' objected Fanny.

The look of mock horror, amazement and resignation with which Sydney received this intelligence threw the whole company into convulsions.

A statesman to whom he was attached was accused of nepotism. 'The Smith of Smiths' defended him thus:

'Such a disposition of patronage is one of the highest inducements to a man of high rank and large fortune to abandon the comforts of private life for the turmoils and disappointments of a political career. Nor does the country suffer by it; on the contrary, a man is much more likely to be able to judge of the competence of his relatives for office than of anyone else. Indeed, I feel so strongly on this point that if by any conceivable freak of fortune I were placed in such a position, I should think myself not only authorised but compelled to give a post to every man of my own name in the country.'

On June 6, 1831, Macaulay went to a large party in order to meet Ramohun Roy, a Brahmin distinguished for his learning and knowledge, who had made a stir by becoming a Unitarian and was paraded about London society for a season and displayed as a curiosity. Ramohun Roy was not present, but Sydney Smith and Rogers were, and Macaulay observed that Sydney was easily the favourite, being incomparably the more amusing. Macaulay advised Sydney to stay in town for the opening of Parliament. 'My flock!' exclaimed the pastor: 'My dear sir, remember my flock! "The hungry sheep look up and are not fed."' He then begged Macaulay to come and see him at Combe Florey: 'There I am, sir, the priest of the Flowery Valley, in a delightful parsonage, about which I care a good deal, and a delightful country, about which I do not care a straw.' Macaulay said that meeting him was some compensation for missing Ramohun Roy. At which Sydney burst forth:

'Compensation! Do you mean to insult me? A beneficed clergyman, an orthodox clergyman, a nobleman's chaplain, to be no more than compensation for a Brahmin; and a heretic Brahmin, too; a fellow who has lost his own religion and can't find another; a vile heterodox dog, who, as I am credibly informed, eats beefsteaks in private! A man who has lost his caste! who ought to have melted lead poured down his nostrils if the good old Vedas were in force as they ought to be.'

No one appreciated Sydney's company more than Thomas Moore, who, though a good diarist, was unfortunately a bad Boswell, either because the great wit's best flights incapacitated him, or because he lacked the power of selection. At any rate he was only able to enter Sydney's lesser flights in his diary, probably because he could not remember what had made him ill with laughing. After all, laughter beyond a certain point is a mental emetic; and the memory, like the stomach, retains the pleasant things, not the things that make one sick. But let us now read what Thomas Moore remembered.

On May 30, 1826, Agar Ellis gave a dinner to several Lords and Ladies, an Archbishop and so on. Moore sat next to Sydney Smith, who in the course of conversation attacked certain demonstrations of aristocracy from Lord Harewood concerning the Parliamentary candidature of one Marshall, a manufacturer. Driving away with Sydney in a hackney coach, Moore remarked how well and good-humouredly Agar Ellis had mixed them all up together. Sydney agreed: 'That's the great use of a good conversational cook, who says to his company "I'll make a good pudding of you; it's no matter what you came into the bowl, you must come out a pudding," "Dear me," says one of the ingredients, "wasn't I just now an egg?" But he feels the batter sticking to him.'

Two years later Moore was at Lady Davy's and met Sydney Smith, who talked of the Irish Protestant Church, pronounced it a nuisance, and said: 'I have always compared it to setting up butchers' shops in Hindostan, where they don't eat meat. "We don't want this," they say. "Aye, aye, true enough, but you must *support our shop*." '

In June, 1831, Moore again dined at Agar Ellis's in company with several peers of the realm and Sydney Smith. Overhearing a conversation between Moore and Miss Berry on the French poet Lamartine, Sydney said he was magnanimous enough to admit that he had never heard of the gentleman and asked: 'Is it another name for the famous blacking man?' Moore said it was. 'Oh, then he's Martin here, La Martine in France, and Martin Luther in Germany,' explained Sydney. He never minded what nonsense he talked, which was one of the reasons why he said so much that was comical. Fanny Kemble recalled a similar piece of absurdity. Seeing him steal on tip-toe from a room where music was being played, she beckoned to him. 'My dear, it's all right,' he whispered; 'you keep with the dilettanti, I go with the talkettanti.'

At a breakfast with Rogers in June, 1831, Sydney was 'beyond anything amusing', but Moore's editor (Lord John Russell) seemed to think he was also unprintable and treated the reader to three asterisks instead. Macaulay's biographer was also writing for a Victorian public and suppressed a scene which promised a rich Rabelaisian repast.

Jan: 6, 1833. Moore and Sydney were staying with Lord Lansdowne at Bowood. Talking of the bread that was about to be made from sawdust, Sydney said that people would soon have sprigs coming out of them. Young ladies, in dressing for a ball, would say 'Mamma, I'm beginning to sprout.'

Nov: 14, 1833. Sydney called on Moore to take him to dinner with the Longman's at Hampstead. Two of the guests were to be Spence and Kirby, the noted entomologists, and Sydney said he had suggested a suitable menu to Mrs. Longman – 'to wit, flea *pâtés*, earthworms on toast, caterpillars crawling in cream and removing themselves, etc, etc.' The road up to Longman's being rather awkward, they told the coachman to wait for them at the bottom. 'It would never do,' said Sydney, 'when your memoirs came to be written, to have it said: "He went out to dine at the house of the respectable publishers, Longman & Co., and, being overturned on his way back, was crushed to death by a large clergyman".'

Sept: 16, 1834. Staying at Bowood. Sydney at breakfast made Moore cry with laughing and caused him to leave the table. His diary that evening explained why: 'In talking of the intelligence and concert which birds have among each other, cranes and crows, etc, showing that they must have some means of communicating their thoughts, Sydney said: "I dare say they make the same remark of it. That old fat crow there (meaning himself) what a prodigious noise he is making! I have no doubt he has some power of communicating, etc, etc." After pursuing this idea comically for some time, he added, "But we have the advantage of them; they can't put us into pies as we do them; legs sticking up out of the crust, etc, etc." The acting of all this makes two thirds of the fun of it; the quickness, the buoyancy, the self-enjoying laugh.'

It is a pity that when Moore was reduced to hysterics, he was also reduced to 'etceteras'.

Two days later Moore ventured the opinion that women felt pain less than men, having less physical sensibility; to prove which he suggested that a hot tea-pot should be brought in, and he was certain the women present would be able to hold it for a much longer time than the men. This started Sydney off on the subject of Moore's cruelty to the weaker sex and the fearsome experiments he had carried out: 'He has been all his life trying the sex with hot tea-pots; the burning ploughshare was nothing to it. I think I hear his terrific tone in a *tête-à-tête*– "Bring a tea-pot".'

April 3, 1836. Dinner with Miss Rogers. 'Sydney highly amusing in the evening. His description of the *dining* process, by which people in London extract all they can from new literary lions, was irresistibly comic. "Here's a new man of genius arrived; put on the stew-pan; fry away; we'll soon get it all out of him." On this and one or two other topics, he set off in a style that kept us all in roars of laughter.'

Such, then, were Moore's entries in his diary. We hear of Sydney being 'most rampantly facetious', 'in full plume and play', 'in full force', and so on, but we are left to content ourselves with a record of other people's convulsions. We learn that Lord Lansdowne did not bore his guests with politics, but provided laughter and good cheer, Sydney Smith administering to the former, the Bowood cook to the latter. Moore, like most poets, paid no attention to the hands of the clock, while Sydney could not cure himself of punctuality. 'Remember, I'm a *prose*-writer, so be ready when I come,' wrote Sydney; and 'I have a breakfast of philosophers to-morrow at ten *punctually*. Muffins and metaphysics, crumpets and contradiction. Will you come?' In March, 1842, they met at Lady Holland's, when Sydney told Moore that his list of dinners was full both at home and abroad for ten days ahead. A day or two later Moore received an invitation to dinner from Sydney and replied that he would willingly have fasted for the chance of dining with him but that, having heard from his own lips there was no chance, he had accepted another invitation. Sydney answered: 'I must explain why my invitation to you came so late. Before I knew you were in town my party was completed; but Lord Carlisle is ill, and I hastened to supply his place from the aristocracy of nature.'

Sydney's high spirits were certainly of no common order, and though they often found expression in mere foolishness – as when Lord Holland sat on and squashed a nosegay of flowers and he exclaimed: 'Oh, dear! Oh, dear! What a pity! Hot-bed! Hot-bed!' – they produced more witty sayings than have been recorded of anyone else. The only thing that ever lowered his spirits was the one thing that usually elevated the spirits of other men – alcohol. Even the large dinners he used to eat failed to make him less cheerful, though he was wise enough to fall asleep with the rest of the party when the action of the gastric juices called for peace and quiet. It is many years now since the nodding and lolling and snoring and snorting of a company of gentlemen at the dinner-table was considered the appropriate conclusion to a hearty meal.

It goes without saying that Sydney had his 'off' days, when the effort to be cheerful cost him more than it was worth. Such periods enabled him to feel sympathy with men who made a profession of amusing people without a natural gift for the business.

> 'No pecuniary embarrassments equal to the embarrassments of a professed wit,' he wrote to his friend Mrs. Meynell: 'an eternal demand upon him for pleasantry, and a consciousness on his part of a limited income of the facetious; the disappointment of his creditors – the importunity of duns – the tricks, forgeries and false coin he is forced to pay instead of gold. Pity a wit, and remember with affection your stupid friend.'

One wonders whether he was thinking here of Theodore Hook, who was invited to meet him at Hayward's chambers in the Temple. Suddenly Lockhart arrived with the information that Hook was priming himself, as usual, at the Athenæum Club with a tumbler or two of hot punch. 'Oh!' exclaimed Sydney, 'if it comes to that, let us start fair. When Mr. Hook is announced, announce Mr. Smith's punch.' Hook arrived and it was soon apparent that he had not drunk enough to be witty; the prospect of meeting a parson had kept him partially sober. Sydney had to do all the talking;

and though they liked one another, the canon came to the conclusion that the wag was a very ordinary sort of person.

However unequal he might feel to the demands made upon him, Sydney was quite incapable of boring people. When he had nothing amusing or novel to say, he said nothing. He had suffered terribly from conversational bores and expressed his feelings freely on the subject in his review of Lister's novel *Granby*. Discussing one of the characters he relieved himself as follows:

> 'Lord Chesterton we have often met with; and suffered a good deal from his Lordship: a heavy, pompous, meddling peer, occupying a great share of the conversation – saying things in ten words which required only two, and evidently convinced that he is making a great impression; a large man, with a large head, and very landed manner; knowing enough to torment his fellow creatures, not to instruct them – the ridicule of young ladies, and the natural butt and target of wit. It is easy to talk of carnivorous animals and beasts of prey; but does such a man, who lays waste a whole party of civilised beings by prosing, reflect upon the joys he spoils, and the misery he creates, in the course of his life? and that anyone who listens to him through politeness, would prefer toothache or earache to his conversation? Does he consider the extreme uneasiness which ensues, when the company have discovered a man to be an extremely absurd person, at the same time that it is absolutely impossible to convey, by words or manner, the most distant suspicion of the discovery? And then, who punishes this bore? What sessions and what assizes for him? What bill is found against him? Who indicts him? When the judges have gone their vernal and autumnal rounds – the sheep-stealer disappears – the swindler gets ready for the Bay – the solid parts of the murderer are preserved in anatomical collections. But, after twenty years of crime, the bore is discovered in the same house, in the same attitude, eating the same soup – unpunished, untried, undissected – no scaffold, no skeleton – no mob of gentlemen and ladies to gape over his last dying speech and confession.'

Sydney coined many phrases that have gone into the language. His facetiæ are to be found scattered throughout the memoirs, diaries, letters and reminiscences of the first half of the nineteenth century. They must be given fresh currency here. If, now and then, the gold seems to have worn a little thin, it is because other wits have made use of it and sometimes debased it. But first let us see how he dealt with other people's coinage.

Exchanging reminiscences with Creevey one day, he described his visit to Sheridan's villa in the country. There was a splendid gathering. No expense had been spared; a magnificent dinner, excellent wines; but not a single candle was to be had to light one's way to bed and the guests had to undress in the dark. Apparently Sheridan thought that in the circumstances candles would only have confused their blindness. In the morning, though the table groaned with delicacies, not so much as a pat of butter was to be seen at breakfast, their host explaining that it was not a butter county. Creevey then described one of his visits. After dinner, when the ladies had left them together, Sheridan drew his chair to the fire and, speaking very confidentially, said that he and his wife had just had a fortune left them. 'Mrs. Sheridan and I,' said he, 'have made a solemn vow to each other to mention it to no one, and nothing induces me now to confide it to you but the absolute conviction that Mrs. Sheridan is at this moment confiding it to Mrs. Creevey upstairs.'

The famous painter of animals, Landseer, asked Scott's biographer, Lockhart, in a patronising manner, whether he would like to sit for his portrait. Lockhart replied: 'Is thy servant a dog that he should do this thing?' Sydney was delighted when he heard this, and, meeting Landseer some days later, said, 'I think I shall take it.' He did take it, repeated it everywhere, and it became known as one of his wittiest sayings.

He also heard a good story about Wordsworth, who, when praised effusively to his face by a disciple from Scotland, said he was the most intelligent and well-informed Scot he had ever met. Sydney inquired whether this story had been told to anyone else, found that it had not, and paid five shillings for the exclusive right of telling it for one week. We may be sure that he made a good thing of it. He was, however, quite capable of inventing good stories of his own, as the following will show.

During his Edinburgh days, the reigning bore was Leslie, the Scottish philosopher, whose favourite subject was the North Pole. Sooner or later, whatever the topic, the North Pole crept into the conversation. No one could escape him or it; Sydney had serious thoughts of inventing a 'slip-button' for such occasions; Jeffrey simply fled when he came in sight. One day Leslie called on the editor of the *Edinburgh Review* and found him just about to set out for a ride. They had not been talking for more than a minute when the North Pole was introduced by Leslie. 'Oh, damn the North Pole!' shouted Jeffrey in a rage, spurring his horse and galloping off. Shortly afterwards Leslie met Sydney and seriously complained of Jeffrey's behaviour. 'Oh, my dear fellow, never mind,' said Sydney consolingly, 'no one cares what Jeffrey says; he is a privileged person; he respects nothing, absolutely nothing. Why, you will scarcely credit it, but, strictly between ourselves, it is not more than a week ago that I heard him speak disrespectfully of the Equator!'

Stories about Sydney and sayings by him are legion. We must select the best.

Someone asked him whether a certain bishop was going to get married. 'Perhaps he may,' was the answer; 'yet how can a bishop marry? How can he flirt? The most he can say is, "I will see you in the vestry after service." '

A turtle had been sent to the house of a friend and the guests gathered round to look at it. Suddenly a child stooped down to stroke the shell of the turtle. 'Why are you doing that?' asked Sydney. 'To please the turtle,' answered the child. 'Why, you might as well stroke the dome of St. Paul's to please the Dean and Chapter,' said Sydney.

An entomologist was boring the company at dinner with his knowledge. From beetles he eventually arrived at flies and remarked in the course of his lecture that the eye of a fly was larger in proportion to its body than that of any other creature. At this point Sydney struck in and flatly denied it. The entomologist was annoyed and asked him what he knew about it. Sydney replied that the common judgment and knowledge of mankind were enshrined in the poetry and nursery rhymes of antiquity. 'What on earth has that to do with it?' demanded the naturalist. ' "I, said the fly, with my *little* eye, I saw him die",' quoted Sydney.

At dinner with the Lyndhursts he defended, for the sake of argument, the Indian custom of suttee. 'But if Lord Lyndhurst were to die, you would be sorry that Lady Lyndhurst should burn herself?' was the sudden and awkward question of one of the guests. 'Lady Lyndhurst,' came the reply, 'would, no doubt, as an affectionate wife, consider it her duty to burn herself, but it would be our duty to put her out; and, as the wife of the Lord Chancellor, Lady Lyndhurst should not be put out like an ordinary widow. It should be a state affair. First, a procession of the judges, then of the lawyers . . .' he paused. 'And the clergy?' insinuated someone. 'All gone to congratulate the new Lord Chancellor,' replied Sydney.

'I have just been with Brougham, and upon my word he treated me as if I was a fool!' complained a baronet one day. 'Never mind, my dear fellow,' said Sydney sympathetically; 'never mind, he thought you knew it.'

To one who expressed a very strong opinion and justified it on the ground that he was a plain man, Sydney retorted, 'I am not aware that your personal appearance has anything to do with the question.'

Hearing his friend, Mrs. Austin, explaining that she was no relation to Jane Austen, he told her that she was quite wrong, adding: 'I always let it be inferred that I am the son of Adam Smith.'

He asked two R.A.'s to advise him as to what paintings he should purchase for his house in Green Street. They went into the matter at some length. Suddenly he interrupted them: 'Oh, I ought to have told you, though, that my outside price for a picture is thirty-five shillings.'

Brougham had a large *B* surmounted by a coronet on the outside of his curious one-horse carriage. 'There goes a carriage,' said Sydney, 'with a *B* outside and a wasp within.'

He was very much concerned about the persecution of the slave abolitionists in America, but Harriet Martineau assured him that it was all for the best as the persecution would try the abolitionists out and test their nerve. 'Now I am surprised at you, I own,' said Sydney; 'I am surprised at your taste for yourself and your friends. I can fancy your enjoying a feather in your cap, but I cannot imagine you could like a bushel of them down your back with the tar.'

Walking down an alley close to St. Paul's Cathedral he heard two women abusing each other from opposite windows and remarked: 'They will never agree, for they argue from different premises.'

Henry Hallam, the historian, was a man who argued for argument's sake. He contradicted everyone and questioned everything. He had a very high opinion of himself and his literary powers, but would not allow other people to have any opinions whatever. 'I think I may assert without fear of contradiction – ' began Lord Melbourne. 'Are you acquainted, sir, with Mr. Hallam?' interrupted Sydney Smith.

Melbourne, by the way, had an irritating manner of damning this and damning that and damning the other; his speech was peppered with 'damns'. Sydney checked him once with: 'Let us assume everybody and everything damned, and come to the subject.'

'He'll let nobody talk but himself,' complained a friend of Macaulay's. 'Who would if he could help it?' retorted Sydney.

'You must take a walk on an empty stomach,' was the advice of his doctor when he was ill. 'Whose?' he inquired.

A lady called on him and spoke of the oppressive heat of the previous week. 'Heat, ma'am,' said he; 'it was so dreadful here that I found there was nothing left for it but to take off my flesh and sit in my bones.' The lady thought this a most uncanonical proceeding and quickly ordered her carriage.

A pretty girl was admiring the flowers in his garden. 'Oh,

Mr. Sydney! this pea will never come to perfection,' she said. 'Permit me, then, to lead perfection to the pea,' he replied, taking her hand.

Managers of theatres used to send him tickets for free admission to their plays. Returning the compliment he sent them tickets for free admission to St. Paul's Cathedral.

Speaking of Jeffrey. 'He has not body enough to cover his mind decently with; his intellect is improperly exposed.'

Of Palmerston: 'His manner when speaking is like a man washing his hands; the Scotch members don't know what he is doing.'

Of a friend: 'He has spent all his life in letting down empty buckets into empty wells; and he is frittering away his age in trying to draw them up again.'

Of another: 'He has no command over his understanding; it is always getting between his legs and tripping him up.'

Of a man who grew excited in argument: 'He is like a barometer; the more you press him, the higher he rises.'

Of someone else: 'In his conversation there are the furrows of long thought.'

Of Charles Lamb: 'He draws so much beer that no wonder he buffoons people – he must have a butt to put it in.'

Of the French: 'A nation grown free in a single day is a child born with the limbs and the vigour of a man, who would take a drawn sword for his rattle, and set the house in a blaze that he might chuckle over the splendour.'

Of political and sociological writers: 'Every man rushes to the press with his small morsel of imbecility, and is not easy till he sees his impertinence stitched in blue covers.'

On cliques that thrive on mutual admiration: 'Surely scholars and gentlemen can drink tea with each other, and eat bread and butter, without all this laudatory cackling.'

To his neighbour at a dinner-party: 'Now I know not a soul here present except you and our host; so if I by chance insult or dishonour any of their brothers, sisters, aunts, uncles or cousins, I take you to witness it is unintentional.'

To someone who had grown fatter: 'I didn't half see you when we met last year.'

To his brother 'Bobus': 'Brother, you and I are exceptions to the laws of nature. You have risen by your gravity, and I have sunk by my levity.'

To Mrs. Grote: 'You have filled me with alarm about money, and I have buried a large sum in the garden; heaven send I may not forget in what bed!'

To Rogers: 'I wish I could write like you. I would write an Inferno, and I would put Macaulay amongst a number of disputants and gag him.'

His definition of marriage: 'It resembles a pair of shears, so joined that they cannot be separated, often moving in opposite directions, yet always punishing anyone who comes between them.'

On the difficulty of convincing a prejudiced man: 'You might as well attempt to poultice the humps off a camel's back.'

'Whewell's forte is science,' said someone. 'Yes, and his foible is omni-science,' added Sydney.

A lady entered dressed in a crimson velvet gown. He started up, exclaiming, 'Exactly the colour of my preaching cushion!' Leading her forward to the light, he pretended to be lost in admiration, saying, 'I really can hardly keep my hands off you; I shall be preaching on you, I fear,' etc.

A few random sayings:

'She has not very clear ideas about tides. I remember her insisting that it was always high tide at London Bridge at 12 o'clock. She referred to me: "Now, Mr. Smith, is it not so?" I answered, "It used not to be so, I believe, formerly, but perhaps the Lord Mayor and Aldermen have altered it lately." '

'The advice I sent to the Bishop of New Zealand, when he had to receive the cannibal chiefs there, was to say to them, "I deeply regret, sirs, to have nothing on my own table suited to your tastes, but you will find plenty of cold curate and roasted clergyman on the sideboard"; and if, in spite of this prudent provision, his visitors should end their repast by eating him likewise, why I could only add, "I sincerely hoped he would disagree with them." '

'Yes, you find people ready enough to do the Samaritan without the oil and twopence.'

'If I ever go to a Fancy-dress Ball, I should go as a Dissenter.'

'My living in Yorkshire was so far out of the way that it was actually twelve miles from a lemon.'

'Don't talk to me of not being able to cough a speaker down: try the hooping-cough.'

'Daniel Webster struck me much like a steam-engine in trousers.'

'In this world the salary or reward is always in the inverse ratio of the duties performed.'

'I once dissuaded a youth from entering the army on which he was bent at the risk of breaking his mother's heart, by asking him how he would prevent his sword from getting between his legs. It quite staggered him; he never solved the difficulty and took to peace instead of war.'

'I don't like dogs; I always expect them to go mad. A lady asked me once for a motto for her dog Spot. I proposed "Out, damned Spot!" but strange to say she did not think it sentimental enough.'

'Death must be distinguished from dying, with which it is often confused.'

'I am not fond of expecting catastrophes, but there are cracks in the world.'

'As regards the prolongation of human life, the invention of gigs has more than counterbalanced the discovery of vaccination.'

'No war for me short of Piccadilly; there . . . I will combat to the death for Fortnum and Mason's, and fall in defence of the sauces of my country.'

'Many in this world run after felicity like an absent man hunting for his hat, while all the time it is on his head or in his hand.'

'It seems quite useless to kill the Chinese. It is like killing flies in July; a practice which tires the cruellest schoolboy.'

'The only way to deal with such a man as O'Connell is to hang him up and erect a statue to him under the gallows.'

'An English mob, which, to the foreigner, might convey the belief of an impending massacre, is often contented by the demolition of a few windows.'

'What two ideas are more inseparable than Beer and Britannia?'

'I never wrote anything very dull in my life.'

CHAPTER XII

DROWSY SLUMBERS

WRITING to John Allen in November, 1830, Sydney Smith referred to 'the drowsy slumbers of my useless old age'. He had fifteen more years to live when he wrote that sentence, during which he contrived to play an important part in the passage of the Reform Bill, to write a smashing and largely successful attack on the Ecclesiastical Commission, to arouse the hostility of the entire Whig party and the hatred of pretty well every bishop in the Church of England, to infuriate the radicals with his views on the Ballot, to incense the commercial world with his remarks on railways, to irritate every pompous person in the country with his unfailing humour, and to enrage the American nation with his criticisms of their debt repudiation. Few people can have slumbered drowsily to such effect.

Sydney was one of those rare mortals who perceive that the truth in anything is the mean between extremes, and that human beings are more important than their beliefs. 'I never heard a story well proved on one side without being equally well proved on the other,' he wrote in early life. That he was a poet would have occurred to few of his contemporaries; and as he neither wrote in verse nor concerned himself with the mystery of the universe, the present age would not rank him with the Shelleys and Wordsworths – for which he would have been devoutly thankful. But he was a poet in the widest meaning of the word; his sense of wonderment, his joy in the glorious pageant of life, were expressed in the poetry of humour, and he looked at life with the eyes of a Shakespeare.

The sensitive and expressive portion of the human race may be divided into three classes – poets, prophets and pessimists – of which we have had three perfect examples in our own literature – Shakespeare, Shelley and Swift. The poets love life for its own sake, the prophets believe that it can be turned into something better, the pessimists regard the whole business of creation as a failure. Sydney, though he spent a good part of his life fighting for social betterment, belonged with his whole soul to the first class. He was not what is commonly called a religious man; he realised that no belief could take the place of life or explain it, that the general effect of religion was to restrict man's outlook and mar his happiness, and that whenever it showed too much concern with another world it was disqualified from enriching man's nature and harmonising his sojourn in this world. He was not a party man; he knew that political parties were founded to promote self-interest, that people were Whigs or Tories or royalists or democrats because it paid them to be so, that very few men acted from disinterested motives, and that there was no panacea for happiness in all the enthusiasms of the reformers and all the programmes of the politicians.

> 'When a nation has become free,' he once wrote, 'it is extremely difficult to persuade them that their freedom is only to be preserved by perpetual and minute jealousy. They do not observe that there is a constant, perhaps an unconscious, effort on the part of their governors to diminish, and so ultimately to destroy, that freedom.'

He believed in freedom; it was probably the only thing he did entirely believe in; but he knew in his bones (what we are only now beginning to find out) that no political party could be trusted with a people's liberties.

Thus we find him attacking Catholics, Dissenters, Whigs, Tories, the Evangelicals and Puseyites of his own Church – every section of the community, in fact, which held an extreme view of anything – and then defending all of them against their opponents. He took no side except that of reason and common sense, which meant that he took no side. One of the most famous passages which he wrote for the *Edinburgh Review* was headed 'Noodle's Oration'. It was amusing enough at the time, and quoted with approbation by all his Victorian admirers, but it was neither so witty nor so amusing as his contemporaries thought. It satirised the mental see-saw of the average politician of every age, who can always be depended upon to say nothing at great length. The interesting point about it is that each party quoted it with delight against the other, which proved that the satire was wasted on both. We need not revive it here, because there are a dozen writers to-day who can expose modern political Noodledom as wittily, because at least a hundred passages already quoted are wittier and more characteristic of Sydney, and because the drowsy slumbers of his useless old age produced far more friction, much better wit, and a more complete portrait of the poet who saw life steadily and enjoyed it all the more for the humorous clarity of his vision.

The Ecclesiastical Commission was established in 1836 by Act of Parliament as a permanent institution for the management of Church business. Sydney Smith objected to its constitution and its recommendations, and wrote three Letters to Archdeacon Singleton (Canon of Worcester and Archdeacon of Northumberland), attacking it with such vigour that many of the recommendations were dropped, and displaying so little regard for the dignity of his superiors that they never forgave him. There was a curious innocence about Sydney, unlooked-for in a man of his uncommon sense. After hitting out right and left at the bishops in their public capacity, he was surprised that they should carry the dispute into private life; and when the battle was over he said that the only quarrel he had with the Archbishop of Canterbury and the Bishop of London was that 'they neither of them ever ask me to dinner'.

The first Letter was published in 1837. He went to the heart of the matter at once. The Commission was crammed with bishops, and all interests not episcopal had been overlooked. He favoured church reform but 'would not have operated so largely on an old and (I fear) a decaying building'. The bishops had suggested forming a Central Fund from the proceeds of confiscated Prebends and enriching the poorer livings with it. Sydney pointed out that the whole income of the Church, equally divided, would only give each clergyman the wages of a nobleman's butler. To remove the general feeling of hatred against the Church, the exorbitant incomes of the wealthier prelates (Canterbury, Durham and London) should be lessened and the idle canons should be made to do parochial work. It was absurd to reduce the incomes of the lesser dignitaries. Men entered the Church because these positions were worth competing for.

> 'Who would go into the Church and spend £1200 or £1500 upon his education, if such were the highest remuneration he could ever look to? At present, men are tempted into the Church by the prizes of the Church, and bring into that Church a great deal of capital, which enables them to live in decency, supporting themselves, not with the money of the public, but with their own money, which, but for this temptation, would have been carried into some retail trade.'

Since the clergy could not be paid equitably, they must be paid by lottery.

> 'This, it will be said, is a Mammonish view of the subject: it is so, but those who make this objection forget the immense effect which Mammon produces upon religion itself.'

He reminded his readers that they were living

> 'not in the age of the apostles, not in the abstract, timeless, nameless, placeless land of the philosophers, but in the

year 1837, in the porter-brewing, cotton-spinning, tallow-melting kingdom of Great Britain, bursting with opulence, and flying from poverty as the greatest of human evils. . . . I must take this people with all their follies, and prejudices, and circumstances, and carve out an establishment best suited for them, however unfit for early Christianity in barren and conquered Judea.'

The alternative would be a set of badly-paid, uneducated fanatics:

'You will have a set of ranting, raving Pastors, who will wage war against all the innocent pleasures of life, vie with each other in extravagance of zeal, and plague your heart out with their nonsense and absurdity: cribbage must be played in caverns, and sixpenny whist take refuge in the howling wilderness. In this way low men, doomed to hopeless poverty, and galled by contempt, will endeavour to force themselves into station and significance.'

Another recommendation by this episcopal Commission was that the livings in the gift of Deans and Chapters should be taken away and conferred upon the bishops. Sydney saw red. Why were the Deans and Chapters singled out for such treatment? Why did not the bishops attempt to take over as well the livings in the hands of the laity? Because the Deans and Chapters were at their mercy, the laity were not. Many people, especially ancient ladies, imagined that the bishops could do no wrong; but 'they have their malice, hatred, uncharitableness, persecution, and interest like other men'. Too often they treated the poorer clergy as Dives did Lazarus, and 'the very essence of tyranny is to act as if the finer feelings, like the finer dishes, were delicacies only for the rich and great, and that little people have no taste for them and no right to them'. A good and honest bishop ought to suspect himself and carefully watch his own heart:

'He is all of a sudden elevated from being a tutor, dining

at an early hour with his pupil (and occasionally, it is believed, on cold meat), to be a spiritual Lord; he is dressed in a magnificent dress, decorated with a title, flattered by chaplains, and surrounded by little people looking up for the things which he has to give away; and this often happens to a man who has had no opportunities of seeing the world, whose parents were in very humble life, and who has given up all his thoughts to the Frogs of Aristophanes and the Targum of Onkelos. How is it possible that such a man should not lose his head? that he should not swell? that he should not be guilty of a thousand follies, and worry and tease to death (before he recovers his commonsense) a hundred men as good, and as wise, and as able as himself?'

Some of the bishops had allowed the Prebends in their own gift to be appropriated to the Fund and it was said that they had made a great sacrifice. True, remarked Sydney, but they had taken more out of the pockets of the Deans and Chapters than they had disbursed from their own.

'Where then is the sacrifice? They must either give back the patronage or the martyrdom: if they choose to be martyrs – which I hope they will – let them give us back our patronage: if they prefer the patronage, they must not talk of being martyrs – they cannot effect this double sensuality and combine the sweet flavour of rapine with the aromatic odour of sanctity.'

The clergy had been warned that if they quarrelled amongst themselves they would all be swept away together by the democrats.

'Be it so; I am quite ready to be swept away when the time comes. Every body has their favourite death: some delight in apoplexy, and others prefer marasmus. I would infinitely rather be crushed by democrats, than, under the plea of the public good, be mildly and blandly absorbed by bishops.'

At this point Sydney introduced one of his favourite parables:

'I met the other day, in an old Dutch Chronicle, with a passage so apposite to this subject, that, though it is somewhat too light for the occasion, I cannot abstain from quoting it. There was a great meeting of all the Clergy at Dordrecht, and the Chronicler thus describes it, which I give in the language of the translation : – "And there was great store of Bishops in the town, in their robes goodly to behold, and all the great men of the State were there, and folks poured in in boats on the Meuse, the Merve, the Rhine, and the Linge, coming from the Isle of Beverlandt and Isselmond, and from all quarters in the Bailiwick of Dort; Arminians and Gomarists, with the friends of John Barneveldt and of Hugh Grote. And before my Lords the Bishops, Simon of Gloucester, who was a Bishop in those parts, disputed with Vorstius and Leoline the Monk, and many texts of Scripture were bandied to and fro; and when this was done, and many propositions made, and it waxed towards twelve of the clock, my Lords the Bishops prepared to set them down to a fair repast, in which was great store of good things – and among the rest a roasted peacock, having in lieu of a tail the arms and banners of the Archbishop, which was a goodly sight to all who favoured the Church – and then the Archbishop would say a grace, as was seemly to do, he being a very holy man; but ere he had finished, a great mob of townspeople and folks from the country, who were gathered under the window, cried out *Bread! bread!* for there was a great famine, and wheat had risen to three times the ordinary price of the *sleich:* and when they had done crying *Bread! bread!* they called out *No Bishops!* – and began to cast up stones at the windows. Whereat my Lords the Bishops were in a great fright, and cast their dinner out of the window to appease the mob, and so the men of that town were well pleased, and did devour the meats with a great appetite; and then you might have seen my Lords standing with empty plates, and looking wistfully at each other, till Simon of Gloucester, he who disputed with Leoline the Monk, stood up among them and said, *Good my Lords, is it your pleasure to stand here fasting, and that those who count lower in the Church than you do should feast and fluster? Let us order to us the dinner of the Deans and Canons, which is making ready for them in the chamber below.* And this speech of Simon of Gloucester pleased the Bishops much; and so they sent for the host, one William of Ypres, and told him it was for the public good, and he, much fearing the Bishops, brought them the dinner of the Deans and Canons; and so the Deans and Canons went away without dinner, and were pelted by the men of the town, because they had not put any meat out of the window like the Bishops; and when the Count came to hear of it, he said it was a pleasant conceit, *and that the Bishops were right cunning men, and had ding'd the Canons well.*" '

Needless to say, the old Dutch Chronicle existed solely in the fancy of the Rev. Canon Sydney Smith, though he made it appear authentic by a footnote explaining that the *sleich* was 'a measure in the Bailiwick of Dort, containing two gallons one pint English dry measure'.

It was unfortunate that the Commission should have consisted almost entirely of bishops, who were utterly out of touch with the feelings and difficulties of the lower clergy.

'Bishops live in high places with high people, or with little people who depend upon them. They walk delicately, like Agag. They hear only one sort of conversation, and avoid bold reckless men as a lady veils herself from rough breezes. . . . What bishops like best in their clergy is a dropping-down-deadness of manner. . . . It would be just as rational to give to a frog or a rabbit, upon which the physician is about to experiment, an appeal to the Zoological Society, as to give to a country curate an appeal to the Archbishop against his purple oppressor.'

The extraordinary partiality for bishops shown by the Commission was 'like those errors in tradesmen's bills of which the retail arithmetician is really unconscious, but which somehow or another always happen to be in his own favour'.

Sydney was well aware that he would be accused of self-interest as the member of a Chapter: 'Be it so. I have been laughed at a hundred times in my life, and care little or nothing about it. If I am well provided for now, I have had my full share of the blanks in the lottery as well as the prizes.' He was on good terms with both the Archbishops: 'I was at school and college with the Archbishop of Canterbury: fifty-three years ago he knocked me down with the chessboard for checkmating him – and now he is attempting to take away my patronage.' As for his friends the Whigs, he did not wish to offend them or anybody else:

> 'I consider myself to be as good a Whig as any amongst them. I was a Whig before many of them were born – and while some of them were Tories and Waverers. I have always turned out to fight their battles, and when I saw no other clergyman turn out but myself – and this in times before liberality was well recompensed, and therefore in fashion, and when the smallest appearance of it seemed to condemn a Churchman to the grossest obloquy and the most hopeless poverty.'

His second Letter was published in 1838. He returned to the subject of prizes in the Church: 'To get a stall, and to be preceded by men with silver rods, is the bait which the ambitious squire is perpetually holding out to his second son.' The prospect of the mitre kept up the courage of curates and attracted the sons of butchers, bakers and publicans:

> 'Young Crumpet is sent to school – takes to his books –

spends the best years of his life, as all eminent Englishmen do, in making Latin verses – knows that the *crum* in crumpet is long, and the *pet* short – goes to the University – gets a prize for an Essay on the Dispersion of the Jews – takes orders – becomes a Bishop's chaplain – has a young nobleman for his pupil – publishes a useless classic, and a serious call to the unconverted – and then goes through the Elysian transitions of Prebendary, Dean, Prelate, and the long train of purple, profit, and power.'

Lord Melbourne had declared that he was quite satisfied with the Church, but that if the public wished to alter it they could do as they pleased. Sydney did not believe in this assumed indifference:

'Our Viscount is somewhat of an impostor. . . . Anyone would suppose from his manner that he was playing at chuck-farthing with human happiness . . . that he would giggle away the Great Charter. . . . Instead of being the ignorant man he pretends to be, before he meets the deputation of Tallow-Chandlers in the morning, he sits up half the night talking with Thomas Young about melting and skimming, and then, though he has acquired knowledge enough to work off a whole vat of prime Leicester tallow, he pretends next morning not to know the difference between a dip and a mould. . . . I am sorry to hurt any man's feelings and to brush away the magnificent fabric of levity and gaiety he has reared; but I accuse our Minister of honesty and diligence: I deny that he is careless or rash; he is nothing more than a man of good understanding and good principle, disguised in the eternal and somewhat wearisome affectation of a political Roué.'

Since his last Letter a Committee of Cathedrals had been formed. But it had over-stated the case for Chapters and adopted such a high tone concerning the rights of property that Sydney was seriously alarmed: 'In the time of Lord

George Gordon's riots, the Guards said they did not care for the mob, if the Gentlemen Volunteers behind would be so good as not to hold their muskets in such a dangerous manner.'

On his appointment the Archbishop of Canterbury had taken an oath to preserve the rights and property of the Church of Canterbury. Yet he was now violating that oath.

> 'A friend of mine has suggested to me that his Grace has perhaps forgotten the oath; but this cannot be, for the first Protestant in Europe of course makes a memorandum in his note-book of all the oaths he takes to do, or to abstain. The oath, however, may be less present to the Archbishop's memory, from the fact of his not having taken the oath in person, but by the medium of a gentleman sent down by the coach to take it for him – a practice which, though I believe it to have been long established in the Church, surprised me, I confess, not a little. A proxy to vote, if you please – a proxy to consent to arrangements of estates if wanted; but a proxy sent down in the Canterbury Fly, to take the Creator to witness that the Archbishop, detained in town by business, or pleasure, will never violate that foundation of piety over which he presides – all this seems to me an act of the most extraordinary indolence ever recorded in history. . . . The attorney who took the oath for the Archbishop is, they say, seized with religious horrors at the approaching confiscation of Canterbury property, and has in vain tendered back his 6/8 for taking the oath. The Archbishop refuses to accept it; and feeling himself light and disencumbered, wisely keeps the saddle upon the back of the writhing and agonised scrivener. I have talked it over with several clergymen, and the general opinion is that the scrivener will suffer.'

He warned the Whigs that they were playing with fire. Once allow the Church to be plundered and mankind would learn from its leaders how to rob on a large scale.

'I am astonished that these Ministers neglect the common precaution of a foolometer, with which no public man should be unprovided: I mean the acquaintance and society of three or four regular British fools as a test of public opinion. Every Cabinet Minister should judge of all his measures by his foolometer, as a navigator crowds or shortens sail by the barometer in his cabin.'

Lord John Russell believed that the recommendations of the Commission were fair, that Church property was not being confiscated but only remodelled and re-divided. Sydney corrected this view of the matter:

'I accuse him not of plunder, but I accuse him of taking the Church of England, rolling it about as a cook does a piece of dough with a rolling-pin, cutting a hundred different shapes with all the plastic fertility of a confectioner, and without the most distant suspicion that he can ever be wrong, or ever be mistaken; with a certainty that he can anticipate the consequences of every possible change in human affairs. There is not a better man in England than Lord John Russell; but his worst failure is that he is utterly ignorant of all moral fear; there is nothing he would not undertake. I believe he would perform the operation for the stone – build St. Peter's – or assume (with or without ten minutes notice) the command of the Channel Fleet; and no one would discover by his manner that the patient had died – the Church tumbled down – and the Channel Fleet been knocked to atoms. I believe his motives are always pure, and his measures often able; but they are endless, and never done with that pedetentous pace and pedetentous mind in which it behoves the wise and virtuous improver to walk. He alarms the wise Liberals; and it is impossible to sleep soundly while he has the command of the watch. . . . Another peculiarity of the Russells is that they never alter their opinions: they are an excellent race, but they must be trepanned before they can be convinced.'

Lord John Russell had written to Sydney after the appearance of the first Letter saying that the arguments in it had not convinced him. Sydney had replied:

> 'You say you are not convinced by my pamphlet. I am afraid that I am a very arrogant person; but I do assure you that, in the fondest moments of self-conceit, the idea of convincing a Russell that he was wrong never came across my mind. Euclid would have had a bad chance with you if you had happened to have formed an opinion that the interior angles of a triangle were not equal to two right angles. The more poor Euclid demonstrated, the more you would not have been convinced.'

The reference to Russell in the second Letter did not therefore take the Whig leader by surprise, but it annoyed him. The passage was quoted against him by the Tories and gained considerable currency. The Whigs were extremely angry at Sydney's outspoken comments on two such prominent members of their party as Melbourne and Russell, and even the easy-going Luttrell was provoked to ask Thomas Moore: 'Could you have conceived any man taking such pains to upset a brilliant position in society as Sydney has been taking lately?'

The third Letter to Archdeacon Singleton appeared in 1839. In the meantime he had been answered by several bishops in the episcopal Billingsgate of that period. The Bishop of London had retorted that, while the parochial clergy were spiritual instructors of the people, the cathedral clergy were only so in a very restricted sense. Referring to the duties of the canons, Sydney agreed with the Bishop on one point: 'A number of little children, it is true, do not repeat the catechism of which they do not comprehend a word.' But he claimed that the cathedral clergy were on the whole more laborious than the parochial clergy, and that, contrary to what might be supposed from the Bishop's remarks, the cathedrals really did teach the Gospel, not chemistry, mechanics, Latin verses and dancing. He again reminded the holy spoliators that justice and economy ought to begin at home with slices off their own incomes; again he emphasised the fact that the Church attracted the better type of man because it held out good jobs for the ambitious:

> 'I am very sorry to come forward with so homely an argument, which shocks so many clergymen, and particularly those with the largest incomes, and the best bishoprics; but the truth is, the greater number of clergymen go into the Church in order that they may derive a comfortable income *from* the Church. Such men intend to do their duty, and they do it; but the duty is, however, not the motive, but the adjunct. If I were writing in gala and parade, I would not hold this language; but we are in earnest, and on business; and as very rash and hasty changes are founded upon contrary suppositions of the pure disinterestedness and perfect inattention to temporals in the clergy, we must get down at once to the solid rock, without heeding how we disturb the turf and the flowers above.'

He referred to 'the gambling propensities of human nature', and answered someone who had called his views materialistic: 'Be it so; I cannot help it; I paint mankind as I find them, and am not answerable for their defects. When an argument taken from real life, and the actual condition of the world, is brought among the shadowy discussions of Ecclesiastics, it always occasions terror and dismay; it is like Aeneas stepping into Charon's boat, which carried only ghosts and spirits.'

Once more he hammered away at the absurdity of equalising the incomes of the parochial clergy. There was not enough money in the whole Church to give a decent living to all its priests. Far better that there should be fat jobs for the ambitious and an incentive to wealthy parents to send capital into the Church along with their younger children.

He warned the Bishop of London that if he gave way to the reformers, it would only mean the beginning of trouble: 'Does he forget that Deans and Chapters are but mock turtle – that more delicious delicacies remain behind?'

And lastly he dealt with the Bishop of Gloucester, who, stung to fury by Sydney's treatment of the Commission, had said that he did not owe his position at St. Paul's to his piety and learning but to his eminence as a scoffer and jester.

> 'Is not this rather strong for a Bishop, and does it not appear to you, Mr. Archdeacon, as rather too close an imitation of that language which is used in the apostolic occupation of trafficking in fish? Whether I have been appointed for my piety or not, must depend upon what this poor man means by piety. He means by that word, of course, a defence of all the tyrannical and oppressive abuses of the Church which have been swept away within the last fifteen or twenty years of my life; the Corporation and Test Acts; the Penal Laws against the Catholics; the Compulsory Marriages of Dissenters, and all those disabling and disqualifying laws which were the disgrace of our Church, and which he has always looked up to as the consummation of human wisdom. If piety consisted in the defence of these – if it was impious to struggle for their abrogation, I have indeed led an ungodly life. There is nothing pompous gentlemen are so much afraid of as a little humour. It is like the objection of certain cephalic animalculæ to the use of small-tooth combs – "Finger and thumb, precipitate powder, or anything else you please, but, for heaven's sake, no small-tooth combs!"'

To read the Bishop a lesson in good manners, Sydney had prepared a reply that would have made every other bishop in the country think twice before bringing any further charges against the incorrigible canon; but his pen was stopped by an appeal the Bishop had made for the prayers of his flock 'to the Father of all mercies, that he will restore to me the better use of the visual organs, to be employed on his service; or that he will inwardly illumine the intellectual vision, with a particle of that Divine ray, which his Holy Spirit can alone impart.'

On which Sydney made this comment:

'It might have been in better taste, perhaps, if a mitred invalid, in describing his bodily infirmities before a church full of clergymen, whose prayers he asked, had been a little more sparing in the abuse of his enemies; but a good deal must be forgiven to the sick. I wish that every Christian was as well aware as this poor Bishop of what he needed from Divine assistance; and in the supplication for the restoration of his sight and the improvement of his understanding, I most fervently and cordially join.'

As a result of these three Letters the Residence and Plurality Bill was considerably modified in Parliament and Sydney was able to tell Lord Lansdowne that a dozen very material points bearing upon the happiness of the parochial clergy, to which he had objected, had been omitted or changed.

Having successfully routed the bishops and ruffled the Whigs, Sydney turned his attention to the radicals. George Grote, the historian, banker and politician, had been urging Parliament to consider the question of the Ballot year after year. Open voting had become an open scandal. At every election there were revelations of bribery and intimidation, and it was felt by the radicals (both the philosophical and the extremist variety) that to vote by ballot would for ever put an end to political corruption. Sydney doubted this and wrote his last pamphlet on the subject.

Broadly speaking, his attitude was that the majority of mankind did not care for whom they voted, so they might just as well vote for the party favoured by their landlords as against them. A great deal of nonsense was talked about the intimidation of the aristocracy. But what about the intimidation of mobs?

> 'Did not the mob of Bristol occasion more ruin, wretchedness, death, and alarm than all the ejection of tenants, and combinations against shopkeepers, from the beginning of the century? and did not the Scotch philosophers tear off the clothes of the Tories in Mintoshire? or at least such clothes as the customs of the country admit of being worn? – and did not they, without any reflection at all upon the customs of the country, wash the Tory voters in the river?'

The real tyranny of the ballot was that it compelled people who hated all concealment to conceal their votes, people who gloried in the cause they supported. The ballot was the friend of cowards.

> 'The present method may produce a vicious act, but the ballot establishes a vicious habit . . . for it must always be remembered and often repeated and said and sung to Mr. Grote that it is to the degraded liar only that the box will be useful.'

Why should honest men fear to advertise their honest opinions?

> 'It is really a curious condition that all men must imitate the defects of a few, in order that it may not be known who have the natural imperfection, and who put it on from conformity. In this way in former days, to hide the grey hairs of the old, everybody was forced to wear powder and pomatum. . . . How beautiful is the progress of man! – printing has abolished ignorance – gas put an end to darkness – steam has conquered time and distance – it remained for Grote and his box to remove the encumbrance of truth from human transactions. May we not

look now for more little machines to abolish the other cardinal virtues?'

He called it the mendacity machine and asserted that it was not necessary that a people should be false in order to be free.

Some politicians, while hating the ballot, had declared that, if bribery and intimidation continued, they would have to vote for it. But then the ballot was no remedy for these evils, and Sydney explained how corruption would continue in spite of it. In addition it would produce greater evils than those it was supposed to cure, and he noted a reasonable analogy:

> 'If (says the physician) fevers increase in this alarming manner, I shall be compelled to make use of some medicine which will be of no use to fevers, and will at the same time bring on diseases of a much more serious nature. I shall be under the absolute necessity of putting out your eyes, because I cannot prevent you from being lame.'

The introduction of the ballot would lead to universal suffrage, which would cure every ill, 'as a teaspoonful of prussic acid is a certain cure for the most formidable diseases'. Government by the many meant the ruin of everything. Majorities were always wrong; or at least they were 'right about as often as juries are right in differing from judges, and that is very seldom'.

Such was his view, and though it has been laughed at for nearly a century, some people are beginning to wonder whether the laugh was entirely on the popular side. The first person to laugh heartily at his pamphlet was Lord Grey, upon which Sydney gravely remarked: 'When I come out with my universal suffrage, I hope to put him in convulsions.'

The arrival of the railway in the West of England in 1842 was hailed by Sydney with delight. He could now get to London in six hours, instead of travelling by coach and spending two nights on the road, and he described it as 'a very serious increase of comfort'. But the monopoly granted to the

Great Western Railway Company was attended by serious disadvantages, and three letters which he wrote to the *Morning Chronicle* in 1842 caused certain boards of directors in the city to meet with unpleasant regularity.

It appears that a few drunken people, as well as certain others of an experimental turn of mind, had taken it into their heads to step out of the trains when in motion and had provided employment for coroners and juries, who had held the railway companies responsible for the actions of these erratic passengers. As a result the Great Western Railway Company had ordered that the doors of all carriages should be kept locked between stations. Recently a terrible railway accident had occurred in France, when a large number of people had been burnt to death because a similar order in that country had resulted in the imprisonment of the passengers in the carriages. Sydney drew attention to the disaster of the Paris train and said that the lives of two hundred sane and sober persons were endangered merely because a few idiots were inebriated or inquisitive. He emphasised the effect of this imprisonment on the imagination and wanted to know why the railway authorities were content with locking doors. 'Why are not strait-waistcoats used? Why is not the accidental traveller strapped down? Why do contusion and fracture still remain physically possible?' In short, 'fools there will be on roads of iron and on roads of gravel, and they must suffer for their folly; but why are Socrates, Solon, and Solomon to be locked up?'

He had talked to several of the directors, but they had pooh-poohed his fears and seemed to think that 'the imagination should be sent by some other conveyance, and that only loads of unimpassioned, unintellectual flesh and blood should be darted along on the Western rail'. Individually, no doubt, the directors were excellent men, 'but the moment men meet in public boards, they cease to be collectively excellent. The fund of morality becomes less as the individual contributors increase in number.' Another reason the directors gave for locking the doors was the 'strong propensity in mankind to travel on railroads without paying', but this did not seem to him a sufficient reason for roasting or crushing or terrifying the mass of more honourable travellers. The railway was too good a thing to be left in the hands of people who adopted such a view, and he mentioned some of its benefits to mankind:

'Railroad travelling is a delightful improvement of human life. Man is become a bird; he can fly longer and quicker than a Solan goose. The mamma rushes sixty miles in two hours to the aching finger of her conjugating and declining grammar boy. The early Scotchman scratches himself in the morning mists of the North, and has his porridge in Piccadilly before the setting sun. The Puseyite priest, after a rush of 100 miles, appears with his little volume of nonsense at the breakfast of his bookseller. Everything is near, everything is immediate – time, distance, and delay are abolished. But, though charming and fascinating as all this is, we must not shut our eyes to the price we shall pay for it. . . . We have been, up to this point, very careless of our railway regulations. The first person of rank who is killed will put everything in order, and produce a code of the most careful rules. I hope it will not be one of the bench of bishops; but should it be so destined, let the burnt bishop – the unwilling Latimer – remember that, however painful gradual concoction by fire may be, his death will produce unspeakable benefit to the public. Even Sodor and Man will be better than nothing.'

The trouble was that the public knew little or nothing of what happened on the line:

'All the men with letters upon the collars of their coats are sworn to secrecy – nothing can be extracted from them; when anything happens they neither appear to see nor hear you. In case of conflagration, you would be to them as so many joints on the spit.'

At first the directors refused to do anything, but at last they gave in, and the doors were left unlocked. This was fortunate, as Sydney had another letter in store for them, in which, he said,

> 'I should have described them gazing with satisfaction on the burnt train of carriages and passengers: 1st carriage – A stewed Duke. 2nd – Two bishops done in their own gravy. 3rd – Three ladies of quality browned. 4th – Lawyers returning from sessions stewed in their own briefs à la Maintenon. 5th – First and second class. A grammar school returning home, legs out of window like a pigeon pie. 6th – A fat woman much overdone. 7th – Two Scotchmen dead but raw, sulphuric acid perceptible.'

Things got better and better. 'Every fresh accident on the railroads is an advantage,' he wrote to John Murray, 'and leads to an improvement. What we want is an overturn which would kill a bishop, or at least a dean. This mode of conveyance would then become perfect.'

Leaving the city gentlemen to their dividends and their turtle soup, he next engaged in controversy with the American nation. This was in 1843. He had written several articles about America for the *Edinburgh Review* and had warmly praised the country and its institutions. He liked the unpretentiousness of its law-courts:

> 'We shall be denounced by the Laureate as atheists and Jacobins,' he wrote in 1818, 'but we must say that we have doubts whether one atom of useful influence is added to men in important situations by any colour, quantity, or configuration of cloth and hair. The true progress of refinement, we conceive, is to discard all the mountebank drapery of barbarous ages.'

He liked the cheapness of American law and compared it,

greatly to its advantage, with the English Court of Chancery, about which he said:

'Nothing can be so utterly absurd as to leave the head of the Court of Chancery a political officer, and to subject forty millions of litigated property to all the delays and interruptions which are occasioned by his present multiplicity of offices. The Chancellor is Speaker of the House of Lords; he might as well be made Archbishop of Canterbury; it is one of the greatest of existing follies.'

He found much to admire in the simplicity of American social life and the economy of its government. In fact, he only had two serious complaints to make against the Americans: their spitting and their slave-trade. Of the former he wrote in 1824:

'We are terribly afraid that some Americans spit upon the floor, even when that floor is covered by good carpets. Now all claims to civilisation are suspended till this secretion is otherwise disposed of. No English gentleman has spit upon the floor since the Heptarchy.'

Slavery he viewed with abhorrence:

'We wish well to America – we rejoice in her prosperity – and are delighted to resist the absurd impertinence with which the character of her people is often treated in this country; but the existence of slavery in America is an atrocious crime, with which no measures can be kept – for which her situation affords no sort of apology – which makes liberty itself distrusted, and the boast of it disgusting.' (1818.)

And again:

'It is impossible to speak of it with too much indignation and contempt; but for it we should look forward with unqualified pleasure to such a land of freedom and such a magnificent spectacle of human happiness.' (1824.)

He prophesied in 1824 that the existence of slavery would (and should) one day 'entail a bloody servile war upon the Americans, which will separate America into slave states and states disclaiming slavery'.

Except for this, and the little expulsive habit already alluded to, he had no quarrel with America – until the State of Pennsylvania repudiated its debts in 1843. Several other states kept it company, but Sydney fastened on to Pennsylvania because it was the richest state in America and because he had personally invested in Pennsylvanian bonds. He was at this time a wealthy man, and the loss of a few hundred pounds meant very little to him, but the coolness of the repudiation irritated him, and his attack opened with a 'Humble Petition' to the House of Congress at Washington, in which he charged America with bad faith and spoke of it as

> 'a nation with whom no contract can be made, because none will be kept; unstable in the very foundations of social life, deficient in the elements of good faith, men who prefer any load of infamy, however great, to any pressure of taxation however light'.

He followed this up with two letters to the *Morning Chronicle*, which had printed his 'Humble Petition'. In these he did not spare the repudiators: 'Men who soar above others in what they say, and sink below all nations in what they do – who, after floating on the heaven of declamation, fall down to feed on the offal and garbage of the earth.' He came to the conclusion that 'there really should be lunatic asylums for nations as well as individuals', and confessed that he never met a Pennsylvanian at a London dinner

> 'without feeling a disposition to seize and divide him – to allot his beaver to one sufferer and his coat to another – to

appropriate his pocket-handkerchief to the orphan, and to comfort the widow with his silver watch, Broadway rings, and the London Guide, which he always carries in his pockets. How such a man can set himself down at an English table without feeling that he owes two or three pounds to every man in company, I am at a loss to conceive: he has no more right to eat with honest men than a leper has to eat with clean men'.

Doubtless the Americans thought themselves very smart, but

'if I had the misfortune to be born among such a people, the land of my fathers should not retain me a single moment after the act of repudiation. I would appeal from my fathers to my forefathers. I would fly to Newgate for greater purity of thought, and seek in the prisons of England for better rules of life'.

Since its fall from financial grace America had become 'the common sewer of Europe, and the native home of the needy villain'. He reminded them that 'it is not for Gin Sling and Sherry Cobbler alone that man is to live, but for those great principles against which no argument can be listened to', and he suggested a reason why the States were behaving so shamefully:

'This new and vain people can never forgive us for having preceded them 300 years in civilisation. They are prepared to enter into the most bloody wars in England, not on account of Oregon, or boundaries, or right of search, but because our clothes and carriages are better made, and because Bond Street beats Broadway. Wise Webster does all he can to convince the people that these are not lawful causes of war; but wars, and long wars, they will one day or another produce; and this, perhaps, is the only advantage of repudiation. The Americans cannot gratify their avarice and ambition at once; they cannot cheat and conquer at the same time. The warlike power of every country depends on their Three per Cents. If Cæsar were to reappear upon earth, Wettenhall's list would be more important than his Commentaries; Rothschild would open and shut the temple of Janus; Thomas Baring, or Bates, would probably command the Tenth Legion, and the soldiers would march to battle with loud cries of Scrip and Omnium, Consols, and Cæsar! Now the Americans have cut themselves off from all resources of credit. Having been as dishonest as they can be, they are prevented from being as foolish as they wish to be. In the whole habitable globe they cannot borrow a guinea, and they cannot draw the sword because they have not money to buy it.'

'I am astonished,' he cried, 'that the honest States of America do not draw a *cordon sanitaire* round their unpaying brethren – that the truly mercantile New Yorkers, and the thoroughly honest people of Massachusetts, do not in their European visits wear an uniform with "S.S., or Solvent States", worked in gold letters upon the coat, and receipts in full of all demands tamboured on their waistcoats, and "our own property" figured on their pantaloons.'

What would be the result of all this?

'Instead of entering with us into a noble competition in making calico (the great object for which the Anglo-Saxon race appears to have been created), they will waste their happiness and their money (if they can get any) in years of silly, bloody, foolish, and accursed war – to prove themselves our equals. John Bull was naturally disposed to love America, but he loves nobody who does not pay him. His imaginary paradise is some planet of punctual payment, where ready money prevails, and where debt and discount are unknown.'

'And now,' he concluded, 'having eased my soul of its indignation, and sold my stock at 40% discount, I sulkily retire from the subject, with a fixed intention of lending no more money to free and enlightened republics, but of employing my money henceforth in buying up Abyssinian bonds, and purchasing into the Turkish Fours, or the Tunis Three-and-a-half per Cent funds.'

With which words he bade farewell to controversy.

But the anger of the Americans knew no bounds. While the repentant ones sent him gifts of cheese and apples, he received quires of paper by every post accusing him of atheism, blasphemy, burglary, etc., etc. The newspapers throughout the States attacked him fiercely. They either called him the Rev. Shylock Smith, or spelt his christian name with an 'i'. For months he continued to receive newspapers and letters 'from the most remote corners of the United States, with every vituperative epithet which human rage has invented'. These he read aloud over breakfast to his family, who greatly enjoyed his humorous comments.

CHAPTER XIII

GROWING OLD MERRILY

UNTIL the last few months of his life, old age did not affect the high spirits of Sydney Smith. If anything, he became more buoyant and more jubilant with the years. Nothing but the country for long periods, or a humorous song, could depress him. He continued, of course, to be bored by fashionable forms of entertainment. Mrs. Meynell asked him to go with a party to the opera. He replied: 'Thy servant is three-score-and-ten years old; can he hear the sound of singing men and singing women? A Canon at the Opera! Where have you lived? In what habitations of the heathen? I thank you, shuddering; and am ever your unseducible friend.' He spoke his mind more fully on the subject to Lady Holland:

> 'I have not the heart, when an amiable lady says "Come to *Semiramis* in my box," to decline; but I get bolder at a distance. *Semiramis* would be to me pure misery. I love music very little – I hate acting; I have the worst opinion of Semiramis herself, and the whole thing (I cannot help it) seems so childish and so foolish that I cannot abide it. Moreover, it would be rather out of etiquette for a Canon of St. Paul's to go to an opera; and where etiquette prevents me from doing things disagreeable to myself, I am a perfect martinet.'

When Mrs. Grote tried to interest him in the theatre, he said:

> 'You cannot excite my envy by all the descriptions of your dramas and melodramas; you may as well paint the luxuries of barley-meal to a tiger, or turn a leopard into a field of clover. All this class of pleasures inspires me with the same nausea as I feel at the sight of rich plum-cake or sweetmeats; I prefer the driest bread of common life.'

He maintained his cheerfulness by constantly shifting his interests from one thing to another and by trying to make other people as cheerful as himself. Long faces were seldom seen at Combe Florey and silent people became talkative in his presence. Believing that nothing produced melancholy so easily as darkness, the room in which he sat every night was 'lighted up like a town after a great naval victory'. He had no relish for conventional talk and even delayed his visit to London after the Queen's marriage in 1840 to avoid 'hymeneal and bridesmaid conversation'.

In order to speed the hours while in the country he apportioned certain duties to each and was most methodical in his habits. Even his favourite daughter Saba had to admit that punctuality with him was rigid enough to be called a vice. The house was run by the clock. Prayers at nine, a carriage drive at ten, lunch at one, dinner at eight, prayers at ten. Then, summer and winter, he visited his horses to see that they were fed and comfortable. Following this a little music, and bed at eleven. He never sat at table after a meal was finished. When children were staying with him, he called them in to lunch or dinner with the speaking-trumpet through which he had bawled instructions to the labourers at Foston. People were seldom unpunctual more than once. In spite of the cherubic countenance, the untidy appearance, the white hair and the humorous mouth of the parson, there was something about the nose, the chin and the black eyebrows that gave point and pregnancy to the momentary frown which greeted late-comers.

Though he found it necessary to keep himself employed, he certainly did not believe in work for work's sake.

> 'There is in England,' he once declared, 'almost a love of difficulty and needless labour. We are so resolute and industrious in raising up impediments which ought to be overcome, that there is a sort of suspicion against the removal of these impediments, and a notion that the advantage is not fairly come by without the previous toil. If the English were in a paradise of spontaneous productions, they would continue to

dig and plough, though they were never a peach nor a pineapple the better for it.'

His natural indolence was at times overcome by ambition, but the older he grew the less did he desire promotion. Already we have seen, in his letter to Russell, that by 1837 he had lost all wish for a bishopric, and at an earlier date he had begged Lord Holland not to make any exertions on his behalf, as he would steadily refuse an offer. At the end of 1832 he wrote to Mrs. Meynell: 'I have come to the end of my career, and have nothing now to do but to grow old merrily and to die without pain.' The last chapter made it clear that he still had quite a lot to do. The present chapter will show that he managed to grow old merrily in spite of pain.

Unlike the large majority of elderly men, Sydney took a keen interest in the younger generation; his mind was perpetually fresh and open to new ideas. He noted two new and interesting figures in the political world and promptly made their acquaintance. One of them, W. E. Gladstone, he met at the house of Henry Hallam in 1833, found him interested in religion, and talked for some time about the clergy. He told Gladstone that the clergy had greatly improved since the last generation, adding, 'Whenever you see a man of *my* age, you may be sure he is a bad clergyman.' In 1844 he read a novel called *Coningsby* and wished to meet the author. A friend arranged a dinner, which included Luttrell, Charles Greville, Lady Morley and Lord Melbourne, and Sydney sat next to Benjamin Disraeli. The dinner was a great success, Disraeli was completely captivated by Sydney, and Disraeli's wife, Mary Anne, thought Mrs. Sydney a very agreeable person. Two foreign politicians were equally delighted with him. Daniel Webster, the American Secretary of State and one of the greatest orators in the history of that country, visited London in 1839 and forgot his perorations when Sydney began to speak. François Guizot, the historian, came to London as French Ambassador in 1840 and marvelled at Sydney's inexhaustible gaiety and optimism, which contrasted strangely with Jeffrey's despondency and disillusionment.

Sydney used to describe himself when in London as 'submerged in a Caspian Sea of soup'. But he found time to encourage young people who were trying to make a living or earn a reputation. In his view the influence of the English aristocracy on literature was oppressive, and though he had hardened himself early and spoken his mind freely before every dunderheaded duke and brainless baron of his time, he felt that it was the duty of writers to support one another in a country where pugilism was glorified and poetry ignored. So we find him advertising all the new books that caught his fancy, mentioning them in letters to friends and talking about them wherever he went. Kinglake's *Eöthen*, Marryat's *Settlers in Canada* and Ruskin's *Modern Painters* were among the books he praised highly on their appearance; in fact, Ruskin declared that he was the first in the literary circles of London to assert the value of *Modern Painters*, speaking of it as a work of transcendent talent which would work a complete revolution in the world of taste.

Unknown musical people were equally sure of his help. Writing from Combe Florey in the summer of 1844, he told Lady Grey:

> 'There is an excellent musical family living in London; and finding them all ill, and singing flat, I brought them down here for three weeks, where they have grown extremely corpulent, and have returned to London with no other wish than to be transported after this life to this paradise of Combe Florey. Their singing is certainly very remarkable, and the little boy, at the age of seven, composes hymns; I mean sets them to music. I have always said that if I were to begin life again I would dedicate it to music; it is the only cheap and unpunished rapture upon earth.'

Sydney wrote to Sir Robert Peel on behalf of a male member of this family and the Prime Minister instantly promised to give the lad a place in some Government office, asking in return 'the privilege of renewing the honour' of Sydney's acquaintance.

He was rather 'curious' about Carlyle, but the Chelsea prophet did not frequent 'the parallelogram' and they never met. Carlyle, however, saw him one day at a distance, shaking his great belly and guffawing in the midst of his admirers, and envied his high spirits and good digestion.

His literary tastes were catholic enough. He liked Shakespeare and Milton, but on the whole poetry made little appeal to him and he definitely drew the line at Wordsworth. He objected to Jeffrey's attacks on Wordsworth, not because they were unfair but because they were unnecessary – the poet did not deserve them and was not worthy of them. Once he publicly confessed his inability to appreciate Wordsworth's poetry. 'There are some things which must be spiritually discerned,' said a lady. Upon which he called her 'a sensible woman', and she considered that he had taken his revenge. In view of the fact that he thought Horace Walpole's correspondence 'the best wit ever published in the shape of letters', it is a little surprising that he should have been one of the first Englishmen to hail the genius of Balzac. He anticipated the verdict of posterity in thinking the poetry of Samuel Rogers overpraised, and his view of Byron had to wait a century before it found an echo in ours. Incidentally, it is noteworthy that the only two people who said anything really unpleasant about Sydney were Byron and George IV. At a distance of four generations we may claim the 'smug Sydney' of the first and the 'profligate parson' of the second to be among the highest compliments ever paid him.

Instances of his thoughtfulness and generosity to younger authors and journalists were countless. We must be content with one. In 1832 a Scottish publisher named William Chambers had issued the first number of *Chambers's Edinburgh Journal*, the pioneer of the cheap popular periodical. In 1844 he was staying in Greek Street, Soho. One day about noon a carriage drove up to the door; not a vehicle of the light, modern sort, but an old family coach, drawn by a pair of sleek horses. From it there descended an aged gentleman, who, from his shovel hat and black gaiters, was clearly an ecclesiastical dignitary. Chambers heard his own name and the name of the visitor mentioned at the door, and then the sound of heavy deliberate footsteps on the antique balustraded stairs. He hastened to receive the celebrated clergyman, who shook hands and said: 'I heard at Rogers's you were in town, and was resolved to call. Let us sit down and have a talk.' They sat by the fire. 'You are surprised possibly at my visit?' the canon went on. 'There is nothing at all strange about it. The originator of the *Edinburgh Review* has come to see the originator of the *Edinburgh Journal*.' Chambers was delighted beyond measure with the good-natured and unceremonious observations of his visitor, who had a lot to say about his collaborators on the *Review*. He spoke with most affection of Horner and referred to Brougham's untrustworthiness, vanity and eccentricity. Next day Chambers breakfasted with Sydney, and the day after they breakfasted with Rogers – 'assuredly the most pleasant conversational treat I ever experienced,' wrote Chambers forty years later in the story of his 'Life'.

To the modern reader, unconcerned with the politics of the past, one of the most interesting facts in Sydney's biography is that he started life as the friend of Scott, who loved him in spite of his Whiggish principles, and ended it as the friend of Dickens, who loved him in spite of his Toryish opinions. We know what he thought of Scott as a novelist; he was an admirer from the start and instantly recognised the exceptional merit of *Waverley*. But he was not quite so quick to recognise the genius of Dickens, whose *nom-de-plume* put him off. By September, 1837, however, he was writing to a friend: 'Read Boz's *Sketches*, if you have not already read them. I think them written with great power, and that the soul of Hogarth has migrated into the body of Mr. Dickens. I had long heard of them, but was deterred by the vulgarity of the name.' A year later he told Sir George Philips: 'Nickleby is very good. I stood out against Mr. Dickens as long as I could, but he has conquered me.'

Meanwhile, Dickens had written to the publisher, Longman,

that of all the men he had ever heard of and never seen, he had the greatest curiosity to see and the greatest interest to know Sydney Smith. By a curious coincidence Dickens was then living in Doughty Street, almost exactly opposite Sydney's first London home. A meeting was arranged, and in June, 1839, Sydney wrote to him:

> 'My dear Sir. Nobody more, and more justly, talked of than yourself. The Miss Berrys, now at Richmond, live only to become acquainted with you, and have commissioned me to request you to dine with them Friday, the 29th, or Monday, July 1st, to meet a Canon of St. Paul's, the Rector of Combe Florey, and the Vicar of Halberton – all equally well known to you; to say nothing of other and better people. The Miss Berrys and Lady Charlotte Lindsay have not the smallest objection to be put into a Number, but, on the contrary, would be proud of the distinction; and Lady Charlotte, in particular, you may marry to Newman Noggs. Pray come; it is as much as my place is worth to send them a refusal.'

The Miss Berrys referred to in this letter were extremely popular in the London society of those days. Horace Walpole, when an old man, had fallen in love with them, and while still in their thirties they had inherited a small fortune from him. Though very attractive they had managed to avoid matrimony and when they were both past seventy their house in Curzon Street was a famous social centre. Sydney had known them in his early London days and on his annual visits to the capital from Foston had seen a good deal of them. They heard him preach in the Palace Chapel of Kensington on several occasions, and in 1810 he helped Mary Berry, who was one year older than her sister Agnes, to prepare the Letters of Madame du Deffand for the press. He criticised her Preface pretty freely; she gratefully adopted all his suggestions and her tranquil reception of his cuttings and slashings earned his praise. In course of time he became their 'most cherished guest'. There was a heartiness and an absence of cant in their drawing-room conversation that appealed strongly to him. The blight of Victorianism had not yet infected the freedom of speech in their circle, and he felt thoroughly at home with them. In 1837 the Elder Berry (as he called her) was seriously ill and Sydney said that if she died he would have to commit suicide: 'To precipitate myself from the pulpit of Paul was the peculiar mode of destruction on which I had resolved,' he told her when the crisis was over. The sisters stayed with him at Combe Florey for five days in August, 1838, and the familiar footing of their intercourse may be gauged from a letter he wrote on April 6, 1841:

> 'Dear Berries, I dine on Saturday with the good Widow Holland, and blush to say that I have no disposable date before the 26th; by which time you will, I presume, be plucking gooseberries in the suburban regions of Richmond. But think not, O Berries! that that distance, or any other, of latitude or longitude, shall prevent me from following you, plucking you, and eating you. Whatever pleasure men find in the raspberry, in the strawberry, in the coffee-berry, all these pleasures are to my taste concentrated in the May-Fair Berries. Ever theirs.'

After that dinner with the Berrys the friendship between Sydney and Dickens became stronger with every meeting. Sydney was the most humorous and inspiring personality Dickens ever met, and one can only explain his absence from the novelist's gallery of portraits by assuming either that his character was too rich and varied for the creator of 'Harold Skimpole' or that Dickens had a greater veneration for Sydney than he had for his own mother and father. There is probably some truth in both assumptions.

By 1842 they were meeting frequently, and a letter of Sydney's in the spring of that year paints the colour of their relationship:

> 'My dear Dickens, I accept your obliging invitation conditionally. If I am invited by any man of greater genius than yourself, or one by whose works I have been more completely interested, I will repudiate you and dine with the more splendid phenomenon of the two. Ever yours sincerely.'

Fanny Kemble, who never enjoyed anything so much as

Sydney's dinners, met Dickens at one of them in the spring of 1843, when there must have been some talk of *Martin Chuzzlewit*, for on January 6th, after the appearance of the first number, Sydney had written to the author:

> 'You have been so used to these sort of impertinences that I believe you will excuse me for saying how very much I am pleased with the first number of your new work. Pecksniff and his daughters and Pinch are admirable – quite first-rate painting, such as no one but yourself can execute. I did not like your genealogy of the Chuzzlewits, and I must wait a little to see how Martin turns out; I am impatient for the next number. Pray come and see me next summer; and believe me ever yours. P.S. Chuffey is admirable. I never read a finer piece of writing; it is deeply pathetic and affecting. Your last number is excellent. Don't give yourself the trouble to answer my impertinent eulogies, only excuse them.'

Then came the famous American chapters, and on July 1st Sydney wrote:

> 'Excellent! nothing can be better! You must settle it with the Americans as you can, but I have nothing to do with that. I have only to certify that the number is full of wit, humour, and power of description. I am slowly recovering from an attack of gout in the knees, and am very sorry to have missed you.'

Sydney's praise meant more to Dickens than anything else (except perhaps the sales) and he told Forster:

> 'I have a great notion to work out with Sydney's favourite (Chuffey), and long to be at him again.'

On December the 2nd, 1843, the Rev. R. H. Barham dined with Dickens in Devonshire Terrace, found Sydney there, and earned our thanks by recording one of his stories. The American publisher Colburn (in those days, by the way, publishers were called booksellers) had come to Sydney with an introduction from Bulwer, had opened the conversation with a delicately conveyed condolence on the canon's recent losses in American securities, and had then proposed, by way of repairing them, the production of a novel in three volumes, for which he would be most happy to treat on liberal terms.

'Well, sir,' said Sydney, after a pause for seeming consideration, 'if I do so, I can't travel out of my own line – *ne sutor ultra crepidam*, you know – I must have an archdeacon for my hero, to fall in love with the pew-opener, with the clerk for a confidant – tyrannical interference of the churchwardens – clandestine correspondence concealed under the hassocks – appeal to the parishioners, etc., etc.'

'With that, sir,' said Mr. Colburn, 'I would not presume to interfere; I would leave it all entirely to your own inventive genius.'

'Well, sir,' returned the canon urbanely, 'I am not prepared to come to terms at present; but if ever I do undertake such a work, you shall certainly have the refusal.'

In February, 1844, Dickens sent his latest work to Sydney, who wrote at once: 'Many thanks for the *Christmas Carol*, which I shall immediately proceed upon, in preference to six American pamphlets I found upon my arrival, all promising immediate payment.' In June of that year they met for the last time. Dickens wished to give a farewell dinner to several carefully chosen friends before his departure for Italy. He had let his house in Devonshire Terrace, and gave the dinner at No. 9 Osnaburgh Terrace. Sydney was one of the select few, among whom, unfortunately, there was no Boswell.

These later years were marked by many new friendships and frequent visits to and from the friends who had stood the test of time. The more he saw of Monckton Milnes the more he liked him, though the manners of that young man did not improve: 'I am just going to pray for you at St. Paul's,' said the canon, 'but with no very lively hope of success.' He met and liked Maria Edgeworth, whose conversation, he said, had the perfume of wit without its pith. Her tribute ran: 'To attempt to Boswell Sydney Smith's conversation would be out-Boswelling Boswell indeed.' She wanted him to visit

Ireland, where his wit would be thoroughly appreciated and where he would be more popular than O'Connell. It is a pity he did not go, for he got on excellently with the Irishmen he met in London. One of them was the eminent Romish dignitary, Dr. Doyle, who, on hearing his assertion that all the trouble in Ireland would be solved if the Catholic priests were paid, retorted that they would not take money from an English Government. 'Do you mean to say,' demanded Sydney, 'that if every priest in Ireland received to-morrow morning a government letter with a hundred pounds, first quarter of their year's income, they would refuse it?' 'Ah, Mr. Smith,' replied Dr. Doyle, 'you've such a way of putting things.'

In 1844 he became friendly with Sir Robert Peel, the Tory Prime Minister, but not, he hastened to inform his Whig correspondents, because he was after a bishopric: 'I have long since got rid of all ambition and wish for distinctions, and am much happier for it. The journey is nearly over, and I am careless and good-humoured.' Other matters, more suitable to his age and nature, were engrossing his attention:

> 'I look back with remorse and regret at the time I have wasted and the late period of life at which my attention has been awakened to esculent investigations,' he wrote to a female friend. 'Let me beg of you to put down on paper any dicta upon the Table which fall from your father, however loosely or carelessly spoken. When his works are published in two Courses, how inestimable will your collection be, how Boswell will fall into the shade! I see a book advertised *Hasty Thoughts on Pickles*. Am I right in my conjecture as to the author?'

One is not surprised to find that Luttrell was a constant guest at Combe Florey and that they saw a good deal of one another when Sydney was in London. They discussed salads with the air of men deciding the fate of nations and the mysteries of *soufflés* in the manner of political conspirators. Withal their wit was losing some of its sting:

> 'Nothing can exceed the innocence of our conversation,'

> Sydney reported. 'It is one continued eulogy upon man-and-woman-kind. You would suppose that two Arcadian old gentlemen, after shearing their flocks, had agreed to spend a week together upon curds and cream, and to indulge in gentleness of speech and softness of mind.'

Other friends were not mellowing so harmoniously. 'Pray give over hunting,' he wrote to Mrs. Meynell. 'Ask Meynell to leave off. He has been pursuing the fox for thirty years. Glory has its limits like any other pursuit.' Sir George Philips had left the neighbourhood of Manchester and was now living at Weston House, Chipping Norton. Sydney went to stay there, but was forced to admit that 'the evils of old age, gout and prolixity of narrative are invading the worthy and recent baronet'. He became less and less inclined to pay visits. Lady Ashburton begged him to come and stay at The Grange, Alresford, but he resisted: 'My health is so indifferent and my spirits so low, and I am so old and half-dead, that I am mere lumber.' She tried again, but he was adamant: 'I am never well when I arrive at a new house. The bread, the water, the hours, the bed, the change of bolster – everything puts me out. I recover in two or three days, and then it is time to depart.' It was probably laziness more than ill-health that kept him from the excitements of house-parties.

> 'I am seventy-two years of age,' he informed Harriet Martineau, 'at which period there comes over one a shameful love of ease and repose, common to dogs, horses, clergymen, and even to Edinburgh Reviewers. Then an idea comes across me sometimes that I am entitled to five or six years of quiet before I die. I fought with beasts at Ephesus for twenty years. Have not I contributed my fair share for the establishment of important truths, and for the discomfiture of quacks and fools? Is not the spirit gone out of me? Can I now mix ridicule with reason, so as to hit at once every variety of opposition? Is not there a story about Gil Blas and the Archbishop of Granada? I am just come from London, where I have been doing duty at St. Paul's, and preaching against the Puseyites – I. Because they lessen the aversion to the Catholic faith, and the admiration of Protestantism, which I think one of the greatest improvements the world ever made. II. They inculcate the

> preposterous surrender of the understanding to bishops. III. They make religion an affair of trifles, of postures, and of garments.'

To a man with Sydney's severely practical view of life, the Tractarian Movement was incomprehensible. He simply saw in it a lot of doctrinal nonsense which had no relation to reason. *To do good and to be happy* – that was his creed. As to whether a certain saint had said or done this or that, or whether a certain Council had determined that or this, what did it matter? It was like appealing from the practical philosophy of Bacon to the theoretical philosophy of Plato. Christianity was a useful creed: it provided the manna for good deeds, not the manner for idolatry. This does not mean that he was a mere materialist. He considered that all speculation not directly concerned with the welfare and happiness of human beings was wasteful and silly; but he knew that all practical systems that ignored the emotional and sentimental side of man were ineffectual and worthless.

'Everybody here is turning Puseyite,' he wrote contemptuously. 'Having worn out my black gown, I preach in my surplice; this is all the change I have made or mean to make.' He described one of his sermons in 1841 to Lady Ashburton: 'I wish you had witnessed the other day at St. Paul's my incredible boldness in attacking the Puseyites. I told them that they made the Christian religion a religion of postures and ceremonies, of circumflexions and genuflexions, of garments and vestures, of ostentation and parade; that they took up tithe of mint and cummin, and neglected the weightier matters of the law – justice, mercy, and the duties of life, and so forth.' The movement progressed and in 1842 he wrote to Lady Davy: 'Mr. Luttrell is going gently down-hill, trusting that the cookery in another planet may be at least as good as in this; but not without apprehensions that for misconduct here he may be sentenced to a thousand years of tough mutton, or condemned to a little eternity of family dinners. I have not yet discovered of what I am to die, but I rather believe I shall be burnt alive by the Puseyites. Nothing so remarkable in England as the progress of these foolish people. I have no conception what they mean, if it be not to revive every absurd ceremony and every antiquated folly which the common sense of mankind has set to sleep. You will find at your return a fanatical Church of England, but pray do not let it prevent your return. We can always gather together, in Park Street and Green Street, a chosen few who have never bowed the knee to Rimmon.'

In the spring of 1839 Sydney Smith published his Collected Works.

> 'I printed my reviews to show, if I could, that I had not passed my life merely in making jokes; but that I had made use of what little powers of pleasantry I might be endowed with to discountenance bad and to encourage liberal and wise principles.'

The volumes were very well received by the critics, one review in particular giving him much satisfaction. 'I honestly confess that the praise and approbation of wise men is to me a very great pleasure.' Incidentally he declared that he had not made as much as £1,500 by his literary labours in the course of his life. The Preface to this collected edition told the story of the *Edinburgh Review*, referred to some of the reforms it had influenced, and concluded:

> 'To set on foot such a Journal in such times, to contribute towards it for many years, to bear patiently the reproach and poverty which it caused, and to look back and see that I have nothing to retract, and no intemperance and violence to reproach myself with, is a career of life which I must think to be extremely fortunate. Strange and ludicrous are the changes in human affairs. The Tories are now on the treadmill, and the well-paid Whigs are riding in chariots: with many faces, however, looking out of the windows (including that of our Prime Minister, Lord Melbourne) which I never remember to have seen in the days of the poverty and depression of Whiggism. Liberality is now a lucrative business. Whoever has any institution to destroy, may consider himself as a commissioner,

and his fortune is made; and, to my utter and never-ending astonishment, I, an old Edinburgh Reviewer, find myself fighting, in the year 1839, against the Archbishop of Canterbury and the Bishop of London, for the existence of the National Church.'

Having launched his complete works upon the world he decided to live in good humour with everybody for the rest of his life and to bury the war hatchet. The older he grew the milder he became, and though he was human enough to write a stinging pamphlet in reply to someone who had attacked him, he was humane enough to realise it would give pain to people who had been kind to him and to fling it into the fire.

In the summer of 1839 his brother Courtenay died suddenly, leaving £100,000 and no Will. A third of this sum went to Sydney:

> 'After buying into the Consols and the Reduced, I read Seneca "On the Contempt of Wealth". What intolerable nonsense! . . . I have been very poor the greater part of my life, and have borne it as well, I believe, as most people, but I can safely say that I have been happier every guinea I have gained.'

Towards the end of 1840 his old friend and benefactor, Lord Holland, died, and he wrote to Mrs. Meynell: 'It is indeed a great loss to me; but I have learnt to live as a soldier does in war, expecting that, on any one moment, the best and the dearest may be killed before his eyes. . . . I have gout, asthma, and seven other maladies, but am otherwise very well.' His health always began to improve late in the year when it got colder. 'I am never happy till the fires are lighted,' he said. But gout had now become a regular visitant, only to be warded off by joyless bouts of abstinence. He called it 'the only enemy that I do not wish to have at my feet' and described it thus: 'When I have the gout, I feel as if I was walking on my eyeballs.' But there were compensations: 'What an admirable provision of Providence is the gout! What prevents human beings from making the body a larder or a cellar but the gout? When I feel a pang, I say, "I know what this is for. I know what you mean. I understand the hint!" and so I endeavour to extract a little wisdom from pain.'

During the last five years of his life he was seldom free from some sort of illness. 'One evil in old age,' he reflected, 'is that as your time is come you think every little illness is the beginning of the end. When a man expects to be arrested, every knock at the door is an alarm.' All the same, illness had its advantages:

> 'It is a bore, I admit, to be past seventy, for you are left for execution and are daily expecting the death-warrant; but it is not anything very capital we quit. We are, at the close of life, only hurried away from stomach-aches, pains in the joints, from sleepless nights and unamusing days, from weakness, ugliness, and nervous tremors; but we shall all meet again in another planet, cured of all our defects. Rogers will be less irritable, Macaulay more silent, Hallam will assent, Jeffrey will speak slower, Bobus will be just as he is, I shall be more respectful to the upper clergy.'

He was often confined to the house: 'Mrs. Sydney has eight distinct illnesses and I have nine. We take something every hour and pass the mixture from one to the other.' There were periods of relative activity, however, when he could say 'We are both tolerably well, bulging out like old houses, but with no immediate intention of tumbling down.' Still, he dared not be too optimistic: 'Mrs. Sydney and I are both in very fair preservation – packed up, however, and ready for palsy or apoplexy or whatever monster of death may be dispatched to us.' Death did not frighten him, though the process of dying left much to be desired: 'I confess myself afraid of the very disagreeable methods by which we leave this world; the long death of palsy, or the degraded spectacle of aged idiotism. As for the pleasures of the world, it is a very ordinary middling sort of place.' During an interval of complete freedom from pain he said that he was 'enjoying life and ready for death'. But he could not count on many such healthy spells and he wrote to John Murray begging him not to put off coming to Combe Florey 'for I am afraid I cannot put off dying much longer'. He complained that Lady Grey suffered from anti-egotism because she did not report the state of her health, and confessed to her: 'When I am ill, I mention it to all my friends and relations, to the lord lieutenant of the county, the justices, the bishop, the churchwardens, the booksellers and editors of the *Edinburgh* and *Quarterly Reviews*.'

In the last years of his life he seemed to relent towards the country. 'Nothing can exceed the beauty of the country; I am forced to own that.' And again: 'I am afraid this country does look enchantingly beautiful; you know the power truth has over me.' On the other hand he applauded the good sense of a young clergyman who had refused the living of Sunbury on the Thames: 'His refusal of the living of Sunbury convinces me that he is not fond of gudgeon-fishing.' He never quite accustomed himself to the mental obtuseness of his neighbours: 'I must do her the justice to say that when my jokes are explained to her, and she has leisure to reflect upon them, she laughs very heartily.' And no one could pretend that life in the country was eventful: 'I saw a crow yesterday, and had a distant view of a rabbit to-day.'

It seems that the lack of excitement in Somersetshire forced him to provide thrills for himself and his friends. Thomas Moore stayed at Combe Florey in the summer of 1843, and a passage in his diary for August the 5th runs:

> 'Sydney drove me out in his gig to show me Sir Thos Lethbridge's place (Sandhill). The day delicious, and the country fine, but neither Sydney Smith's horse nor his driving were such as to allow me sufficient ease for any enjoyment of the scene. The horse, which had evidently been better fed than taught, took at last to rearing, and I (as the safer break-neck expedient of the two) jumped out and walked the remainder of the way home. Sydney's wit and eke his good sense (i.e. upon paper) nobody doubts, but to trust himself with such a horse is stark staring foolish.'

Moore sang a good deal for them in the evenings, and

Sydney, now in his seventy-third year, was learning to sing some of Moore's Irish melodies.

In the autumn he received what he considered a very great honour: Jeffrey's collected essays were dedicated to him. That same year he was invited by the Prime Minister, Sir Robert Peel, to meet the King of Saxony at a select dinner in Whitehall Gardens of the leading figures in literature, science, painting and politics. But it was the last big public function he attended.

> 'I am retiring from business as a diner-out,' he wrote to Georgiana Harcourt, daughter of the Archbishop of York: '. . . I suppose you will soon be at Bishopthorpe, surrounded by the sons of the prophets. What a charming existence to live in the midst of holy people, to know that nothing profane can approach you, to be certain that a dissenter can no more be found in the Palace than a snake can exist in Ireland, or ripe fruit in Scotland. To have your society strong and undiluted by the laity, to bid adieu to human learning, to feast on the Canons, and revel in the Thirty-nine Articles. Happy Georgiana!'

Instead of dinners he now gave breakfasts at his house in Green Street. He was delighted with his London residence and spent much time beautifying it, adding marble chimney-pieces in the drawing-rooms to please his wife. The move from Combe Florey to London was a great event and he usually packed up about ten times as many things as he wanted. A favourite haunt towards the end of his life was the Athenæum Club, where he could button-hole bishops and make them laugh so much that they became almost human. Here he would listen to old gentlemen reliving the days that were no more, talking of the good old times and wondering what the world was coming to. Sydney had the misfortune of perpetual youth in a decaying body. He lived in the present and the future, never in the past; and a letter he wrote to the press on 'Modern Changes' compared the old days very unfavourably with the new. He enumerated the improvements that had taken place in his own life-time – gas, steam-boats, railways, macadamised roads, wooden pavements, the police force, cabs, umbrellas, braces, quinine, carriage-springs, clubs, the penny-post, to say nothing of humane laws, the sobriety of the gentry and the safety of the streets. Yet, in spite of the horrors of the past, 'I lived on quietly, and am now ashamed that I was not more discontented, and utterly surprised that all these changes and inventions did not occur two centuries ago.'

In 1843 he made his Will. It was a characteristically businesslike document, containing no reference to the Almighty, no pious hope that he would be transported to a state of blessed felicity, no mention of his immortal soul, no proclamation of faith, and nothing about the Thirty-nine Articles. Except for a few bequests to his old servants he left practically everything to his wife. After her death the bulk of the property was to go to their son, Wyndham, who was to receive £200 a year during Mrs. Sydney's life, paid quarterly, on one condition, viz.: that he lived apart from his mother.

The unaccountable reticence of Victorian chroniclers concerning the boy Wyndham suggested to the present biographer a visit to Somerset House, where a glance through the Last Will and Testament of Sydney Smith revealed this skeleton in the family cupboard. We learn from Fanny Kemble that Sydney's younger son was known in London society as 'the assassin' and that he preferred the turf to wit. We learn from an unpublished letter of Sydney's to Lord Melbourne, asking him to give the boy a job in some public office, that Wyndham had taken his degree at Cambridge in 1836 and was a nervous youth, difficult to handle. But that is all. He is scarcely mentioned by name in the official *Memoir*. Knowing little we must assume little. The clause in the Will makes certain of one thing: Sydney wished to protect his wife from the society of his son when he was no longer there to protect her. We may make what we like of it.

With his two daughters Sydney remained on excellent terms, seeing a lot of Saba when in town, sometimes staying at Munden House, Watford, with Emily, and frequently entertaining both their families at Combe Florey. He loved returning home and seeing a dozen or more of his descendants tearing about the house and grounds, delirious with happiness and high spirits. After one such home-coming he wrote: 'I found . . . many grandchildren, all of whom I whipt immediately – never give any reason; it increases their idea of power and makes them more obedient.'

On New Year's Day, 1844, Sydney was walking with a friend in his garden. Suddenly he saw a crocus, which had somehow managed to fight its way through the frozen earth. He stopped, gazed at it for several seconds in silence, then, touching it with his stick, said solemnly: 'The resurrection of the world.' It was perhaps the only kind of resurrection he could entirely believe in. The resurrection of the soul was founded on hope. His health that month was not too good: 'I look as strong as a cart-horse, but I cannot get round the garden without resting once or twice, so deficient am I in nervous energy.'

In the spring he went up to London for duty at St. Paul's, where he preached the sermon on war by Channing to which allusion has been made. Though the words were not his own, the subject was one upon which he felt deeply and the delivery over-taxed his strength. 'I think I could write a good sermon against war,' he told Lady Grey, 'but I doubt if I shall preach any more. It makes me ill; I get violently excited and tire myself to death.' He still took a faint interest in politics, and suggested an extension to Lord Shaftesbury's Ten Hours Bill, then before Parliament: 'When he brings forward his Suckling Act, he will be considered as quite mad. No woman to be allowed to suckle her own child without medical certificates. Three classes – viz., free sucklers, half-sucklers, and spoon-meat mothers. Mothers whose supply is uncertain, to suckle upon affidavit.'

A French critic wished to write about Sydney's works in the *Revue des Deux Mondes* and requested personal details, which were supplied:

'I am seventy-four years of age; and being Canon of St. Paul's in London, and a rector of a parish in the country, my time is divided equally between town and country. I am living amongst the best society in the Metropolis, and at ease in my circumstances; in tolerable health, a mild Whig, a tolerating Churchman, and much given to talking, laughing, and noise. I dine with the rich in London, and physic the poor in the country; passing from the sauces of Dives to the sores of Lazarus. I am, upon the whole, a happy man; have found the world an entertaining world, and am thankful to Providence for the part allotted to me in it.'

Charles Greville, the diarist, asked him to dinner in May and received this reply: 'On the 23rd (if you will allow me to bring thirteen people to dinner) I shall be most happy to dine with you, but as I can hardly calculate on such expanded hospitality, I must, I fear, decline your kind invitation, and try to entertain my thirteen in Green Street.' In June he was laid up with the gout and one of his callers, Thomas Moore, was amused and surprised to find him studying French, a copy-book open upon the table with all the verbs, their moods and tenses, written out neatly in his own hand. Moore thought it an odd pastime for a septuagenarian.

On July the 28th he preached for the last time in St. Paul's Cathedral. He was troubled by a presentiment at the close of the sermon and finished with the words: 'I never take leave of anyone, for any length of time, without a deep impression upon my mind of the uncertainty of human life, and the probability that we may meet no more in this world.'

August was spent at Combe Florey, where he had several visitors, among them his brother 'Bobus' and Henry Hallam, and arrangements were made to receive a very famous personage:

'Lady Holland has not yet signified her intentions under the sign manual; but a thousand rumours reach me, and my firm belief is she will come. I have spoken to the sheriff, and mentioned it to the magistrates. They have agreed to address her, and she is to be escorted from the station by the yeomanry. The clergy are rather backward; but I think that, after a little bashfulness, they will wait upon her. Brunel, assisted by the ablest philosophers, is to accompany her upon the railroad; and they have been so good as to say that the steam shall be generated from soft water, with a slight infusion of chamomile flowers.'

The musical family, of whom mention has been made, were also staying with him this month, and they were surprised to see the crowds of poor people that swarmed into his work-room after breakfast every morning, asking for help and advice in their domestic affairs, for food and medicines. He suffered much from languor and said: 'I feel so weak both in body and mind that I verily believe, if the knife were put into my hand, I should not have strength or energy enough to slide it into a Dissenter.' His physician and son-in-law, Dr. Holland, was anxious to have a full account of every symptom. He obliged:

'I ought to have answered your letter before, but I have been so strenuously employed in doing nothing, that I have not had time to do so. . . . I saw the other day, in midday, a ball of fire, with a tail as long as the garden, rush across the heavens, and descend towards the earth; that it had some allusion to me and my affairs I did not doubt, but could not tell what, till I found the cow had slipped her calf: this made all clear.'

At the end of August he took his wife to Sidmouth.

'We are at Sidmouth,' he wrote to Lady Grey on the 29th. 'It is extremely beautiful, but quite deserted. I have nothing to do but to look out of window, and am *ennuied*. The events which have turned up are, a dog and a monkey for a show, and a morning concert; and I rather think we shall have an invitation to tea. I say to everyone who sits near me on the marine benches that it is a fine day and that the prospect is beautiful, but we get no further. I can get no water out of a dry rock. There arrived the other day at New York a Sydney Smith. A meeting was called and it was proposed to tar-and-feather him; but the amendment was carried that he should be invited to a public dinner. He turned out to be a journeyman cooper. My informant encloses for me an invitation from the bishop of the diocese to come and see him, and a proposition that we should travel together to the Falls of Niagara.'

Back at Combe Florey by the middle of September, he pictured his dissolution in a letter to Lady Holland:

> 'It is a sad scene, the last – the last act of life – to see beauty and eloquence, sense, mouldering away in pain and agony under terrible diseases, and hastening to the grave with sundry kinds of death – to witness the barren silence of him who charmed us with his exuberant fancy and gaiety never to be exhausted – to gaze upon wrinkles and yellowness and incurvations where we remember beautiful forms and smiles and smoothness and the blush of health and the bloom of desire, to see – but here I recollect I am not in the pulpit, so I stop.'

At the beginning of October he had a severe attack of giddiness and the local doctor, thinking the trouble proceeded from the stomach, dieted him. Dr. Holland travelled down at once and advised him to come to London as soon as he could stand the journey. The medical consultation on his health amused him: 'I rather think that last week they wanted to kill me, but I was too sharp for them,' he wrote to Lady Grey. 'I am now tolerably well, but I am weak, and taking all proper care of myself; which care consists in eating nothing that I like and doing nothing that I wish. . . . See what rural life is: –

Combe Florey Gazette

> Mr. Smith's large red cow is expected to calve this week.
>
> Mr. Gibbs has bought Mr. Smith's lame mare.
>
> It rained yesterday, and, a correspondent observes, is not unlikely to rain to-day.
>
> Mr. Smith is better.
>
> Mrs. Smith is indisposed.
>
> A nest of black magpies was found near the village yesterday.'

On October 21st he was in London and writing to Lady Carlisle:

> 'From your ancient goodness to me, I am sure you will be glad to receive a bulletin from myself, informing you that I

am making a good progress; in fact, I am in a regular train of promotion: from gruel, vermicelli, and sago, I was promoted to panada, from thence to minced meat, and (such is the effect of good conduct) I was elevated to a mutton-chop. My breathlessness and giddiness are gone – chased away by the gout. If you hear of sixteen or eighteen pounds of human flesh, they belong to me. I look as if a curate had been taken out of me.'

On November 7th he sent the latest bulletin to Lady Grey:

'I have been seriously ill, and I do not think I am yet quite "clear of the wood", but am certainly a good deal better. My complaints have been giddiness, breathlessness, and weakness of the digestive organs. I believe I acted wisely in setting off for London on the first attack; it has secured for me the proximity and best attentions of Dr. Holland, and the use of a comfortable house, where a suite of rooms are perfectly fitted up for illness and death.'

Until about Christmas he was able to take a drive in his carriage every day and to see his friends, but he was kept on a low diet and felt very weak. 'Ah, Charles!' he said one day to General Fox, 'I wish I were allowed even the wing of a roasted butterfly'.

At the end of December his symptoms became more alarming and Dr. Holland urged that a specialist should be called in. Sydney unwillingly consented; he had no great faith in a multitude of doctors, and was quite satisfied with his son-in-law's perfect bedside manner. At last it became apparent that he was suffering from water on the chest, caused by heart-disease, and though every possible remedy was applied there was no hope of recovery. Realising this, he told his old maid and nurse, Annie Kay, that he wished to be buried by the side of his son, Douglas, in Kensal Green Cemetery; and from that moment he maintained a cheerful demeanour before his family, so that they should not perceive he was aware of his condition. He had a dread of long and sorrowful faces.

The moment it became known that he was dangerously ill messages from friends and strangers were received every day from all parts of the country. Lady Grey, whose husband was also on his death-bed, wrote to Mrs. Sydney:

> 'Lord Grey is intensely anxious about him. There is nobody of whom he so constantly thinks; nobody whom, in the course of his own long illness, he so ardently wished to see. Need I add, dear Mrs. Sydney, that, excepting only our children, there is nobody for whom we both feel so sincere an affection.'

The front-door bell of No. 56, Green Street was ringing, morning and afternoon, with few intervals. Sometimes he felt well enough to see friends, especially those, like Monckton Milnes, who begged daily for admission to the sick-room. Milnes, admitted at last, wished to know what sort of night he had passed. 'Oh, horrid, horrid, my dear fellow!' exclaimed Sydney: 'I dreamt I was chained to a rock and being talked to death by Harriet Martineau and Macaulay.' A cloud seemed to be passing over 'the parallelogram' and people spoke of 'dear Sydney' with something between a sob and a giggle. He was 'dear Sydney' to everyone who knew him, from his earliest friend Jeffrey to his latest friend Dickens; a summary and a fitting epitaph.

Mental inactivity was hateful to him and he studied several books on music, saying that he would like to know something about it. He asked his regular correspondents to return his letters; several did so and he destroyed them, giving the reason that they might be misunderstood by any but those to whom they were addressed. On the same principle he had always destroyed letters to himself.

> 'It is hardly a fair practise to keep letters', he once wrote. 'It ought not to be done if the correspondent does not like it, and that nobody does like it is clear, for it would put an end to any correspondence, or render it not worth keeping up.'

Towards the end he suffered much but spoke little. Once, when he was semi-delirious, he was heard to say: 'We talk of human life as a journey, but how variously is that journey performed! There are some who come forth girt, and shod, and mantled, to walk on velvet lawns and smooth terraces, where every gale is arrested, and every beam is tempered. There are others who walk on the Alpine paths of life, against driving misery, and through stormy sorrows, over sharp afflictions; walk with bare feet, and naked breast, jaded, mangled, and chilled.' It was a passage from one of his own sermons.

Sometimes, when he was only half-conscious, the cry of 'Douglas, Douglas!' escaped his lips. His dead son was constantly in his thoughts, and once or twice he mistook Wyndham for Douglas.

But there were lucid intervals. His brother 'Bobus' came to say 'good-bye', and then left for his own death-bed. One of the canon's last acts was to bestow a small living of £120 a year on a poor and friendless clergyman, a Tory in politics, who had struggled for many years on a third of that sum. Full of gratitude the clergyman wished to thank his benefactor. 'He must not thank me; I am too weak to bear it,' said the dying man, but he allowed him to come in and gave him a few words of advice. There was a flash of the old humour during another lucid moment. In looking for his medicine the nurse found half a bottle of ink in the place where it ought to have been, and said jokingly that he had probably taken a dose of ink the previous time by mistake. 'Then bring me all the blotting paper there is in the house,' said Sydney.

The end came on the evening of Saturday, February the 22nd, 1845. Not perhaps too soon, for a serious age had already dawned, and Falstaff and Merry England were out of date.

Two days later Charles Greville heard the news that had spread a gloom over Foston, Combe Florey and Mayfair, that had plunged Jeffrey into an agony of grief, shaken Lord John Russell, silenced Macaulay, caused Lady Holland to forget her ailments, made Samuel Rogers sentimental, stopped the pen of Dickens, saddened the home of Grey, forced Brougham to think for a moment of someone beside himself, reddened the eyes of Thomas Moore, and upset Luttrell's dining arrangements. Taking up his pen, Greville drew the character of Sydney Smith in his diary, closing the entry with these words:

> 'I do not suppose he had any dogmatic and doctrinal opinions in respect to religion . . . in his heart of hearts he despised and derided all that the world wrangles and squabbles about; but he had the true religion of benevolence and charity, of peace and goodwill to mankind, which, let us hope (as I firmly believe) to be all sufficient, be the truth of the great mystery what it may.'

POSTCRIPT

The Smith of Smiths was published in January 1934. As biographies go, it was a success, and I received many letters about it. One was from Sydney Smith's great-grandson, Lord Knutsford, who as a boy had known Sydney's only surviving son Wyndham. He told me that Wyndham, a short tubby man who resembled Napoleon I in appearance, was called 'the assassin' because he fought a savage dog unarmed, that he was a deep drinker, had many illegitimate children, and generally speaking was 'a bad lot'. Lord Knutsford also reported a saying of Wyndham Smith's: 'I remember vividly his telling me I should never be a man till I could drink a bottle of port at a sitting. As I have lived seventy-nine years as a total abstainer it seems to me his information was inaccurate.'

Lord Knutsford showed me a number of Sydney's letters in his possession, one of which the original editor had quite spoilt by leaving out the last sentence. 'I may see as many crosiers in the clouds as I please,' wrote Sydney after he had decided to build a rectory for his Yorkshire living, 'but when I sit down seriously to consider what I shall do upon important occasions, I must presume myself rector of Foston for life.' Then followed this characteristic phrase, perforce omitted from my book: 'God in his mercy grant that this may be pure hypothesis.'

Although I am usually accurate over dates and places and such-like details, I made two slips in my Life of Sydney Smith. The first was simply unaccountable. I gave his birthplace as Woodbridge, Suffolk, instead of Woodford, Essex, and can only guess that I had been reading the letters of Fitzgerald, who had lived at the former. The second error was excusable and due to ignorance. It was pointed out to me by Mr. Arthur H. Pollen, who wrote me a most appreciative letter in the course of which he said, 'If you will pardon a self-evident remark, it is a book which must obviously take its place amongst the classical biographies,' but went on to express his surprise that his friend Mr. Gilbert Chesterton should have passed my reference in Chapter 10 to 'the Immaculate Conception', when it was clear that what I had meant to say was 'the Virgin Birth'. Wishing to know whether my ignorance was shared by others or peculiar to myself, I asked the next twenty educated people I met if they knew the difference. Not one of them was aware of it.

Viscount Charlemont wrote to say that when Sydney Smith declared 'the Catholics must be kept in subjection in order that Sir Phelim O'Callaghan may whip Sir Toby M'Tackle' he was confusing the Protestant and Catholic nomenclatures, and that the surnames should have been the other way about. 'I hope, however,' wrote Lord Charlemont, 'that you will take it as a real compliment that I – an Orangeman and possibly the descendant of those whom Sydney Smith believed to be addicted to whipping their Catholic neighbours (and worse) – should show a practical desire to rivet the chains of guilt on the right necks!'

Mr. C. F. Moysey, writing from Torquay, favoured me with the 'last edition' of Sydney's famous *Receipt for Salad*, which the author had given in verse and prose to Mr Moysey's great-uncle in January 1843:

Two large potatoes, passed through kitchen sieve,
Unwonted softness to the salad give;
Of mordent mustard, add a single spoon,
Distrust the condiment which bites so soon;
But deem it not, thou man of herbs, a fault,

To add a double quantity of salt:
Three times the spoon with oil of Lucca crown,
And once with vinegar, procured from town;
True flavour needs it, and your poet begs
The pounded yellow of two well-boiled eggs;
Let onion atoms lurk within the bowl,
And scarce suspected, animate the whole;
And lastly, on the flavoured compound toss
A magic tea spoon of anchovy sauce:
Then though green turtle fail, though venison's tough,
And ham and turkey are not boiled enough,
Serenely full, the Epicure may say –
Fate cannot harm me, – I have dined to-day.

A WINTER SALAD

Two well boiled Potatoes, passed through a sieve; a tea spoonful of Mustard; two tea spoonsful of Salt; one of Essence of Anchovy; about a quarter of a tea spoonful of very finely chopped Onions, well bruised into the mixture; three table spoonsful of Oil; one of Vinegar; the yolk of two Eggs, hard boiled. Stir up the Salad immediately before dinner, and stir it up thoroughly.

N.B. As this Salad is the result of great experience and reflection, it is hoped young Salad makers will not attempt to make any improvements upon it.

With regard to Sydney Smith's scathing attack on the State of Pennsylvania for having repudiated its debts in 1843, Mr. Franklin S. Edmonds (of Philadelphia), who had served in the Legislature of Pennsylvania from 1921 to 1927, sent me sufficient evidence to prove that in later years the State had 'paid the principal and interest of its bonds in full'. As a native of Pennsylvania Mr. Edmonds was interested in the credit of his State and hoped that in future editions of the book 'you can see your way clear to add a footnote which would indicate that later Pennsylvania justified in full the confidence of its friends'.

One more item from my correspondence must be quoted.

Miss Muriel Dudley Smith sent me a letter in her possession which had been written by Sydney Smith to his niece:

MY DEAR MARY,
Your friend in collecting autographs should confine herself to the signatures of great and good persons, not covet the scrawls of unmeaning Clergymen. I send my Epitaph as well as my Autograph –

Beneath this Tombstone Sydney's ashes lie
Born but to eat and drink and sleep and die
His autograph is asked we know not why.

Your affec'ate Uncle,
SYDNEY SMITH.

April 12, 1840.

Hesketh Pearson, *Thinking It Over* (1938)

AUTHORITIES

Unpublished Correspondence.

A Memoir of The Reverend Sydney Smith, by his daughter, Lady Holland, with *A Selection from His Letters*, edited by Mrs. Austin, 2 vols., 2nd ed., 1855.

The Life and Times of Sydney Smith, based on Family Documents and the Recollections of Personal Friends, by Stuart J. Reid, 4th and revised ed., 1896.

Sydney Smith, by George W. E. Russell (*English Men of Letters*), 1904.

The Works of the Rev. Sydney Smith, a New Edition, 1869.

The Wit and Wisdom of the Rev. Sydney Smith, New Edition, 1865.

Bon-Mots of Sydney Smith and R. Brinsley Sheridan, edited by Walter Jerrold, 5th ed., 1904.

Essays in English Literature, 1780–1860, by George Saintsbury, 3rd ed., 1896.

Memoirs, Journal and Correspondence of Thomas Moore, edited by the Right Hon. Lord John Russell, M.P., 8 vols., 1856.

Monographs: Personal and Social, by Lord Houghton, 1873.

Selected Essays, by A. Hayward, vol. 1, 1878.

The Life, Letters and Friendships of Richard Monckton Milnes (first Lord Houghton), by T. Wemyss Reid, 1890.

The Life and Letters of Lord Macaulay, by G. O. Trevelyan, New Edition, 1881.

The Life and Letters of the Rev. Richard Harris Barham, by his Son, 2 vols., 1870.

The Greville Memoirs, vols. 3 and 5, a New Edition, 1888.

Letters to 'Ivy' from the First Earl of Dudley, by S. H. Romilly, 1905.

Records of Later Life, by Frances Anne Kemble, 3 vols., 1882.

Further Records, by Frances Anne Kemble, 2 vols., 1890.

Harriet Martineau's Autobiography, 3 vols., 1877.

Life, Letters and Journals of George Ticknor, 2 vols., 1909.

The Dictionary of National Biography.

The Life and Times of Henry, Lord Brougham, written by Himself, 3 vols., 1871.

Memorials of His Time, by Henry, Lord Cockburn, 1856.

Journal of Henry Cockburn, 1831–54, 2 vols., 1874.

Life of Lord Jeffrey, by Lord Cockburn, 2 vols., 1852.

The Pope of Holland House (Selections from the Correspondence of John Whishaw and his friends, 1813–40), edited by Lady Seymour, 1906.

An Account of the Friday Club, written by Lord Cockburn (The Book of the Old Edinburgh Club, vol. 3), 1908.

Archibald Constable and his Literary Correspondents. A Memorial by his Son, Thomas Constable, 3 vols., 1873.

Correspondence of Two Brothers: The eleventh Duke of Somerset and Lord Webb Seymour, Lady Gwendolen Ramsden, 1906.

The Holland House Circle, by Lloyd Sanders, 1908.

Holland House, by Princess Marie Liechtenstein, 1874.

A Book of Famous Wits, by Walter Jerrold, 1912.

Miscellanies of the Philobiblon Society, vol. 15, 1884.

Samuel Rogers and His Circle, by R. Ellis Roberts, 1910.

Rogers and His Contemporaries, by P. W. Clayden, 2 vols., 1889.

Recollections of the Table-Talk of Samuel Rogers, edited by A. Dyce, 1856.

Memoirs and Correspondence of Francis Horner, M.P., edited by his brother, Leonard Horner, 2 vols., 1853.

Memoirs of the Life of Sir James Mackintosh, edited by his son, R. J. Mackintosh, 2 vols., 1835.

The Journal of the Hon. Henry Edward Fox (afterwards fourth and last Lord Holland), 1818–30, edited by the Earl of Ilchester, 1923.

A. W. Kinglake, by the Rev. W. Tuckwell, 1902.

Life and Letters of Thomas Campbell, edited by William Beattie, 3 vols, 1849.

The Creevey Papers, edited by the Right Hon. Sir Herbert Maxwell, Bart., 3rd ed., 1905.

A History of the Thirty Years Peace, by Harriet Martineau, 4 vols., 1877.

Early Correspondence of Lord John Russell, 1805–40, edited by his Son, Rollo Russell, 1913.

The Personal Life of George Grote, by Mrs Grote, 1873.

Diary, Reminiscences and Correspondence of Henry Crabb Robinson, 2 vols., 1872.

An Embassy to the Court of St. James's in 1840, by F. Guizot, 1862.

Memoir of Thomas, first Lord Denman, formerly Lord Chief Justice of England, by Sir Joseph Arnould, 1873.

Autobiography of Sir Henry Taylor, 2 vols., 1885.

Memoirs of the Life and Correspondence of Henry Reeve, by J. K. Laughton, 2 vols., 1898.

Henry Fothergill Chorley: Autobiography, Memoir and Letters, compiled by Henry G. Hewlett, 2 vols., 1873.
Story of a Long and Busy Life, by W. Chambers, LL.D., 1882.
Extracts of the Journals and Correspondence of Miss Berry, 1783–1852, edited by Lady T. Lewis, 3 vols., 1865.
Recollections of Past Life, by Sir Henry Holland, 1872.
Reminiscences by Thomas Carlyle, edited by J. A. Froude, vol. 2, 1881.
Carlyle, by D. A. Wilson, vol. 4, 1927.
Journal of Washington Irving, 1823-4, edited by Stanley T. Williams, 1931.
The Letters of Daniel Webster, edited by C. H. Van Tyne, 1902.
Letters of David Ricardo to Hutches Trower and Others, 1811–23, edited by James Bonar and J. H. Hollander, 1899.
Further Memoirs of the Whig Party, 1807–21, by Henry Richard Vassall, third Lord Holland, 1905.
Lord Beaconsfield's Correspondence with his Sister, 1832–52, 1886.
The Letters of Charles Dickens, edited by his sister-in-law and his eldest daughter, 2 vols., 1880.
Mrs. Brookfield and Her Circle, by Charles and Frances Brookfield, 1906.
Memoirs of the Life of Sir Walter Scott, by J. G. Lockhart, 1836–8.
Life of Dickens, by John Forster, 1872-4.
Sheridan, by W. Fraser Rae, 2 vols., 1896.
Diary of W. C. Macready, 1912.
Critical and Historical Essays, by Lord Macaulay.
The Spirit of the Age, by William Hazlitt.

INDEX

THE HOGARTH PRESS

A New Life For A Great Name

This is a paperback list for today's readers – but it holds to a tradition of adventurous and original publishing set by Leonard and Virginia Woolf when they founded The Hogarth Press in 1917 and started their first paperback series in 1924.

Now, after many years of partnership, Chatto & Windus · The Hogarth Press are proud to launch this new series. Our choice of books does not echo that of the Woolfs in every way – times have changed – but our aims are the same. Some sections of the list are light-hearted, some serious: all are rigorously chosen, excellently produced and energetically published, in the best Hogarth Press tradition. We hope that the new Hogarth Press paperback list will be as prized – and as avidly collected – as its illustrious forebear.

A list of our books already published, together with some of our forthcoming titles, follows. If you would like more information about Hogarth Press books, write to us for a catalogue:

40 William IV Street, London WC2N 4DF

Please send a large stamped addressed envelope

HOGARTH FICTION

Death of a Hero by Richard Aldington
New Introduction by Christopher Ridgway

Epitaph of a Small Winner by Machado de Assis
Translated and introduced by William L. Grossman

Chance by Joseph Conrad
New Introduction by Jane Miller

The Whirlpool by George Gissing
New Introduction by Gillian Tindall

Mr Weston's Good Wine by T. F. Powys
New Introduction by Ronald Blythe

Catharine Furze by Mark Rutherford
Clara Hopgood by Mark Rutherford
The Revolution in Tanner's Lane by Mark Rutherford
New Introductions by Claire Tomalin

Christina Alberta's Father by H. G. Wells
Mr Britling Sees It Through by H. G. Wells
New Introductions by Christopher Priest

Frank Burnet by Dorothy Vernon White
New Afterword by Irvin Stock

HOGARTH HUMOUR

The Amazing Test Match Crime by Adrian Alington
New Introduction by Brian Johnston

Mrs Ames by E. F. Benson
Paying Guests by E. F. Benson
Secret Lives by E. F. Benson
New Introductions by Stephen Pile

Vestal Fire by Compton Mackenzie
New Introduction by Sally Beauman

HOGARTH LITERARY CRITICISM

Seven Types of Ambiguity by William Empson

The Common Pursuit by F. R. Leavis

By Way of Sainte-Beuve by Marcel Proust
Translated by Sylvia Townsend Warner
New Introduction by Terence Kilmartin

The English Novel from Dickens to Lawrence by Raymond Williams

The Common Reader, First Series by Virginia Woolf
Edited and introduced by Andrew McNeillie

HOGARTH POETRY

The Complete Poems 1927-1979, Elizabeth Bishop

Collected Poems, C. P. Cavafy
Translated by Edmund Keeley and Philip Sherrard
Edited by George Savidis

Collected Poems, William Empson

HOGARTH TRAVEL

Now I Remember: A Holiday History of England by Ronald Hamilton

The Spanish Temper by V. S. Pritchett
New Introduction by the Author

The Amateur Emigrant by Robert Louis Stevenson
New Introduction by Jonathan Raban

HOGARTH CRIME

The Beckoning Lady by Margery Allingham

Hide My Eyes by Margery Allingham

Dead Mrs Stratton by Anthony Berkeley

The Baffle Book edited by F. Tennyson Jesse

Death by Request by Romilly and Katherine John

The Saltmarsh Murders by Gladys Mitchell

The Hand in The Glove by Rex Stout

HOGARTH BIOGRAPHY AND AUTOBIOGRAPHY

The Journal of a Disappointed Man & A Last Diary by W. N. P. Barbellion
Original Introduction by H. G. Wells and New Introduction by Deborah Singmaster

Samuel Johnson by Walter Jackson Bate

Still Life: Sketches from a Tunbridge Wells Childhood by Richard Cobb

Ivor Gurney: War Letters
A selection edited by R. K. R. Thornton

Being Geniuses Together, 1920-1930 by Robert McAlmon and Kay Boyle
New Afterword by Kay Boyle

The Smith of Smiths by Hesketh Pearson
New Introduction by Richard Ingrams